Practice Skills in

Social Work & Welfare

2nd edition

2nd edition

Practice Skills in
Social Work & Welfare

MORE THAN JUST COMMON SENSE

Edited by
Jane Maidment & Ronnie Egan

ALLEN & UNWIN

Allen & Unwin
83 Alexander Street
Crows Nest NSW 2065
Australia
Phone: (61 2) 8425 0100
Fax: (61 2) 9906 2218
Email: info@allenandunwin.com
Web: www.allenandunwin.com

National Library of Australia
Cataloguing-in-Publication entry:

National Library of Australia Cataloguing-in-Publication entry:

    Practice skills in social work and welfare : more than just
    common sense / editors, Jane Maidment, Ronnie Egan.

    2nd ed.

    978 1 74175 714 9 (pbk.)

    Includes index.
    Bibliography.

    Social services–Australia.
    Social services–New Zealand.
    Public welfare–Australia.
    Public welfare–New Zealand.

    Maidment, Jane.
    Egan, Ronnie.

    361.320994

Internal design by Midland Typesetters, Australia
Index by Jon Jermey
Set in 10.5/13 pt Garamond Book by Midland Typesetters, Australia
Printed in Australia by Ligare Book Printer

10 9 8 7 6 5 4 3 2 1

CONTENTS

TABLES AND FIGURES

TABLES

FIGURES

ACKNOWLEDGMENTS

The need for a social work practice skills text which uses both relevant and local material has been disucssed by social work educators and students on both sides of the Tasman. We acknowledge those discussions in the development of the text. We thank the authors who generously gave their time, energy and knowledge to this text. The richness of their work has contributed greatly to the diversity of material throughout the book. We thank the many students we have taught, and who in turn have taught us. Their feedback and ideas have greatly influenced the development of this text. We also thank the Knowledge Media Division of Deakin University for producing the *Practice Skills* DVD and our social work colleagues who kindly gave their time to the filming project. Finally, thank you to Elizabeth Weiss and Lisa Boxsell at Allen & Unwin, who supported and guided us along the way.

Jane Maidment,
Deakin University

Ronnie Egan,
Victoria University

CONTRIBUTORS

Jim Anglem is a Senior Lecturer in the School of Social Work and Human Services and a cultural adviser to the College of Arts and College of Science. He is a Ngai Tahu Maori and an adviser for the Violence Research Centre on matters related to culture. He teaches diversity, biculturalism and multiculturalism, and writes on matters related to racism.

Lynne Briggs is a Senior Lecturer for the University of Otago, New Zealand where she is responsible for teaching Mental Health and Specialist Practice, Advanced Counselling and Interpersonal Practice papers on the MSW program. Lynne has had many years of clinical practice in mental health, and in her clinical role heads the Canterbury District Health Board's Refugee and Migrant Mental Health Service.

Wendy Bunston is manager of the Community Group Program and Addressing Family Violence Programs in the Mental Health Service of Melbourne's Royal Children's Hospital. She has published work in the area of child protection, childhood trauma, child/adolescent sex offending, family violence and groupwork. Wendy has co-developed national award winning specialist groupwork programs for children and their parents affected by family violence called 'PARKAS', as well as 'The Peek a Boo Club' for infants and mothers.

Helen Cleak has worked as a social worker in health care and family mediation, and is currently a Senior Lecturer and Director of Field Education in the School of Social Work and Social Policy at La Trobe University. She teaches in social work skills and interdisciplinary professional practice and has written a book on supervising students on placement, *Making the Most of Field Education*.

Lesley Cooper is the Dean of Social Work at Wilfrid Laurier University in Ontario, Canada. Prior to this, she was Head of the School of Social Administration and Social Work at Flinders University. She researches in the area of social housing, Indigenous health and social work education. At Flinders, she taught social planning and social work ethics.

Yvonne Crichton-Hill is a Senior Lecturer with the School of Social Work and Human Services, University of Canterbury. She is a registered social worker and has experience in social work practice, social work education and in social work with Pacific communities. Yvonne currently serves on the New Zealand Social Workers Registration Board. Her research interests include family violence, fieldwork and culturally responsive social work practice.

Ronnie Egan is a Lecturer in Social Work at Victoria University. She teaches in the skills, organisational context and human development aspects of the course and provides consultative supervision across fields of practice in the human services sector.

Mark Furlong is a Senior Lecturer in the School of Social Work at La Trobe University where he coordinates the 'Direct Practice' and 'Diversity' sequences. Prior to taking up this position, Mark practised for twenty years, including the last ten years as Senior Social Worker/ Clinical Coordinator at Bouverie Family Therapy Centre. As well as extensive practice research in the fields of child protection, mental illness and acquired brain injury, Mark's research concentrates on social connectedness and relationally based practice.

Alison Lewis-Nicholson is a social worker and family therapist who works in Geelong. She works in a practice where the main emphasis is on using strengths-based principles. Her main interest is working with couples and families. She enjoys working with them as it involves degrees of complexity, and demands creativity and flexibility. Alison also provides external supervision and has taught with Ronnie Egan at Victoria University for a number of years.

Jane Maidment is a Senior Lecturer in Deakin University's School of Health and Social Development. She has been involved in teaching social work practice skills for fourteen years, in both Australia and New Zealand. Her main research interests are focused on social work education, the health and welfare of older people, and most recently using domestic craft as a vehicle for social connectedness.

Ken McMaster is based in Christchurch, New Zealand. He works as a principal trainer/facilitator with Hall McMaster & Associates Ltd, which is involved in the design and delivery of training and supervision programs for workers in the human services. Ken himself is well known in the social services sector, having worked extensively in the family violence and sexual abuse area, in addition to having lectured part-time in the Department of Social Work, University of Canterbury. He has a thorough understanding of social justice issues, but more significantly has eighteen years' experience delivering groupwork programs in the addictions, violence and sexual abuse areas. Ken has published two books on violence and recently co-edited *Will They Do It Again? Assessing and Managing Risk* (HMA Books, 2006). He is known for his innovative practice ideas and his ability to translate theory into practice.

Robyn Miller is a social worker and family therapist with over 25 years' experience in the field. She has worked in the public and private sectors as a therapist supervisor, consultant and trainer for a range of organisations and academic institutions. She has been a member of the Victorian Child Death Review Committee for the past five years and was the recipient of the inaugural Robin Clark Memorial PhD scholarship. For the past two years, she has provided practice leadership as the Principal Practitioner in the Children, Youth and Families Division of the Department of Human Services in Victoria.

Christine Morley currently works as a Senior Lecturer in social work at the University of the Sunshine Coast, Queensland. She has been a social work practitioner and academic for the past ten years. Her practice experience has been predominantly in the fields of grief and loss, and sexual assault. Her main teaching and research passions include critical social work, anti-oppressive theory and practice, and critical reflection. She has published widely in these areas.

Delia O'Donohue has a Masters in Social Work from Monash University. She is currently working as a program manager at Jesuit Social Services in Victoria, managing a pre-employment training program for young people with complex needs and a dual diagnosis counselling and outreach program. Before joining Jesuit Social Services, Delia worked as a Lecturer in Social Work at Monash University for seven years. She has extensive experience working with disadvantaged young people, and has undertaken research and evaluation work in relation to their health and vocational training needs.

Daryle Rigney is an Associate Professor in the Yunggorendi, First Nations Centre for Higher Education and Research at Flinders University in Adelaide. His research interests include theoretically informed transformative strategies for the political, social, economic and cultural advancement and development of Indigenous/Ngarrindjeri people.

PART I

Preparing to learn practice skills

1

INTRODUCTION: THE INTEGRATED FRAMEWORK

Jane Maidment and Ronnie Egan

This text is primarily aimed at teaching and learning practice skills for social work and welfare students in Australia and New Zealand. In writing, collecting and editing these chapters, we have used material that reflects contemporary practice issues, debates and dilemmas students are likely to encounter in their field placements. Nine practitioners and six academics have contributed to this second edition of the text, and changes that have been made reflect recent shifts in the human service sector in Australia and New Zealand. The various case studies highlight the diversity of practice settings and challenges in the current human service context. Many of the specific interpersonal skills we discuss throughout the text will be helpful for students, not only in their professional capacity as future practitioners, but also in day-to-day encounters with colleagues, peers, family and friends. Although the content of the text is important, we believe the process for teaching and learning these skills is equally significant. We have therefore also aimed to create a 'culture of learning' within the text that will challenge, motivate and inspire students to actively experiment with practice styles and critically examine their own values.

Our subtitle, 'More than Just Common Sense', suggests that there are problems with relying on the veracity of what is called 'common sense'. Further, it suggests that we need more than common sense in our practice. We believe it is important to have both an understanding of what common sense is and its limitations. Limitations, if unrecognised, can have a profound negative impact upon practice. Common sense assumes a sound practical perception or understanding that we share. The difficulty with this view is that there is an underlying notion that common sense accords with the dominant cultural view. The implications of such a view, if left unchallenged or unacknowledged, can lead to misunderstandings between people. This is especially the case between people of differing groups, each of whom may have a markedly different understanding of common sense. These different understandings reflect human roles, social norms and values. In this text, we encourage students to look beyond this dominant notion and recognise the impact of diverse cultural understandings in our practice. Further, students will explore beyond common sense by grappling with different ideologies, theories, skills and phases of the work, as highlighted in the Integrated Framework used in this text.

In this chapter, we wish to explain the Integrated Framework, which has underpinned the foundation, content and theoretical approaches used throughout the text. This framework is significant as it will help students to understand how we have interpreted and presented the use of certain skills within an explicit ideological perspective, drawing on different practice theories to assist in our understanding and work with clients. Next, we identify some similarities and differences between the Australian and New Zealand contexts when it comes to working in welfare. We identify several debates and potential tensions related to the application of practice and use of theory that students may encounter in their field placements and subsequent workplaces. These tensions will be flagged and discussed in order that they can be related to the ensuing case scenarios and exercises. Finally, we examine some of the impacts on both countries of the current global sociopolitical context for practice. In this discussion, we address nomenclature to ensure consistent language (with reference to clients and workers) between the Australian- and New Zealand-authored chapters.

THE INTEGRATED FRAMEWORK

Figure 1.1 illustrates the Integrated Framework we have used to understand, write about and teach practice skills for social work and welfare in this text. There are five components to the framework. These include anti-oppressive practice (AOP) as the foundation of the framework, the practice theories, the skills, the phases of the work and the organisational context. The framework is three-dimensional in that the foundation, skills, phases of helping, theoretical perspectives and organisational context are entirely interwoven. All aspects of the helping transaction are understood in relation to each other, and none of the five components of the matrix can be applied to practice in isolation. The framework is underpinned by an anti-oppressive foundation. This foundation is used throughout the text as a means of understanding and analysing the application of theory to practice, and for guiding the use of micro-skills in work with individuals, families and groups. Each dimension of the framework will now be defined and explained.

Figure 1.1 The Integrated Framework

ANTI-OPPRESSIVE PRACTICE

Our understanding of teaching and learning practice skills is predicated on the notion that the source of individual problems is located within the wider societal context. Appreciation of this involves the worker understanding oppression, inequity and the impact of marginalisation on individuals, groups and families. This entails the worker developing self-awareness in order to identify how her or his own values and the mandate of the agency could further contribute to, or challenge, oppression.

Oppression is the domination of subordinate groups in society by more powerful groups who have vested interests in maintaining the inequitable structures and social relations that ensue. We understand oppression as operating across and between three levels. These levels are structural oppression, cultural oppression and personal oppression (Dominelli, 1997; Thompson, 1998; Mullaly, 2002).

Structural oppression refers to the means by which powerlessness and marginalisation are institutionalised in societal relations. This type of oppression concerns the ways that social institutions, laws, policies, social processes and practices work together in favour of the dominant group at the expense of the subordinate group or groups within society (Mullaly, 2002, p. 49). Cultural oppression refers to those dominant sets of knowledge, values, behaviours and customs that are privileged at the expense of others in any given society. Cultural dominance and oppression can be understood as occurring across broad social divisions, and are not limited to analysing issues of ethnicity. Discrimination occurs on the basis of gender, class, sexuality, ability or age. Personal oppression refers to the negative impact of interpersonal relationships, attitudes and actions between people.

Anti-oppressive practice entails workers both acknowledging and challenging these three levels of oppression—structural, cultural and personal—in their daily practice. This understanding is incorporated into social work and welfare practice with clients by actively using strategies to bring about change at all three levels. Workers who are anti-oppressive in their practice recognise that they personally may reproduce oppressive practices which need to be challenged. Similarly, they will also recognise that the agency mandate under which they operate may be oppressive. The process of critical reflection, described later in the chapter, enables us to explore these tensions further.

Our focus in this text is on work with individuals, groups and families. We have used the notion of empowerment to translate anti-oppressive ideas into practice. In order to do this, we have drawn upon strengths-based theories (Saleebey, 1992) to demonstrate how skills can be used in emancipatory practice. The strengths-based theories are embedded in an understanding of social, environmental, economic and cultural influences that impact on individuals. Strengths-based theories challenge traditional models, which focus on problem identification and individual deficits, by instead identifying and building upon client strengths and resources that can be used to address personal concerns.

We have encouraged all authors in this book to locate the learning of practice skills and the application of theory within broad cultural dimensions. As noted above, these dimensions include understanding age, gender, class, indigeneity and cross-cultural dynamics within the context of helping relationships. The application of theoretical perspectives discussed in the following chapters has therefore been strongly embedded within a broad structural analysis of power, oppression and the marginalisation of particular client groups. This ideology forms the foundation of the Integrated Framework of Practice.

UNDERSTANDING DIVERSITY

Australian and New Zealand practitioners differ in the emphasis they bring to work with Indigenous and migrant populations. In Australia, practice is located in a more culturally diverse context where emphasis has been given to understanding the delivery of welfare from this perspective. In New Zealand, a commitment to the development of bicultural practice and the principles of the Treaty of Waitangi has become a major organising construct for practice (Connolly, 2001b, pp. 26–7). For the purposes of teaching and learning practice skills, we have asked authors to focus case studies and exercises on scenarios that address issues from both bicultural and culturally diverse perspectives. You will find in these chapters an emphasis placed on tackling issues of culture. This focus is not confined to examining questions of ethnicity. We have endeavoured to incorporate examples that highlight diversity in terms of working with age, gender, sexuality and class. In essence, understanding diversity from this broad perspective challenges students to examine assumptions, investigate their world-view and in the process become critically reflective practitioners. Chapter 3 provides an overview of how AOP is incorporated with strengths-based theories.

THEORY AND PRACTICE

Much has been written exploring the divide between theory and practice in social work and welfare delivery (Barbour, 1984; Papell, 1996). This debate has seen tutors and academics labelled as being out of touch with practice (Marsh & Triseliotis, 1996, p. 61), while workers have been described as 'practical folk' (Howe, 1986, p. 2). We believe both theory and practice can only be understood in relation to the broad social context in which services are delivered. This context will influence social norms and expectations, political ideology and ideas of legitimacy. While there has been long-standing debate between students, academics and practitioners about the ascendency of either practice or theory, we have conceptualised the use of skills, theory, ideology, phases and organisational context of practice as a whole, where each aspect of the framework influences the other (see Figure 1.1). In this way, we do not believe that practice should be a slave to theory, or that certain skills should only be used within specific practice settings. We consider the relationship between theory and practice to be symbiotic, ever-changing and reflexive. Differing theories may inform practice, but at the same time theoretical perspectives can be contested, developed further and changed in light of practice outcomes. This iterative process between revising practice and adapting theory is called praxis (Ife, 1999). We invite you to grapple with the tensions inherent in understanding the relationship between theory and practice over the course of learning these practice skills.

Workers use sets of ideas and principles to guide and inform their practice, and together these form specific theoretical viewpoints. Practitioners rarely adhere to just one particular theoretical perspective in their work with clients. Most workers explain their practice as being informed by a blend of ideas originating from several theoretical approaches. In this text, we include explanations and the application of a number of practice theories. These include predominantly strengths-based practice approaches including solution-focused, narrative, ecological/systems theory and crisis intervention.

MICRO-SKILLS

This term refers to a large set of individual verbal and non-verbal communication techniques that, when combined, form the basis for the way we communicate with others. In the second part of this text you will learn about using the following micro-skills:

listening	reflecting	clarifying	conflict
responding	paraphrasing	negotiation	management
using empathy	using silence	prioritising	affirming
summarising	assertiveness	normalising	using immediacy
questioning	goal-setting	challenging	boundary-setting

conciliation	interpreting	universalising	confronting
transfer and	verbal and		recording
referral	non-verbal cues		

Learning how to recognise and use these skills takes practice. You will find discussion on the ways to learn practice skills in Chapter 2. For the purposes of understanding the place of micro-skills within the Integrated Framework, it is sufficient to note that all personal interactions are composed of an inventory of many techniques. In this text, we focus on using a selection of those techniques to facilitate and understand our communication with and among clients, and in community settings. That is, the skills demonstrated throughout each chapter are transferable across the micro/macro continuum of practice.

PHASES OF THE HELPING PROCESS

We have used a generic model to discuss the various phases of the helping relationship. The notion of phases breaks down the helping process into discrete parts, in order to readily identify the components and purpose of each phase. There are four main phases of the helping process, and these include the beginning of the helping relationship, (engagement and collaborative assessment), taking action, intervention and termination. Different types of evaluation procedures occur throughout the process. Each of these phases signposts a different stage of the helping process, although it can never be assumed that the worker and client transaction proceeds in a linear fashion from engagement through to termination. The micro-skills we have listed above will be used in all phases of helping, but some skills may be used more than others at different stages. For instance, during the initial meeting and engagement with a client, the worker will be predominantly listening, reflecting and beginning to use questioning. Later, during the intervention phase, goal-setting, immediacy and confronting micro-skills are more likely to be used. In this way, the use of micro-skills and phases of the helping process are linked.

ORGANISATIONAL CONTEXT

The final component of the Integrated Framework is the organisational context. This refers to the organisation in which human services practice occurs. This component provides the parameters that govern practice.

In summary, the Integrated Framework provides a template for conceptualising the interrelationship between practice skills, phases of the helping process, the organisational process, theory and ideology. It is a framework that must be understood in relation to the specific context in which the welfare services are being delivered. All authors have located the case studies and exercises within an Australian or New Zealand cultural milieu. While these countries share some similarities in terms of the models used and ways in which current welfare services are delivered, the cultural context of each is quite unique. Acknowledging and working with the shades of difference between these two countries has been a significant challenge in compiling this text.

THE CONTEXT FOR WELFARE DELIVERY IN AUSTRALIA AND NEW ZEALAND

In order to have an appreciation of the current challenges of the human service sector experienced by individuals and communities in both Australia and New Zealand today, it is critical to understand the links between the historical antecedents and the present social conditions. Both countries share a history that has been shaped by nineteenth-century European colonisation and immigration. This feature has impacted greatly on the Indigenous populations of both countries, acting as it has to dispossess both Maori and Aboriginal people of their land and fracturing these cultures through a process of 'spiritual and intellectual colonization' (Matahaere-Atariki et al., 2001, p. 128). In both countries, the long-lasting and continuing effects of dispossession and alienation are evident. Indicators for social wellbeing show that both Maori and Aboriginal people are currently disadvantaged in most aspects of daily living. This includes having lower life expectancy, higher rates of hospital admissions, lower levels of education and qualification attainment, and greater levels of imprisonment compared with the non-Indigenous populations (Federal Race Discrimination Commissioner, 1997; Te Puni Kokiri, 2002). Reasons for the inequity between Indigenous and non-Indigenous populations are complex. Mainstream systems of education, health and employment dominate and perpetuate the continued marginalisation of Indigenous populations and their culture.

Australia and New Zealand therefore share a history of early and ongoing colonisation. Meanwhile, practitioners in both countries are in the process of developing new and different practice responses to address the influence of contemporary social trends. In recent years, both countries have experienced an exponential growth in the aged population, refugee immigration, escalating crime rates, increases in reported cases of child abuse, homelessness, alcohol and drug addiction and mental illness (Council for Aboriginal Reconciliation, 1995; Povey, 2002). Within this context, the paradigm of risk-assessment has grown in popularity and use.

In New Zealand, the Treaty of Waitangi, signed in 1840, provides a touchstone from which contemporary Maori are acknowledged as *tangata whenua*, or 'people of the land'. As such, Maori are able to contest current land ownership, test legislation and use the principles of the Treaty to legitimate their rightful place as equal participants in agency and citizenship. As a result, practitioners in New Zealand are alert to approaching client concerns and analysis of current issues from a bicultural perspective. This bicultural stance is further strengthened through the competency assessment process required from those practitioners wishing to become members of the Aotearoa New Zealand Association of Social Work (ANZASW). Indigenous Australians have no equivalent of the Treaty of Waitangi in Australian law.

Authors have used material in their chapters that examines practice from both bicultural and cross-cultural perspectives. In Chapter 5, for example, Lesley Cooper and Daryle Rigney focus on a historical view of Indigenous oppression. Such a focus is in line with anti-oppressive practice and provides a template for students to examine their understanding of personal, cultural and structural levels of oppression. Chapter 14 demonstrates a bicultural model in working with Maori men in a group setting. Further chapters on learning practice skills incorporate work with both Maori and Australian Indigenous clients, and address Indigenous concerns as they relate to practice. Meanwhile, Chapters 11 and 12 include material that explores practice from a cross-cultural perspective. Reflections of these shades of difference between Australian and New Zealand society are evident in the case studies. Nevertheless, all case study material, exercises and discussion in this text are relevant to students learning practice skills from either Australia or New Zealand. There are many individual and community struggles common to both countries, and the material in the following chapters has been designed to address issues that students are likely to encounter in the field.

ADDRESSING STRUCTURAL INEQUALITY IN THE CURRENT CONTEXT

The current context of welfare delivery in both Australia and New Zealand is characterised by widening social inequities and uncertainties between the dominant rich and the subordinate poor (Weeks & Quinn, 2000). Such inequities reflect the broader politics of globalisation dominated by wealthy corporations, institutions and states which set the agenda for the distribution of resources. This agenda supports the liberal-humanist notion of redistributive justice, which has become the dominant methodology in human service provision (Mullaly, 2002). Relationships between workers and clients increasingly have become conceptualised in terms of procedural, legal and administrative issues, resulting in an emphasis on contracted, time- and cost-limited service provision (Howe, 1998). In conjunction with these changes, there has been an increasing emphasis on meeting service agreement targets with concrete outcomes, while risk-assessment protocols have become a key strategy to use in prioritising resources (Parton, 1996). In a context of rising litigation, more intense public scrutiny in service provision and competition for government funding (Beddoe & Randal, 1994; Egan, 2005), practitioners require a strong structural analysis to maintain a position of ethical and practice integrity.

QUESTIONS OF ETHICS

All workers will encounter ethical dilemmas in their daily practice, and these are evident in the case scenarios presented in each chapter. Both Australia and Aotearoa New Zealand Associations of Social Work (AASW and ANZASW) have a Code of Ethics to guide practice. Chapter 3 discusses the overlap between the AOP, strengths-based approaches and professional practice. On their own, codified standards are not sufficient to equip practitioners for negotiating complex case scenarios and decision-making processes. Throughout the text, students are invited to consider the tensions generated by competing demands, scarce resources, different ideological viewpoints and the mandates for intervention that form the context of diverse practice settings. Balancing the need to be challenging and confronting with some clients against a desire to practise in a way that acknowledges structural inequality is a dilemma that workers frequently negotiate. The Western notion of building rapport and trust with clients while maintaining 'professional boundaries' is a further contestable area of practice. Conducting a mandated mental health assessment while at the same time trying to facilitate client empowerment can appear contradictory. Similarly, the mandatory attendance of justice clients presents a challenge to the practice of anti-oppressive principles. Endeavouring to practise in a way that takes account of cross-cultural difference when we can never fully know or understand another person's culture provides yet another challenge for the worker. These dilemmas are further compounded when workers find themselves practising in environments that can be hostile to social work or welfare intervention, lacking in staff resources and in a political climate characterised by risk management.

In the following chapters, we have attempted to expose students to the practice tensions, contradictions and dilemmas that will be faced in field placement and in the years ahead.

PRACTICE CONTRADICTIONS AND DILEMMAS

Practitioners encounter a range of contradictions and dilemmas in their daily practice. We believe these can be summarised under two central tensions. The first tension addresses the issue of whether social work and welfare delivery are acts of care or control. The second tension is concerned with the question of where current practitioners focus their change efforts. Should workers be most intent upon bringing about individual or structural change, and what are the implications in terms of practice for each of these positions? These dilemmas are briefly discussed below.

Care versus control

When people apply to undertake studies in welfare or social work, they often do so because they are motivated to help others. However, as you read through and consider the material in this text, the question of whether the worker facilitates care or control in their practice with clients will be raised many times. For overt examples of social control, consider the role practitioners play in juvenile justice, corrections, child protection or mental health secure units. In these settings, some practitioners will be using lock and key or security pins every day to keep their clients separated from the rest of society. This practice has all the hallmarks of social control. Are workers in these settings simply ameliorating the impacts of social control, or do they serve to humanise a process that might otherwise be entirely disempowering?

In Chapters 8 and 15, where work with involuntary clients is discussed, this dilemma is explored further. While the juvenile justice and mental health settings provide overt examples of situations where workers appear to carry out functions of social control, we need to remember that control can occur in much more subtle ways. Take, for example, the worker in aged care who gently persuades an older person to go into a residential facility, or the worker in a primary school who uses techniques of behaviour modification to help improve a child's performance in the classroom. Are these acts of care or control? Essentially, both situations demonstrate subtle forms of social control, yet they are likely to be motivated by the worker's desire to facilitate a good outcome for the client. In this debate, the degree to which client choice and self-determination have been factored into the helping process impacts on where the workers' actions lie on the care and control continuum.

Individual or social change?

In the above examples, the challenge for the worker is to strike a balance between addressing the immediate practical or psychosocial needs of the client, while also tackling the macro social inequities that impact on individuals in a negative way. For example, we know that people with mental health issues are more likely to be on low incomes and have fewer social networks (Bland, cited in Alston & McKinnon, 2001). We also know that the growing numbers of older people in society have fuelled a mounting industry in aged care housing, the production of disability products and personal security alarm systems. This industry is essentially ageist in its focus, having been founded upon making profit from promoting notions of safety and security in a climate of fear. A tension therefore exists for the worker in addressing the immediate concerns of the client and their family, when it is clear that broader social pressures and structures are exacerbating individual problems. Apart from community development workers, the majority of practitioners are employed by agencies to intervene at an individual, group or family level. This leaves the worker little time to address the macro concerns that cause individual problems. In the following chapters, we ask students to think about the structural inequalities that impact on the people we work with, and consider how to go about addressing these in daily practice. This approach to working with clients is referred to as anti-oppressive, and in its own way it presents a further challenge or contradiction for practitioners to deal with. We believe critical reflection provides a way to assist students to work productively with these tensions.

CRITICALLY REFLECTIVE PRACTICE

Critical reflection is a specific technique and process which workers can use to examine their own professional and personal responses in relation to situations encountered in the field. It is possible to facilitate critical reflection in a number of ways. Often field educators use this process within supervision, and students will critically reflect upon how their own attitudes impact on their work with clients. Jan Fook (1999) explains that the process of critical reflection involves 'the ability to locate oneself in a situation through the recognition of how actions and interpretations, social and cultural background and personal history, emotional aspects of experience, and personally held assumptions and values influence the situation' (1999, p. 199).

Critical reflection is therefore a deeply personal process that can lead to workers developing greater self-awareness and changing the way they see themselves in relation to practice, broader social issues, questions of ethics and interpersonal relationships. Engaging in critical reflection also entails thinking about how practice relates to theory and considering how theory may in turn be reshaped to reflect contemporary and changing social contexts. It is therefore a process that fosters an integration of self, theory and practice in a way that is dynamic, sharpening our view and understanding of factors that influence the way we think and behave towards others.

As a student, you can facilitate your own critical reflection by keeping a journal of your reactions and decision-making processes, significant practice events and the dilemmas that might trip you up during the course of your studies. Over time, you may see patterns emerging in terms of issues that you find testing, areas of particular interest, and recurring questions about notions of individual or social change. A journal such as this will provide you with a rich learning resource, which you can use to trace your development as a practitioner.

HOW TO USE THIS TEXT

The material in this text has been divided into six sections. Part I, 'Preparing to Learn Practice Skills', includes five chapters that can be used in teaching and learning micro-skills. These chapters cover topics related to the experience of learning practice skills in a group setting and preparation for client contact. They aim to provide an overview of the micro–macro practice approaches used in work with clients and should be read in the beginning weeks of the semester. The material presented in Chapters 1, 2 and 3 focuses on the first session together. Part II, 'Phases of the Helping Relationship', focuses on students' learning specific practice skills related to the different stages of service delivery with clients. This section begins with an introductory chapter to each phase of the helping relationship, followed by chapters with related case material. Each chapter in Part II identifies a set of practice skills and uses a case study to demonstrate how workers may apply these skills. The case studies are written to present realistic scenarios that students could encounter on field placement. Each chapter in this part also includes discussion on a particular theoretical perspective, and contains a set of exercises students can use to learn the micro-skills, and consider the broader social and ethical issues raised from the case study material. The final part of the book sums up its themes in a conclusion.

We have designed the text to be used in a linear fashion during the course of the semester, where students begin at Chapter 1 and work their way forward as the weeks progress. In order to cover all the material in one semester, it will be necessary for students to complete some of the exercises and reading as homework. This way, classroom time can be used to focus on discussion, demonstration and practice of the micro-skills, and having summary discussion and debates about case material presented. Most chapters include exercises that students can also do in pairs or groups during the class session, and that also be adapted for online distance education.

LANGUAGE

There is a range of terminology used in the naming of workers and clients. Workers will be referred to as social workers, service providers, welfare workers, service coordinators, youth workers, practitioners or human service workers. Throughout this text, we have chosen the generic terms 'worker', 'practitioner' or 'human service worker' to describe those in the role of delivering the service. Similarly, clients are referred to by differing titles depending on the context. Clients may also be called 'patients', 'service users', 'consumers' or 'customers'. We have mainly used the term 'clients' to describe those people accessing services. Throughout this text, students will encounter terminology that is unique to human service work. We are mindful that learning to practise involves gaining an understanding of how language and specific terminologies are used in relation to providing services to clients. We have been careful to include definitions of specific terms such as 'risk-assessment' or 'contracting' in the context of social work and welfare practice.

Needless to say, language is a strong indicator of ideology, and of the approach and understanding of worker and client agency. We received a potent reminder of this when we were considering the use of the terms 'voluntary' and 'involuntary' client. From an anti-oppressive perspective, what client could ever truly be defined as 'voluntary'? Who would choose to be burdened with poverty or mental ill-health, discrimination or issues of violence? These conditions are the products of structural inequality and, as such, the distinction between voluntary and involuntary clients appears to be somewhat spurious. Mostly we have referred to 'involuntary' clients as being mandated clients—that is, they have no choice about being service recipients.

CONCLUSION

In this introduction, we have set the scene for learning about practice skills. In the first instance we explained the Integrated Framework (see Figure 1.1), which provides the conceptual scaffolding on which the rest of the text is based. We examined the similarities and differences between Australian and New Zealand practice contexts, and aired the tensions, debates and questions of ethics that students are likely to encounter in the field. Finally, we discussed using critical reflection as a means to deconstruct and grapple with the thorny issues that make social work and welfare practice both exciting and memorable. In the next chapter, you will find material that highlights some of the principles of successful learning in this subject.

We wish you well with your studies, and hope that you enjoy working through the text. We have certainly enjoyed putting these chapters together, and feel confident that the material reflects the diversity of practice environments and types of cases you will encounter in your field placements and future career.

No single book can provide guidelines to encompass the range of situations that can arise in practice. While we have provided general information about skills you need to develop and typical practice situations, clearly practitioners need to use their own discretion and exercise caution in their work. If you have concerns about a practice issue, there is no substitute for discussing this with a supervisor or colleagues.

2

SKILL-BASED LEARNING

Jane Maidment

Have you ever seen a photo of yourself that you just detest? Alternatively, have you ever seen and heard yourself on video and cringed? For many students, confronting self-perceptions about how they look, speak and act with others is the biggest hurdle embedded in learning practice skills. The purpose of this chapter is to closely examine the challenges inherent in undertaking practice skills education, with the aim of ensuring this learning process is both safe and supportive, while remaining exciting and stimulating.

This chapter begins with a brief discussion about notions of collaborative peer learning and teamwork, which are the vehicles for the iterative teaching and learning process in this subject area. Next, some of the strategies commonly used in learning practice skills are outlined. These include the use of technologies such as video and audio recording, practising role-plays and giving and receiving feedback. Students are introduced to the notion of working with diversity, and provided with guidelines for working with interpreters. This is followed by a discussion about the assumptions we bring to social service work.

The teaching and learning of interpersonal communication skills in a Western cultural context involves:

- students being involved in collaborative learning activities with their peers

- frequent use of audio-visual equipment, such as audio and video/ DVD recordings
- giving and receiving constructive feedback between students and between the class facilitator and the student group.

Learning practice skills is therefore a participatory process, where students are constantly engaged in listening, observing, reflecting upon and practising their own interactions with others. Some students retreat from this learning for fear that they may make a fool of themselves in front of others. It is also important to acknowledge that not all students will necessarily have been educated in a Western system. As such, the capacity of some students to actively experiment and demonstrate skills in peer groups could be challenged. It is not unusual for adult students to feel self-conscious, shy and sometimes anxious about engaging in skills group learning. Given this context, the critical first task for the group is to create a 'safe' learning environment where a culture of trust, respect and support is promoted and nurtured throughout. The role of the facilitator at this stage is to work with the group to generate shared understandings of how the group will work together, fostering principles that underpin collaborative peer learning and teamwork. We recommend that all practice skills teachers who choose to use this text complete the exercises before using them with students. Using these exercises, as a teacher, highlights the points of contradiction in practice. As we found in developing many of these exercises and in our own experience in the classroom, completing the exercises before the class makes the material live for the business of learning.

COLLABORATIVE LEARNING

In brief, learning practice skills collaboratively involves students in a wide range of activities. These may include observing and reflecting upon role-plays, offering constructive and immediate feedback to peers regarding interview performance, designing and making case presentations, recording video and/or audio tapes of role-plays, writing case reports and doing mock risk-assessments. Self-evaluation and observation of others at work, practising, reflecting and giving feedback are techniques used to reinforce the learning.

The group itself is the most valuable and dynamic resource to use in learning practice skills. Each student has a wealth of experiences, insights and observations that they can contribute to strengthen the learning of others. Peer learning and the development of teamwork skills do not develop automatically just because a group is formed to work and learn together. First, it is important for students to begin to explore what they hope to learn from being part of the group and to be clear about their own personal strengths and weaknesses in terms of engaging in an interactive learning environment. We acknowledge that this might be difficult for students to do; nevertheless, this process engenders a culture of developing self-awareness.

Exercise 2.1

- In pairs, discuss your past experiences of being part of a participatory, collaborative learning environment. What did you like about it? What didn't you like about it? Write down these likes and dislikes.
- In discussion with your partner, identify what personal strengths you will bring to the participatory learning group. Write these down.
- Next, identify what areas you believe you need to develop in terms of your own practice skills, and also your own ability to work as part of a team. Note these down.
- As a class, share these likes, dislikes, strengths and areas for development. While having this discussion as a class, also focus on strategies for addressing the dislikes and thinking about ways of addressing the individual areas of development.
- Keep a record of this discussion, individual contributions and class strategies. Use this baseline information as one tool for evaluating the learning and group process at the end of the semester.

Giving and receiving continuous feedback is one of the primary ways for learning how to demonstrate practice skills, and therefore it needs to occur in an ongoing way during class.

GIVING, RECEIVING AND USING CONSTRUCTIVE FEEDBACK

In some educational contexts, feedback is conceptualised and packaged as a 'gift' in the learning process (Askew & Lodge, 2000). Nevertheless, we have all experienced occasions when the 'gift' has not been what we want. In recognition of the ambivalence most feel about giving and receiving feedback, others have endeavoured to reframe the process of feedback as a mechanistic model which needs to be used with great delicacy. In particular, discussion about attempts to use feedback would be incomplete without acknowledging and exploring notions of honesty, truth and compassion (Rubin & Campbell, 1998).

Exercise 2.2

- Take a moment to think about a time when you received some very constructive feedback about something on which you could improve. What had you done? Try to remember your feelings, thoughts and actions at the time. Identify these and write them down.
- Now think about a time when you were given feedback about something you did not do well and the feedback was given in an unhelpful way. What was the feedback? What form did it take? How did you feel? What did you do? Note down your responses to these questions.
- Discuss these incidents with a partner. Jot down specifically what was helpful about the feedback you received in the first instance and what was not helpful about the feedback you received in the second instance. Now as a whole group, and drawing from your own experiences, create a list of helpful and unhelpful ways in which to give feedback.

From this exercise, it will become clear that there are both hurtful and helpful ways to give feedback to others. Learning some principles and techniques about giving feedback will be one of the first skills developed in the collaborative group setting. Some principles of giving feedback are listed below.

Feedback:

- describes rather than evaluates behaviour;
- shares perceptions rather than offers advice;
- identifies specific current behaviours rather than recalls incidents from the past;
- reports positive behaviours as well as points to improve;
- keeps pace with the student's readiness (Miley et al., 2001, p. 311).

Giving the feedback, is just half of the equation, however. How do you receive feedback? It is not uncommon to feel defensive about receiving feedback. Most people can think of occasions when they have felt or reacted badly to what has been constructive feedback. Addressing immediate negative feelings and reactions to constructive criticism is one of the challenges you will quickly confront in learning practice skills. Acknowledging the personal vulnerability and the humanness of defensive responses within the group setting will normalise these reactions.

The next step in the process of learning to work with feedback is to conceptualise feedback as a tool and a resource we all use in our daily lives to adapt our behaviour, refine our skills and learn more about how to practise effectively. Whenever you are in a position of receiving feedback in class, at home or in the workplace, try to do so by:

- being open and non-defensive;
- listening carefully to what the person is saying to you;
- being aware of your own self-talk (the dialogue we have with ourselves) that is occurring at the same time as the feedback is being received;
- acknowledging the feedback in a positive way.

There are many texts that give advice on how to give, receive and use feedback (Myers Kirst, 2000; Cleak & Wilson, 2004). In each of them, the message is clear: the result we are hoping to achieve is a process of exchange, whereby feedback acts as a tool for learning more and better ways of doing things.

One of the problems that can arise in supportive class settings is that students may be unwilling to give feedback to other students about practice skills that can be improved. In this way, students may overcompensate for the nervousness of their peers by only giving positive feedback. However, the conceptualisation of feedback as a tool and resource for learning links directly with the notion of 'use of self' in practice. Use of self entails drawing from your own knowledge, experience and perceptions in a way that contributes to the learning or helping context (Harms, 2007). The process of giving balanced feedback to peers is a concrete example of the 'use of self' in social work practice.

Receiving feedback from others is one way to learn how to judge and modify our own practice skills. Using technologies that allow for self-evaluation is another way to develop an awareness of strengths and areas to modify when learning practice skills.

USING AUDIO-VISUAL/DIGITAL RECORDING

For several decades, video/digital technology has been used to assist students to learn practice skills across a range of disciplines (Cassata et al., 1977; Bauman, 1981; Munson, 1993; Hulsman et al., 2004). Currently, most social work and welfare courses will have access to video or digital systems, and this section has been written with that in mind. With the development of digital recording facilities, it is possible for students to record role-plays and presentations and upload them on to the web for viewing. Viewing would, of course, be restricted by password to other class members. In this way, distance education students can have better access to the work of on-campus peers, while the facilitator can also view the work of distance students more readily than work sent by mail and viewing of conventional video tapes allow.

Typically, the atmosphere of the group changes immediately the first time a video or digital camera and monitor are set up for use in the classroom. There are exclamations of horror and it is not hard to see that students feel exposed by these technologies. Nevertheless—like feedback—the use of the camera and recording technology in this type of education is an invaluable learning tool. However, it is true that while practitioners acknowledge the very useful role video/digital and audio recording has in developing and reviewing practice skills, many dislike using these technologies themselves (Shulman, 1993). This is because numerous current practitioners can recall various humiliating experiences of viewing themselves when the use of the technology and the feedback processes were not managed with compassion. We know, however, that the use of audio-visual recording enables students to carry out self-assessment (Barrie, 1996), sets the pace for their own learning (Bauman, 1981) and provides clear evidence of original student work (Marsh & Triseliotis, 1996). While the technology helps us to develop critiques of our work and enables us to acquire better practice skills, recording client sessions for analysis in supervision also enhances professional transparency and accountability in human service work (Maidment, 2000).

The task, therefore, is to use recording technologies with established guidelines for how feedback and viewing will be managed. Listed below are some strategies to sustain a supportive learning environment while using these technologies:

- There needs to be group agreement about how recordings will be stored and who will have access to them.

- Confidentiality is highlighted and discussion regarding any student recording made in the sessions is confined to the classroom or online discussion noticeboard.
- Students need a hands-on demonstration and instruction in the first session about how to access, set up and use the recording equipment.
- Students have the first opportunity to provide self-evaluative feedback on their own performance before others comment.
- All students need to play the worker role as often as possible in order to maximise the amount of practice and feedback individuals receive in each session.

Before students attempt to do role-plays on tape, it is preferable for the facilitator to first demonstrate being the worker in a role-play, while having the session recorded. By doing a role-play, viewing the recording, providing self-evaluation and reflection, and then receiving feedback from the class, the facilitator is modelling the process that will be used throughout. Recordings should be short in the first instance so that there is a quick turnover of practice, observation, reflection and feedback to keep all class participants actively involved. Students may like to use their own videotape or DVD so that personal skill development in the worker role can be captured over time as a sequence of recordings and used to develop a recorded portfolio of work.

Exercise 2.3
Different teaching institutions will have access to a variety of audio-visual technology. In groups of three or four, take turns at setting up the video/digital equipment. Record a short conversation between two students and then play this conversation back on the monitor.

It is not uncommon for people to experience 'stage fright' at first when recording. This might take the form of not being able to think of something to say, or laughing at the wrong moment. When this happens, it is important for the facilitator and other group members to act as a 'live supervision team'. This means grouping together with the student who is in the worker role to form strategies about how the taped interview may proceed. Strategies could include giving possible suggestions for the next worker statement in the interview, or reflecting on how the client may be feeling at this particular point in the interview. These approaches are integral to using role-play in teaching and learning practice skills for welfare and social work.

USING ROLE-PLAYS FOR LEARNING

Using role-plays to learn social work and welfare practice enables us to:

- develop interpersonal skills in a way that will not have any negative impacts on real clients;
- grapple with client issues that could emerge from a range of diverse agency contexts;
- demonstrate the application of theoretical knowledge in practice;
- pace the learning so that more complex scenarios are introduced incrementally;
- experiment with different approaches to working with 'clients';
- model ways to be transparent about practice;
- have opportunities to reflect upon 'worker' and 'client' responses.

Role-plays in the classroom setting should *not* be:

- treated as a public theatrical performance;
- used to examine current, authentic personal problems;
- used as a means to shame any individual.

From these checklists, it is possible to recognise the potential richness and dangers inherent in using role-play to learn in the group setting. It is a medium that can quickly expose individual values, along with strengths and limitations, in practice. Students can also find role-playing difficult because they may not see it as 'real'. For these reasons, students are understandably cautious and often reticent to participate, so it is important from the first session to determine with the group the educational objectives and purpose of using role-play (Errington, 1997), and to demonstrate how role-plays work. This may be done by setting up a role-play in the group with the facilitator playing the 'worker' role, or by showing snippets of role-plays that have been recorded for teaching purposes.

To become familiar and more at ease with using role-play, it is necessary for students to frequently and consistently engage with the medium using relevant scenarios. Expectations in terms of how long the role-play will be, and how the feedback and reflections will be facilitated, need to be discussed before practice begins.

It is also essential to map out the role of the observers. Observers play an active part in contributing to the role-play analysis, and ideally should have a checklist of skills and other matters to focus and make notes on during the role-play.

Exercise 2.4

In groups of four (one worker, one client and two observers), role-play the following scenario.

Role-play scenario: You are a worker at a City Mission emergency relief centre. An older woman comes in and asks for a food parcel. You notice that even though it is a cold winter day, she is not dressed warmly and she has a hacking cough. Role-play the beginning of your conversation with the client, where you endeavour to find out whether there is more you could do to assist the woman.

Before beginning the role-play, jot down four aspects of the role-play the observers need to make notes on. For example, what are the responses given by the worker, or what are the verbal and non-verbal cues given by both worker and client?

Commence the role-play with characters staying in role for five minutes. At the conclusion of the role-play, debrief the characters, give and receive the feedback, and discuss the issues raised in the role-play. Specifically, identify how the person in the worker role demonstrated particular skills, and select one area where the 'worker' could change aspects of the exchange with the 'client' so as to make it more constructive.

Earlier in this chapter, we discussed the necessity for developing a supportive, empathic ethos to learn practice skills in the group. Nevertheless, there may be instances when individual group members demonstrate values in the role-play or discussion that are not consistent with a social work or welfare ethos. Examples of this would be if a group member made racist, ageist, sexist or homophobic comments. In these situations, it is the role of the facilitator and peers to challenge these values and statements in a fair and constructive way. This challenging is likely to take the form of raising student awareness about attitudes, providing information, and investigating underlying assumptions and beliefs while identifying the origins of these values. In particular, when discussing values, it is critical to identify the systemic sources of structural oppression and their impact on the lives of marginalised individuals in the community. This process of making explicit the links between personal problems and political issues is fully discussed elsewhere (Burke & Harrison, 1998; Lee, 2001). Nevertheless, as outlined in Chapter 1, an anti-oppressive foundation that situates individual difficulties within the political dimensions of oppression underpins the way we understand using skills. This perspective therefore has particular relevance for interpersonal communication with client groups who are in some way different from ourselves.

HONOURING DIFFERENCE AND DIVERSITY

Understanding difference in terms of culture or ethnicity is a key component to learning how to work with people who are in some way unlike ourselves. In practice, workers have contact with diverse groups of people. In order to communicate and work effectively with others it is necessary to understand something of the culture of different groups in society.

Exercise 2.5
- In groups of three or four, formulate definitions that demonstrate the difference between the terms 'culture' and 'ethnicity'.
- Next, as individuals, recall a time when you have been immersed in a culture that is completely different to your own. Discuss with the others in the group what you did, and how you felt.

Lum (2001) offers the following definition of culturally diverse practice:

> Culturally diverse social work practice recognises and respects the importance of difference and variety in people and the crucial role of the helping relationship. Its primary focus is on people of color ... who have suffered historical oppression and continue to endure subtle forms of racism, prejudice, and discrimination. In working with an individual, family, group and or community, practitioners draw on the positive strengths of diverse cultural beliefs and practices and are concerned about discriminatory experiences that require approaches sensitive to ethnic cultural environments. (2000: 11)

In this definition, Lum identifies the primary focus being on people of colour. For the purposes of learning practice skills, we would like to extend that definition to include those people who are marginalised on the basis of ethnicity, gender, class, sexuality, ability or age. Recognition that practitioners adopt a strengths perspective and honour difference is at the heart of Lum's definition, and it is this ethos that influences our approach to teaching and learning practice skills.

Some students will have had little or no contact with people from outside their own cultural context. If this is the case, it is not unusual for them to feel self-conscious and somewhat anxious about attempting to understand and communicate effectively with people who are different from them. In the first instance, it is important to gain something of an understanding of the lives and experiences of a diverse range of people. There are numerous ways of going about this, which include differing degrees of engagement.

- Volunteer some time in agencies that work with a client group different from yourself. This requires commitment on your part to meet the requirements and obligations of working in an agency setting.
- Read personal accounts or biographies of people who have addressed adversity and/or oppression in their lives such as:
  - *Black Chicks Talking* by Leah Purcell
  - *A Child Called It* by Dave Pelzer
  - *Becoming an Ally* by Anne Bishop
  - *Hiam* by Eva Sallis
  - *An Angel at My Table* by Janet Frame
  - *The Fox Boy* by Peter Walker
  - *The Whale Rider* by Whiti Ihimaera
  - *Just Another Little Murder* by Phillip Cleary
  - *Snake Dreaming* by Roberta Sykes
  - *My Place* by Sally Morgan
  - Films: *Yol*; *Rabbit Proof Fence*; *Once Were Warriors*; *Ruby and Rata*; *Ngati*; *The Black Balloon*; *Ten Canoes*.
- Develop personal networks with people and agencies with which you may be able to consult on matters of diversity.
- Explore internet sites that focus on fields of practice such as substance abuse, mental health, Indigenous issues or aged care.

By engaging with difference in the above ways, we are attempting to gain an understanding of the culture of a range of groups in society. Acquiring an appreciation of diverse cultural contexts is a complex process that entails learning about 'different life patterns related to conduct, beliefs, traditions, values, language, art, skills and social/ interpersonal relationships' (Lum, 1990, p. 80). Anthropologists have formulated typologies setting out characteristics that can differ between cultures. These include understanding how the following concepts are played out in daily life:

- *Time.* What is the main orientation to time? Is it past, present or future? Do people need to complete tasks, meet deadlines and adhere to plans? If so, this is related to a monochronic understanding of time. Alternatively, are people very flexible with time commitments, can they tackle a series of tasks at once, and are they more committed to people and relationships than completing tasks? These approaches suggest a polychronic understanding of time.
- *Power.* On what basis is power recognised and distributed? What are the formal and informal systems of power distribution? How does class, age, gender, sexuality, ethnicity or religion influence the way power is experienced?
- *Activity.* What sort of activity is valued in the culture: 'being there' or 'doing things' and accomplishing set goals?
- *Relationships.* How are relationships organised—on an individual or collective basis?
- *Space.* How are notions of territory understood? How is space used to communicate different messages? (Gannon, 2001, pp. 17–23)

In Chapter 5, Lesley Cooper and Daryle Rigney provide guidelines for learning specifically about local Indigenous communities. Along with the above suggestions, a commitment to and groundwork in learning about diversity are necessary to become an effective practitioner in your community. Rather than feeling daunted by the prospect of stepping out of the comfort of your own familiar world, consider these explorations as a personal challenge that, when undertaken in a respectful way, will lead you into discovering the individual and collective strengths diversity brings into community living. It is likely that, through undertaking these investigations, you will have some of your cultural assumptions challenged. In the same way, learning practice skills is a time to examine some of your own assumptions about notions of helping.

WORKING WITH INTERPRETERS

If you are working with clients for whom English is a second language or with people who have sensory impairment (such as being partially or totally deaf), it is possible that you will need to engage the services of an interpreter. The role of the interpreter is to translate, and not to act as a cultural adviser. Chapter 11 cautions against using family members, particularly children, or friends of the client to provide translation—with good reason. If sensitive matters are to be discussed, this can be embarrassing for the client and compromising for the client's friend or family member. An unfair burden of responsibility for positive outcomes can be placed on children who translate for their parents, while this arrangement can also lead to a disruption of lines of authority within the family structure (Frey et al., 1990). Generally, professional interpreters adhere to a code of ethics and standards of practice, remain impartial, have excellent language skills and have no former relationship with the client.

A number of the case studies in this book involve work with people who come from cultural backgrounds that will be different from your own. It is quite possible when you consider how you might work with these clients that you would like to contract the services of an interpreter. If this is the case, you may wish to refer to the following checklist to consider before engaging an interpreter:

- What language is required and is there a specific dialect needed?
- Are there political or religious sensitivities that must be considered?
- What level of language skill is required?
- Does the interpreter require specialist knowledge or experience in, for example, psychiatric services?
- Is the gender of the interpreter an issue?
- Has enough time been allocated? Interviews using an interpreter will take twice as long. (Frey et al., 1990, p. 59.)

It is possible you may be able to use telephone interpreting services if you have hands-free or dual-handset telephone facilities. These services are usually more readily accessible and less intrusive. In some situations, however, telephone interpreting is problematic. Where there is a need for a lengthy consultation, the signing of documents or work to be done with several family members, using a telephone interpreting service is not feasible. Some clients may be unfamiliar with or frightened of using the telephone, or may have conditions which make a telephone interview impractical (Frey et al., 1990).

In practice, whoever you find yourself talking to in the role of student or worker, the principle remains the same. Your goal is to facilitate quality communication between yourself and the person you are attempting to assist. To do this, it is important to assess what is needed in a safe and accepting environment. When working with people who are different from ourselves, we need to be particularly careful that we do not let our own assumptions about the client or the situation obstruct our understanding of the client's needs.

Exercise 2.6

Read the following transcript of a real supervision session. The student and the field supervisor are discussing work with older people.

Scenario: The student is working on a hospital ward with elderly people. The discussion is focused on how working with older people is different to work with other client groups.

Field Educator: So what are the things you've noticed about working with elderly clients?

Student: Speak very clearly.

Field Educator: Yes. Because . . .?

Student: Because their hearing is not as good as a younger person. Being quite clear about what you are doing and also just in general interaction with them, being quite clear.

Field Educator: Uh huh. And what's that based on?

Student: I guess trying not to confuse them.

Field Educator: Are you saying that your experience of older clients is that they are confused?

Student: No, most of them have been alert.

Field Educator: So does this confusion picture fit? I'm intrigued.

Student: Not sure.

Field Educator: On the one hand you're saying that older people you've met have been alert, and on the other hand you're saying you need to be very clear about what you're doing because they'll get confused easily.

Student: I guess it's more where I come from. The way I do things, that come across . . . yeah, I guess it's more me than them. I like to be clear for me.

Field Educator: So you like to be clear for you.

Source: Maidment and Cooper (2002, p. 403). Reprinted with the kind permission of the editor, *Social Work Education.*

- What were some of the assumptions that this student had about working with older people?
- What point do you think the supervisor is trying to make in this conversation?
- What are some of the assumptions you might have about working with different client groups, such as youth offenders, or people with addictions?

IDENTIFYING ASSUMPTIONS ABOUT HELPING AND LEARNING PRACTICE SKILLS

Learning practice skills is also a time to examine your own assumptions about notions of helping. Being able to identify our own conscious and sometimes subconscious assumptions about 'helping' and using practice skills is a major challenge in this type of learning. In terms of engaging in welfare and social work, some assumptions may be:

- *To be of any use as a worker I have to provide a resource, solve the problem and help in some tangible way.* This is one of the most common assumptions people bring to welfare and social work. While in some crisis situations the worker does need to be very proactive in mobilising immediate resources, other situations call for a more reflective approach where just being there and spending time actively listening to the client is the most effective intervention. In the current climate of economic rationalism, it is easy to feel pressured into believing providing good service involves the delivery of certain tangible inputs, products or resources that will enable future client performance and progress to be measured. However, time is the most precious resource workers have to share with a client. To feel valued and to make progress, sometimes all clients need is to have another person to talk to—a person who will listen and enable them to tell their story in a way that is unhurried. At times in our work, this is all that is needed for clients to draw their own conclusions about the best way ahead.
- *Because I have experienced a certain crisis (e.g. homelessness, sexual abuse, domestic violence, addiction), then I know what it is like and I can help.* Without a doubt, some of the best helpers are those who have experienced for themselves the issues clients bring them to work on. Having experienced certain life events can give

unique insight into both the pain and strategies that may help others in similar situations. However, not all 'survivors' of life crisis have resolved these issues to the extent that they are able to assist others without letting their own experiences colour the judgment, discretion and direction in which they work with clients.

- *Learning these skills will provide a 'toolkit' for me to use in the field.* The skills you learn for practising welfare or social work cannot be applied in a way that is context free. As outlined in Chapter 1, the application of these skills needs to occur within a framework that acknowledges structural oppression, while seeking empowerment for clients. Without acknowledgment of the context, the skills or toolkit you put together will be a collection of simple, mechanistic formulas that, used on their own, cannot bring about positive change in any meaningful or enduring way. In our role as workers, the goal is not simply problem-solving, but working towards helping people to empower themselves. In this way, using practice skills must be embedded within a context of understanding and raising awareness about social, political, economic and cultural factors impacting upon the client or client group.

- *Clients will welcome and be grateful for my help.* Two attitudes are inherent in this assumption: first, that all people want to be helped; and second that clients are appreciative of input from workers. Many people are motivated to work in human services because of a desire to help others. However, not all clients necessarily want input from the social service sector. Some, who are mandated to attend programs via a court order, can be actively hostile about worker intervention. Others, who may come to the attention of an agency through a third-party referral mechanism, may simply regard worker input as interfering or unnecessary. The notion of the client being 'grateful' begs the question of whose needs are being met in the client–worker transaction. A distinct power differential is also inherent in this assumption, where the client is somehow beholden to the worker. This position is contrary to an empowerment approach to work with marginalised people, where the worker and client join as partners against oppression (Lee, 2001, p. 63).

CONCLUSION

This chapter has examined some of the obstacles and challenges that students may encounter in learning practice skills, and some strategies have been outlined to address these. In particular, we have focused on the process of learning in a peer group setting where role-play, feedback and audio-visual technologies are used to develop practice skills. Students are encouraged to actively participate and to challenge themselves and others in this learning. Engaging with people from a range of different cultural contexts is central to gaining an understanding and increasing a working knowledge of how to practise in diverse settings. During these encounters, it is likely we will experience challenges to our own assumptions about diversity, culture and the process of what constitutes helping. It is these challenges that make this particular learning unpredictable, life-changing and memorable.

After facilitating a class on learning practice skills one semester, I asked the students to jot down an observation or piece of advice to give to the next group of students who were about to embark on the course. In closing, I would like to offer the following student observations about learning practice skills:

- Get involved and participate as much as you can; it's the best way to learn.
- Do the relevant readings, otherwise it's hard to keep up.
- Practise, practise, practise . . . soon you forget about the video camera even being on.
- This class involves learning in a different way; it is fun but also scary at times.
- We learned from each other, and the more you put in the more you get out of it.

3

ANTI-OPPRESSIVE AND STRENGTHS-BASED PRACTICE

Ronnie Egan and Alison Lewis-Nicholson

The Integrated Framework introduced in Chapter 1 (see Figure 1.1), has an anti-oppressive practice (AOP) foundation to inform work with individuals, families and groups. This chapter will provide an overview of strengths-based approaches and associated skills which will be used throughout the text. It will draw links between an antioppressive perspective in social work and welfare, and strengths-based practice approaches. In the chapter, we will locate strengths-based practice approaches within a historical view of delivering helping services, and highlight the professional value base informing social work and welfare practice in both Australia and New Zealand. Strengths-based practice will be the generic term used; this approach includes solution-focused and narrative approaches. The key skills and processes associated with these approaches will be defined through the use of practice examples.

Anti-oppressive practice provides the foundation in the Integrated Framework because this approach acknowledges the inevitability of structural constraints, and recognises that service users' lives are affected by social structures and systems. Further, AOP acknowledges the cultural and personal forms of oppression experienced by service users and legitimises the interpersonal part of the work in addressing these oppressions. AOP has emerged as a dominant framework in critical social work.

Anti-oppressive practice has, however, been critiqued due to its failure to offer strategies for how change can occur at the interpersonal level, the level at which most social work practice is played out (Healy, 2005). For this reason, strengths-based approaches have been used to integrate AOP into practice with service users. In this text, two strengths-based practice approaches will be used: solution-focused and narrative. Each of these challenges service providers to learn, develop and reflect on 'the subtle ways in which our attitudes and language as helping professionals can be used to enable or conversely, to disempower service users' (Healy, 2005, p. 167). Solution-focused and narrative approaches have been chosen to illustrate how strengths-based practice challenges dominant discourses about professional expertise, and represents a shift in promoting collaborative relationships between service providers and users.

The history of strengths-based approaches has been summarised by O'Hanlon and Weiner-Davis (2003), who identified three waves of therapy that influence the way helping professions approach practice. The first wave was identified as problem-focused, with an internalised view of behaviour influenced by psychodynamic understandings of pathology. This wave had its roots in modernist understandings, and its translation into practice was informed by the notion of 'helper as expert'. The helper as expert assumption continued into the second wave, but the focus shifted beyond individual pathology to a focus on systems and circumstances surrounding clients that needed to be changed. The third wave, identified as strengths-based practice, was significantly different. This approach resulted in a re-evaluation of traditional casework and counselling practices, shifting the emphasis away from the worker with expert knowledge to acknowledge the strengths of the service user. The value of this approach is that it repositions the service user. The AOP worker stays alert to the possibility that their role and knowledge may undermine the agency of service users. There exists an inevitable power imbalance between service user and provider because of the assumed power of agencies and institutions, and the mandated nature of the helping encounter.

McCashen (2005) comments on the ever-present temptation to use power over service users rather than a more collaborative stance that adopts power with them: 'This occurs when an individual, group or institution assumes the right to control or colonise others. There is an over-arching sense of superiority found in beliefs that negate or limit the right and access to resources, participation and self-determination . . .

Constantly there is a need to overt the practices which enhance the possibility of effective connection.' (2005, p. 31) For example, many service users feel powerless in the face of bureaucratic policies and processes that they experience as confusing and frustrating. If service users have a sense that service providers are trying to work collaboratively with them, that they understand and hear service users' frustration about service systems and are prepared to advocate for them, then they are more likely to collaborate with the worker.

Acknowledging the power differential between service user and provider, whilst trying to empower service users, is consistent with the professional value base of both social work and welfare in Australia and New Zealand. Fook (2000) notes the fundamental values of social work practice as 'driven by a mission of social justice and change to balance inequities and to create a more enabling society' (2000, p. 129). Both Australian and New Zealand core social work and welfare professional values include respecting the person, promoting social justice, empowerment and autonomy, valuing people's strengths and resilience and being authentic (Harms, 2007). Table 3.1 summarises McCashen's (2005) comparison between aspects of practice that demonstrates power with service users as opposed to practice that demonstrates power over service users.

Table 3.1 A strengths approach to power

Power over	Power with
• relies on dominant knowledge to diagnose and describe people and imposes that view on the client	• avoids imposition of dominant knowledge, stories and labels
• validates and acknowledges people's experience but interprets experience according to particular models	• validates people's unique experience and respects the meaning they give to their experience
• tends to ignore or minimise structural and cultural contexts and under-value people's knowledge and meanings	• acknowledges the structural and cultural contexts of people's lives and the uniqueness of their experience
• ignores or minimises the value of people's strengths and capacities, relying primarily on the worker's skills and expertise	• seeks to recognise and mobilise people's strengths and capacities as a central focus in change efforts
• is driven by organisational, state and professional priorities	• values people's aspirations and goals over other agendas

Table 3.1 A strengths approach to power *(continued)*

Power over	Power with
• expects people to meet workers on their ground and expects people to adapt to their context	• enables professionals to form partnerships and adapt to people's contexts
• relies on professional interpretations, concepts and language	• enables professionals to enter into people's worlds and landscapes, and honours their language
• confines practice to therapeutic or social work models, conventions and traditions	• creates a context of discovery and action, improvising and trying new things
• relies on worker expertise and gives weight to professional knowledge and skill	• relies on the shared expertise and knowledge of all stakeholders and gives priority to inclusive, transparent and consultative practice
• believes in objective knowledge—knowledge that is removed from the client	• values diversity of knowledge and acknowledges subjectivity
• relies on having to know the answers and tends to blame people for failure, framing them as uncooperative, resistant or hopeless if things don't work out	• relies on the finding the right questions and a team approach where responsibility is shared
• enables processes and outcomes to be determined by professionals	• enables processes and outcomes to be determined in partnerships

Source: McCashen, (2005, p. 24).
Reprinted with the kind permission of Innovative Resourses © Innovative Resources 2005

Essential to this way of working is the notion of empowerment of the service user. Healey (2005) notes that empowerment is the bridge between strengths-based approaches and anti-oppressive approaches because it contains the core elements of *both* perspectives. Strengths-based approaches acknowledge and build on service users' capacities, while anti-oppressive practice is predicated on the social and structural origins of service users' problems. Saleebey (1992) labelled his notion of empowerment as strengths-based. As the architect of strengths-based approaches, its underpinnings are:

- respecting client strengths that can be mobilised to improve lives;
- fostering motivation by building upon and utilising service user strengths;
- gaining cooperation through the process of acknowledging strengths;

- focusing on strengths to enhance service user personal agency and capacity to act in particular situations.

Strengths-based approaches challenge the tendency for workers to hold domain-specific knowledge of a problem and design a treatment that best fits the service users' diagnosis. As noted above, this text uses two strengths-based approaches to practice: solution-focused and narrative practice.

SOLUTION-FOCUSED PRACTICE

Solution-focused practice (SFP) provides an approach that emphasises and respects people's ability to be their own agents of change. SFP as a practice approach had its origins in the work of De Shazer (1994) and DeJong and Berg (1998, 2007). The approach focuses on what service users want to achieve rather than on their problem(s). Using this approach, the worker does not dwell on the past, but instead focuses on the present and future. The worker uses respectful curiosity to invite the service user to clearly identify a preferred future, and then together the worker and service user plan small incremental steps required to achieve this. This approach to practice recognises that often there is a need for additional resources to be factored in, and this can easily be accommodated. Table 3.2 contrasts the difference between strengths-focused approaches as opposed to problem-focused practice. Further, Table 9.2 in Chapter 9 provides a comparison between strengths-based models of assessment and problem-based models of assessment.

Table 3.2 Contrasting problem- and solution-focused approaches to practice

Problem-focused	Solution-focused
Asks what is wrong and why	Asks what the client wants to change, and how
Explores historical causes and present difficulties in order to find a remedy	Opens space for future possibilities through a focus on exceptions and resources
Searches for underlying issues—that is, the 'real' problem	Invites client to clarify main issues and priorities for counselling
Elaborates on emotional experience of client	Continuously channels client affect towards goals or desired actions
Assumes client is deficient, resistant, misguided or naïve	Assumes client is competent, resilient and resourceful
Labels/categorises clients in problem-saturated ways	Views clients as unique and maintains a positive view of curiosity

Table 3.2 Contrasting problem- and solution-focused approaches to practice
(continued)

Problem-focused	Solution-focused
Views counselling as treatment or remediation	Views counselling as conversation that opens up new possibilities
Focuses on assessment and intervention	Focuses on a process of collaborative inquiry
Identifies client with his/her problems	Sees client as oppressed or restricted by problems
Privileges counsellor's voice and expertise	Privileges client's voice and expertise
Utilises counsellor's model and language	Builds on client's ideas and language
Often tends to be directive, strategic or mysterious	Seeks to be open, collaborative and respectful
Considers good counselling to be hard work, painful and long	Considers good counselling to be time-effective, hope-generating and often enjoyable
Asks how many sessions will be needed for this problem to be resolved	Asks whether enough has been achieved to end

The worker's primary task is to facilitate a helping relationship in which the client is hopeful about possible change, motivated to try making changes and engaged in discovering how to make useful changes. The approach is based on the following assumptions:

- Change is constant and inevitable: therapeutic change is most likely to be rapid.
- There are many ways to solve any problem, since there are always various possibilities for personal choice, regardless of the situation.
- People always have untapped resources for coping, learning and problem-solving that can be accessed and focused toward therapeutic change.
- The helping relationship is facilitated by respecting client's emotional experience (pain) and their potential for change (hope).
- Life is a learning process that often involves two steps forward and one back. Useful helping focuses on how to get on track, and stay on track.
- To solve a problem, one needs to know more about possible solutions, not more about the problem. It is easier to start a solution

process than stop a complaint process. Focusing on goals, potential solutions and future possibilities opens up intrapersonal and inter-personal space for therapeutic change.

- People generally want to change, and tell us behaviourally how to cooperate with them. The helper's job is to join with them in a way that motivates change and helps service users discover how to make changes.
- Service users must be the ones who define the problems and goals they are willing to address, as well as the most fitting ways to achieve these goals. They are always the experts on their own lives.
- Complex problems do not necessarily need complex solutions. Small changes often lead to bigger changes, since change in any part of a system influences change throughout the entire system. Change is most likely when the focus is on small, concrete, practical, achievable and observable goals.
- Seldom does anything happen all the time. 'Exceptions' to problems contain strengths, resources and abilities that can help with solution development.

These assumptions generate a set of skills for the worker to use. These skills include developing scaling, coping, exception and miracle questions, along with goal-setting.

Scaling questions

Service users are invited to put their observations, impressions about their past experiences and predictions of future possibilities on a scale from one to ten. This technique is a versatile, simple and useful tool that can be asked of anyone old enough to understand numbers. Scaling can help in many difficult situations such as when a problem is vague, or where there is a series of distinct disagreements, as might occur in some families. Scaling questions can be used to measure less definable things such as hope or confidence. For example, Jan and Peter differ in their approaches to parenting their adolescent children. It is useful for the worker to understand the complexity of these differences so she might ask both parents: 'When you think about your own and your partner's parenting, how confident, on a scale of one to ten, are you that the ideas we have discussed can be implemented?' This question is then a reality check as to the viability of change, and the service users' degree of hopefulness.

Coping questions

These questions can be useful when service users are discouraged and stuck in their difficulties. Coping questions provide a way of gently challenging the service user's belief system and their feelings of helplessness, while at the same time orienting them towards a sense of success (Miller et al., 1996, p. 89). For example, a worker might say:'I am amazed that despite all these difficulties you have managed to keep attending school. Can you tell me how you have done this?'

Exception questions

These questions help the service user locate and appreciate moments in their past when the present problem had less influence or was absent (Berg, 1994). Exceptions may be present and predictable, or they may be random. They may even need to be constructed hypothetically as a means of establishing the possible presence of something different. For example, when working with families, a worker might ask: 'When you think about getting to work on time, is there any difference between when you go to work in the term time or in the school holidays?' This question then opens up the possibility for exploration as to why there might be reasons for the differences. Or a worker might inquire hypothetically:'If you were to do something different before the children went to bed, what would you experience when you all get up for school in the morning?' This question is designed to encourage the client to explore the difference if the problem is not present. The difference might relate to her or his behaviour, thinking, actions or experiences.

Goal-setting

Goal-setting is used to assist a service user to define what they are trying to achieve. Goals are usually co-constructed between the worker and service user. The miracle question may also be utilised to help develop goals that may be hypothetical (see below).

The miracle question

This type of question is useful when the service user is unable to describe an alternative future. The miracle question provides an opportunity for the service user to think about how the problem could be different, and how the future can be different when the problem is no longer present, without having to think of the processes required to get there. The detail of the question can be adapted to the context in which it is used but the basis of it is: 'Suppose our meeting is over, you go home, and do whatever you planned to do for the rest of the day. Then, some time in the evening, you get tired and go to sleep. In the middle of the night, when you are fast asleep, a miracle happens and all the problems that brought you here today are solved, just like that. But since the miracle happened overnight, nobody is telling you that the miracle happened. When you wake up the next morning, how are you going to start discovering that the miracle happened?' This explanation is then followed up by the worker eliciting as much detail as possible about this description, with the intent of developing a picture of what the service user *will* do, rather than a continuing conversation around what the service user *cannot* do. Chapters 6, 8, 11, 12, 14, 17 and 18 provide further examples of these skills in action.

Exercise 3.1

- In pairs, interview one another about the following:
  Consider a real concern/worry/issue that you have experienced— one that you don't mind sharing in pairs.
- Ask your partner a scaling question:
  'How far on a scale of 1–5 are you in sorting out the problem?'
  'Have you ever been higher or lower on the scale in sorting out this problem?'
  'What was the difference at these times?'
- Ask your partner an exception question:
  'Have there been times when the issue has not been so much of a problem?'
  'What's been happening at those times?'
  'What's different about those times?'
- Practise using the miracle question specifically in relation to the concern your partner has raised.

A solution-focused approach to practice can be summarised into four phases which coincide with the generic phases in the Integrated Framework used in this text.

1   In the first phase of the social work process, the service user and worker build rapport and develop the contract for working

together. In this stage, information is gathered, a communication style appropriate to the individual service user is developed, expectations are defined, issues are delineated and the formulation of appropriate and achievable goals occurs. This is the beginning of the helping relationship, the *engagement* phase. Chapters 6, 7 and 8 explore this phase further.

2 In the second phase of the process, the service user and worker will each search for and identify exceptions—that is, times when the service user does not have the problem. These may be existing and predictable exceptions, or random exceptions. The exceptions may need to be created hypothetically. This is the phase where shared goals for change are developed, often referred to as the *assessment* phase. Chapters 9, 10, 11 and 12 explore this phase further.

3 In the third phase of the social work process, changes will be encouraged. Exceptions will be amplified and genuine compliments will be used to encourage the positive change. Small steps of progress will be noted, and scaling will be used to monitor levels of confidence and hope in achieving the goals. In this stage, the resources needed will be identified, and possible homework suggestions may be discussed. This is the phase where change is undertaken, the *intervention* phase. Chapters 13, 14 and 15 explore this phase further.

4 The final stage will integrate changes made by the service user into their current living situation. Plans will be discussed about possible relapse prevention, future changes may be discussed and these possible changes will be rehearsed. This is the *ending* phase. Chapters 16, 17 and 18 explore this phase further.

Narrative practice is the other strengths-based approach used in this text. Its origins are both Australia in the work of Michael White and New Zealand in the work of David Epston (White & Epston, 1990).

NARRATIVE PRACTICE

Narrative practice focuses on personal stories as a way to guide how people think, act and feel, and how they make sense of any new experience. These guiding stories have the effect of organising the information of a person's life, and the ability to refocus on previously unnoticed or denigrated pieces of information that can assist service users to 're-author' their lives (White & Epston, 1990).

Underlying this approach is the belief that identity is malleable and is co-created in relationship with others, as well as by one's own history. Thus our identity is socially constructed. Service users are encouraged to use alternative stories of identity to overcome obstacles to achieve their preferred ways of life. For example, there may be a shift from identifying as a 'victim' to identifying as a 'survivor'. A narrative practice approach places the experiences of the person in a central position, with an interest in exceptions rather than the 'rules' and specific *context*. Stories we have about our lives shape how we think and behave, how we make sense of ourselves and the world around us. Stories filter and focus our understandings, the meanings we make of things and our feelings. Sometimes these stories can blind us to ways of feeling, thinking and behaving that do not fit with the interpretation we have of our lives. We all have key stories about ourselves that we hang on to tightly. These stories have been developed jointly by ourselves and the important people who have influenced our lives, and by the wider community. We do not have to passively accept the stories we have lived with, or those that are imposed upon us. The worker's primary task in narrative practice is to help service users recognise that these stories can be rewritten. The dominant story does not have to define or constrain a person's way of being in the world.

A narrative practice approach is based on the following assumptions (Morgan, 2000):

- The problem is the problem. (The person is not the problem.)
- People have expertise about their own lives.
- People can become the primary authors of the stories of their own lives.
- By the time a person consults a worker, they will have already made many attempts to reduce the influence of the problem in their lives and relationships.
- Problems are constructed in cultural contexts. These contexts include power, relations of race, class, sexual preference, gender and disadvantage.
- The problems for which people seek consultation usually cause them to reach conclusions about their lives and relationships. Often these conclusions have encouraged them to consider themselves as deficient in some way, and this view makes it difficult to access personal knowledge, competencies, skills and abilities.
- These skills, competencies and knowledges can be made available to service users to assist with reclaiming their lives from the influence of the problem.

- There are always occasions in a person's life where they have escaped the influence of a problem. Problems never successfully claim 100 per cent of people's lives or relationships.

These assumptions generate two key skills in narrative practice—externalising the problem and reauthoring:

- *Externalising* locates problems as products of culture and history, with problems being understood to have been socially constructed and created over time and outside of the individual. This means that workers encourage the service user to locate the problem outside of themselves so that it is not 'them' that is the problem, but an externalised problem. For example, a person experiencing anxiety may be encouraged to wonder how anxiety (external to them) has begun to have power over them.
- *Reauthoring* recognises that sociocultural forces, norms and alleged truths become embedded in the internalised stories of individuals. This shapes and determines how service users understand their lives. This can lead to self-defeating behaviours. Reauthoring allows a service user to review the history they have accepted and re-evaluate their story from a different perspective. This process can foster a greater sense of agency and recognition of the overwhelming power of structural constraints.

Chapters 8, 11, 12, 14, 17 and 18 provide further examples of these skills in action.

Exercise 3.2: Externalising conversation

Consider a characteristic or trait, quality or emotion that you dislike in yourself.

Give the characteristic, trait, quality or emotion a name (x), then answer the following questions:

- How does x impact on your life?
- What would things be like if x were not in control?
- What kinds of things happen that typically lead you to x?
- What are the consequences for your life and relationships of being x?
- How is your self-image different when you are x?

Note the overall effect of answering those questions.

• How do you feel?
• What seems possible?
• What seems impossible?

This chapter has provided an overview of how the Integrated Framework in this text incorporates an anti-oppressive foundation and uses strengths-based practice approaches and associated skills to understand practice. The remainder of the text provides rich material for understanding how this process occurs in practice with individuals, families and groups. This chapter ends with a caution about using strengths-based practice approaches without an appreciation of the broader structural, cultural and personal oppressions impacting on the people we work with (Rossiter, 2000; Egan, 2005; Healy, 2005). Simply using the word 'strengths' in our work with clients does not translate into anti-oppressive practice. AOP practice requires an understanding of the oppressive aspects of us as service providers, as well as our clients' circumstances and social structures. This requires service providers to prepare for practice. Preparation for practice includes the intellectual preparation of incorporating the knowledge informing practice, and the ethical basis of social work practice which then forms the basis for tuning into the service user's world. Chapter 5 details the rationale for preparing for practice. It uses the experience of Indigenous Australians as a way of tuning into the complexity of clients' worlds before interaction with service users begins.

4

DELIVERING HELPING SERVICES ONLINE AND OVER THE TELEPHONE

Jane Maidment

While there is an established tradition of telephone helpline services in both Australia and New Zealand, this medium for providing services has grown at an exponential rate in recent years with the development of large call centre operations. These centres are responsible for the delivery of diverse services, including but not limited to income support advice, parenting help, emergency poisons information, smoking cessation support and employee assistance programs. Simultaneously, internet communication technology has been adopted quickly in both countries, with mobile phone and computer ownership increasing at a rapid rate alongside growing daily use of the internet for accessing services and social connections (World Internet Usage Statistics, 2007).

As a consequence, social workers are now routinely providing intervention with clients using the telephone and online facilities, rather than engaging in face-to-face encounters. It is no longer unusual for workers to be located in one geographical region providing telephone or internet input to service users several hundred kilometres away. We therefore think it is important to consider how social work and welfare services are delivered specifically in these environments, since future practitioners are likely to spend more of their time communicating with clients in cyberspace or on the telephone. This chapter is focused on three dimensions:

- the ways in which online and telephone forums are now utilised by clients and practitioners;
- the transferability of traditional micro-skills for use in telephone and online modalities; and
- the provision of guidelines for service delivery using the telephone or online environment.

TELEPHONE AND ONLINE SERVICES

Telephone help lines

Telephone help lines have been a feature of service delivery for some time, with Lifeline Australia commencing its operation in 1963 and its counterpart in New Zealand starting in 1967. Since these early days, many thousands of volunteer helpers have been trained through Lifeline and other non-government organisations in both countries to respond to calls for assistance in areas mainly related to emotional or practical needs. In response to the changing economic and political conditions in both Australia and New Zealand, human service organisations have come under increasing pressure to deliver more service at less cost (Baines, 2006), while service users have become better informed about their rights to access quality professional assistance and information.

Within this context, call centres and telephone advice lines have burgeoned as a way to maximise access to expertise, while rationalising costs associated with staff time used for travel and face-to-face consultations. Recent statistics indicate that Plunket Helpline New Zealand received 55 000 calls during 2006, while Kids Help Line in Brisbane provided telephone support to 44 554 young people throughout Australia. During 2006, the number of calls to Lifeline Australia and New Zealand totalled 1 073 460 (Lifeline Australia and New Zealand, personal communication, 17 July 2007). Picking up the telephone or mobile and dialling for information and advice is becoming the strategy of choice for many, particularly those individuals on low incomes or living in isolated communities who are physically or financially unable to visit a health or social service facility. Meanwhile, there is empirical evidence to suggest that proactive telephone support and counselling can be a particularly effective intervention to address explicit issues such as smoking cessation (Meites & Thom, 2007). Research findings also indicate that many clients actually have a preference for participating in telephone rather than face-to-face service delivery, due to ease of access and convenience, while maintaining a greater sense of control during the helping transaction (Reese et al., 2006). Not surprisingly, costs associated with both delivering and receiving telephone counselling are less than those for face-to-face interactions.

These developments have meant professionals from a diverse range of disciplines are now engaged in consultations with clients at a distance using telephone, video and web conferencing technology. Delivery of health services using these technologies is fast becoming mainstream, and is now referred to as 'telehealth' or 'telemedicine'. These forms of service delivery practised in local, national and even global contexts draw together expertise and assistance from disparate locations to address client issues (Wootton & Batch, 2005). Such developments have been welcomed in rural and remote communities, where access to health services and information has been especially problematic, as well as in urban areas where services may in fact be available but not necessarily with an expert knowledge base in less common fields of practice (Starling & Dossetor, 2005). Telephone helplines are increasingly being used to address client issues on a number of levels, including providing professional advice and counselling services, befriending and support, promoting advocacy and information-giving. Bringing together clients with similar issues who live in geographically disparate locations to engage in groupwork over the telephone has also been tried and tested with some success (Rosenfield & Smillie, 1998).

Bearing in mind that that practitioners will spend a good amount of time either providing direct services to clients via the telephone or using the telephone to supplement in-person consultations, we believe it is important for students to be both effective and confident in using this form of communication. While people routinely use the telephone or mobile phone several times a day, most have not been trained to use this medium for the purposes of developing a helping relationship. Therefore, we have collated the following guidelines as a starting point for learning how to work with clients effectively over the telephone.

Guidelines for effective use of the telephone for support, advice, counselling and groupwork include the following:

• Ensure you are able to manage the technical features of the telephone in terms of transferring a call or putting a person on hold in order to consult with another worker.

- If possible, make a toll-free number available to increase client accessibility to your service.
- When initiating a call, the worker needs to ensure at the outset that they are speaking to the intended client, and that the call is not being listened to or recorded by someone other than the client.
- Smile when you are greeting and speaking with a client on the telephone. The client can 'hear' that you are smiling.
- Provide your name in the opening statement made to the client, and if you know the client's name refer directly to the client by name during the course of the conversation.
- Listen very carefully and concentrate during the phone conversation; have pen and paper to make notes of key points.
- Practice skills of opening and closing conversations effectively, especially in relation to attending to group process.
- In the absence of non-verbal cues, it is important to remain responsive to the changing tone, flow and pace of the conversation.
- Be mindful of your own tone in the conversation. Increased volume and rhythm in your voice conveys interest, while downward changes in volume and tone suggest boredom, frustration or fatigue.
- Stay calm when responding to an angry client and be mindful of your own tone; acknowledge the client's feelings and do not get drawn into an argument. Demonstrate empathy, ask questions and listen carefully to the answers.
- When facilitating a group over the telephone, make a list with the names of the people attending and tick off each time a person contributes to the conversation. This way, in the absence of visual cues, you can keep track of those people who may need to be invited or encouraged into the group conversation.
- When ending a group discussion over the telephone, be mindful that once the client has hung up, he or she may be sitting in silence, alone with just the telephone. Prepare group participants for this 'silence' by discussing what they will do once the group conversation is over. (These guidelines were developed with reference to Ferguson (2005), Kenny & McEachern (2004) and Leon (1999).)

To protect client privacy, caller display details should not be available to workers when one of the stated aims of the service is for clients to remain anonymous should they wish to do so. Providing services on the telephone also means that workers will need to practise how to manage a range of 'difficult' calls. These include responding to people with suicide ideation, hoax and abusive callers, and inappropriate sexual calls.

On a practical note, if telephones without headsets are being used routinely for consultations by a number of people, they need to be cleaned regularly with hygienic anti-bacterial wipes. Headsets should be provided for people spending long periods of the day on telephone consultations to prevent neck, shoulder and arm muscle strain.

As we explained in Chapter 2 of this text, using role-plays is a common way to develop practice skills. In this next exercise you are asked to role play a series of telephone conversations.

Exercise 4.1: Telephone helpline role-plays

Jacqui calls the parent support line at 5.15 am. She is a first time mother with a four-week-old baby boy. Jacqui is crying on the phone, saying she has been having real trouble settling her baby. She has had little uninterrupted sleep since the birth and the baby is crying loudly in the background. Jacqui's partner works on night shift and is not home.

Place two chairs back to back and role-play this case scenario between the client, Jacqui and telephone parent support counsellor, Meg.

1   What did you notice about listening and talking to Jacqui over the telephone?
2   How did you convey to Jacqui that you were really listening to her concerns?
3   How might this interaction be different if you were speaking to Jacqui:
    (a) at her own home during a home visit; or
    (b) in your office?
4   What do you think some of the advantages might have been for Jacqui calling the helpline?
5   What might you have done if Jacqui was new to the country and from a non-English-speaking background?
6   What skills would you have needed to use more in the conversation if Jacqui was speaking English on the telephone but you found her accent difficult to understand?

Exercise 4.2

You are a worker in an agency that provides free online and telephone counselling services to youth. Ben calls on the telephone one evening saying he feels like 'ending it all'. He and his girlfriend have just broken up and he says he cannot get out of feeling really down. Ben's speech is slurred and he is clearly having difficulty concentrating.

Place two chairs back to back and role-play this telephone conversation between the client, Ben, and the youth worker.

1   What skills did the worker use to engage with Ben over the telephone?
2   What clues did Ben provide during the conversation about his support system?
3   How did the worker go about gauging the level of risk Ben might pose to himself or others?
4   How did the worker use pace and voice tone during the conversation?
5   What strategies and micro-skills did the worker use when concluding the conversation with Ben?

Exercise 4.3: Telephone groupwork

You work as a social worker in an aged care assessment team that serves a large, geographically isolated area. Once a month, you facilitate a telephone conference with a group of five people who care for either their spouse or a parent who has dementia. The carers have come to know each other over the telephone, but have never met. They are:

*   Bill, aged 78, who cares for his wife at home;
*   Sandy, aged 47, who has her mother living with her along with two adolescent children and her husband;
*   Mary, aged 68, whose mother has just recently been placed in nursing home care;
*   Norm, aged 55, whose wife has early-onset dementia and is still at home;
*   Nancy, aged 75, who cares for her husband at home.

Place six chairs with their backs to the inside of the circle so none of the group participants or the facilitator can have eye contact. Role-play:

- beginning the group;
- discussing with the group feelings about placing a family member in care. This conversation relates to Mary's recent change of circumstances with her mother moving into nursing care;
- discussing arrangements people have made for upcoming Christmas Day celebrations;
- ending the group.

1   What observations did you make about how the group was facilitated?
2   What was it like being one of the clients in the group?
3   What was it like facilitating a groupwork process over the telephone?
4   What specific skills did the facilitator need to use to keep everyone on track in the group?
5   In what way did the facilitator need to use the same or different skills as those used facilitating a group in a face-to-face setting?

Online counselling services

Online counselling can occur via asynchronistic email exchange and message boards or through synchronistic (real-time) text chat. While this mode for providing service is well embedded in North America, it is still in its infancy in Australia and New Zealand. Kids Help Line is one of the most established services of this kind in Australia, with its nation-wide web-based counselling service commencing in 1999 (Reid & Caswell, 2005). Serving a client group of young people between the ages of five and eighteen years, during 2006 the service received 32 932 online contacts, with 8 733 web counselling sessions conducted, and a further 10 354 email responses being given (Kids Help Line, 2007). Clients of this service report that the advantages of engaging with a counsellor online included increased anonymity, having time to reflect upon and construct email questions and responses, satisfaction with the 'journalling' and written recording of the email exchange over a period of time (Rawson & Maidment, forthcoming). Even so, most social work and welfare practitioners are not familiar with this mode of working.

Online counselling is more resource intensive than telephone counselling, requiring the worker to receive, read and construct in text an appropriate reply, with written communication being more time consuming than speech.

Exercise 4.4: Consumer self-help

Go online and find three consumer self-help sites dealing with different issues (e.g. health, gambling, ageing or sexuality). Note what resources they offer to users, conditions of use and etiquette for communication between users.

It is generally reported in the literature that no matter what modality is being used for service delivery—whether online, over the telephone or face-to-face—similar sets of micro-skills are utilised by practitioners (Stople & Chechele, 2004). Even so, the online environment does require additional skills to refine accuracy of communication in the absence of visual and verbal cues (Fenichel, 2004). Some argue that there can be no substitute for the type of therapeutic alliance developed in the face-to-face counselling transaction, and that 'it would not be possible or even desirable to develop a computer mediated therapeutic relationship' (Robson & Robson, 1998, p. 39). Others caution that in fact counsellors may become too reliant on the visual and non-verbal cues offered in face-to-face counselling, pointing out that this can lead to questions remaining unasked and assumptions being made by the counsellor regarding the client's situation (Murphy & Mitchell, 1998). Clearly, the efficacy of online counselling is still hotly contested.

In response to this debate, recent research has been conducted to ascertain whether and how an online therapeutic alliance can be developed. As a result, some clear parallels have been drawn between traditional counselling concepts such as demonstrating warmth, genuineness and empathy, and ways in which these same constructs are facilitated during email counselling sessions. Consumers report that factors such as the counsellor taking time to construct lengthy and thoughtful replies, remaining engaged in the counselling process over a period of time, careful use of emoticons and techniques such as 'emotional bracketing', and the tone of email exchanges all contribute to the building of online rapport between counsellor and client (Rawson & Maidment, forthcoming; Murphy & Mitchell, 1998). For some clients, the degree of anonymity afforded by web-based counselling can generate a level of openness and even disinhibition that may well be absent in face-to-face encounters. Clients particularly ambivalent about developing levels of intimacy can paradoxically find that synchronistic and asynchronistic conversations provide the means for clear, honest communication while generating the distancing effect of text-based communication (Suler, 2004). Factors such as the anonymity and invisibility embedded in online transactions, along with the status-neutralising effects of web communication, can contribute to increased levels of disinhibition. In this way, it seems that the features which significantly differentiate face-to-face from online counselling may actually contribute to the forming of successful text-based relationships. As such, these features add to our understanding of ways to develop the therapeutic alliance online.

Guidelines for fostering the *therapeutic alliance* during asynchronistic communication include the following:

Expectations and boundaries

- Establish from the outset provisions for privacy and security of online communications, and establish realistic, manageable timeframes to provide written responses to emails.
- Be reliable in terms of responding within the timeframes you have stated and ensure an automated message is dispatched indicating that you have received the sender's email or web message.

Process

- Take care to write responses with clarity, responding to both cognitive and emotional content using a reading level that will be understood by the client, without spelling or grammatical errors.
- Use descriptors to illustrate your engagement with the presenting issues—for example, 'As I was reading about the way your week unfolded . . .'
- Use emotional bracketing to explain the context in which you are writing your response—for example, 'I was wondering why I hadn't heard from you in some time (feeling pushy about asking).' This conveys the tone and intent of what is being written.
- Pay attention and respond to both the overt and covert messages you discern in the previous email counselling messages sent by the client.
- Use the opening paragraph of your responding email to prepare and focus the client for your response.

- Avoid use of colloquialism, slang, humour or innuendo, especially in the early stages of engaging with the client and with clients from a culture that may be different from your own.
- Draw upon literary techniques in email responses such as use of metaphor, simile, storytelling and poetry to convey a level of emotional engagement with what the client has written.
- Encourage consumers to use the content of previous email exchanges to reflect upon patterns of behaviour and issues raised.
- Take notice of the changing tempo and tone of emails from clients, and use these cues to guide your own responses.
- Make use of the message peripherals such as the sender's user name, subject line, the tone of the greeting and the way the email communication is signed off to provide clues about what the client may be thinking and feeling.
- Construct new subject lines for each email you send that capture the 'essence' of the message you wish to convey back to the client.
- Carefully construct 'new' replies, making direct reference to text passages provided by the client, using changed font colour, emoticons and text size to emphasise aspects of your reply. Avoid simply pressing the reply key and typing a response at the top or bottom of the message sent by the client. (This list of guidelines was constructed with reference to Suler (2004), Stofle & Chechele, (2004) and Murphy & Mitchell (1998).)

Not surprisingly, online counselling lends itself to creative use of journalling, analogy and constructing metaphor for text-based self-examination and expression. These written genres can feel less threatening for some, compared with direct verbal communication in a face-to-face setting.

The practice skills commonly used during face-to-face encounters are also deployed in working with people over the internet. These include *reflecting back* the emotional and practical content about what you understand the client has said; *asking* open and closed questions; *reframing* the client's perspectives or responses; *gently confronting* when there appear to be anomalies in the client story or incongruity between what the client is saying and what they subsequently do; *using clarification* when you are not certain of the facts or of how a client is feeling; *normalising and universalising* when a client feels they are not handling a situation as well as others; assisting the client with *goal-setting; summarising* complex situations and plans; *affirming* client progress; and *facilitating* some form of client evaluation of service delivery at the close of the helping transaction. Each of the above skills is also utilised when delivering a service over the telephone.

Other ways to use the internet

As practitioners, there are many ways we can use the internet to inform service delivery while also providing additional resources for service users to access, outside of the professional helping relationship. While it is self-evident that the internet can be used to quickly source credible information about differing fields of practice and modes of intervention, there are also plenty of examples where both practitioners and consumers have used the internet to facilitate advocacy and promote social justice agendas (Friess, 1999), access self-help groups (Hsiung, 2000), address social and professional isolation (Kurzydio et al., 2005; Haythornwaite, 2000) and provide educational development and supervision opportunities (Russell & Perris, 2003). These web-based initiatives have enabled people to connect with others across the world who are concerned about similar issues or experiencing related difficulties. The degree of personal and political empowerment afforded individuals and groups through these activities is well documented in the literature (Hill & Hughes, 1998; Leaffer & Mickelberg, 2006). As such, the internet can provide a rich source of ongoing cost-effective support to both practitioners and consumers outside of the time spent during the client–worker transaction.

Exercise 4.5: Online activism

Go online and find three sites where the internet is providing a forum for political advocacy on particular issues. What are these issues? How has the advocacy been organised? Who are the stakeholders in the process? What are the 'rules' stated on these sites for participating in the online advocacy activity?

MAKING LINKS WITH THE STRENGTHS PERSPECTIVE AND ANTI-OPPRESSIVE PRACTICE

Web- and telephone-based human services can be used to develop client strengths and address micro, meso and macro forms of oppression.

According to Glicken (2004, pp. 51–6), dimensions of the worker–client relationship based upon a strengths perspective include a number of specific features. First, a strengths perspective is charac-terised by the *absence of the power differential between the client and worker.* We know from earlier research on web-based counselling that clients do identify with a greater sense of control and privacy afforded by working online or over the telephone (Rawson & Maidment, forth-coming). In and of itself, this is not enough to ensure the transaction between the client and worker remains on an equal footing; however, it is a good start. It has been noted that some clients can be intimidated by office surroundings and attributes of status such as publicly displayed qualifications (Suler, 2004), while these artefacts of the built environment are absent during online or telephone communication.

Other features of the helping relationship that characterise a strengths-based approach include ensuring *active and attentive listening; building early rapport; encouraging independent client solutions; focusing on the positives* and *identifying exceptions* (Glicken, 2004). Each of these elements can be integrated into working online or over the telephone, despite the absence of physical presence and non-verbal cues.

It is also possible to generate some principles for client engagement and assessment from an anti-oppressive practice perspective that can be integrated into web and telephone worker–client transactions. These include *ensuring openness and honesty in all communication;* fostering a process where both workers and clients *share values and concerns;* acknowledging the *structural context* in which individual client issues are located more broadly; facilitating interactions *where the different narratives of all people involved are taken into account*; and maintaining a position of *critical questioning and examination* (Dalrymple & Burke, 2006, pp. 210–11), while also ensuring that dimen-sions of power and authority are acknowledged and addressed constructively throughout the process (Burke & Harrison, 1998).

Perhaps somewhat surprisingly, the online and telephone environ-ment can in fact add empowering dimensions to the helping relationship. The client is not dependent upon worker appointment schedules, and can make contact when he or she wishes using asynchronistic web counselling. As such, the client can be proactive in setting the agenda and timing for engagement with the worker. During telephone and synchronistic web counselling sessions, the client also has greater control over the duration of any given session compared with the face-to-face interview. The client is able to put the telephone receiver down or log off when they wish, whereas extracting oneself abruptly from an office setting can be more problematic. Furthermore, the provision of online and telephone services has enhanced access to specific cohorts of people who traditionally have had difficulty tapping into information, support, education and professional expertise for a range of reasons. These include people who live and work in rural and remote regions, those with mobility problems, people with social anxiety, and those without access to private or public transport (Haas et al., 1996). It is therefore not difficult to see how telephone- and web-based service provision may be used as a means to resource people who may otherwise remain marginalised.

Even so, a chapter about providing web and telephone helping services would not be complete without referring to the limitations and even dangers associated with these modes of working.

LIMITATIONS OF WEB- AND TELEPHONE-BASED HELPING SERVICES

Not surprisingly, one of the major criticisms about providing helping services over the telephone or online is the lack of non-verbal communication cues available to the worker. Given that we know that the major contribution to meaning-making in communication is non-verbal cues (Matsumoto & Juang, 2004), concern about the absence of visual prompts is justified, despite claims that digital writing to convey emotional content is a developing art form.

The well documented digital divide between those people who do have ready access to information communication technology and those who do not must also be considered from an anti-oppressive practice perspective. While online delivery does bring support, information and professional expertise into the homes of many who have previously not had access to these services, some client cohorts still remain under-represented in terms of access to computer hardware and internet services on the basis of age, income, ethnicity and geography (Guillen & Suarez, 2005).

The burgeoning of telephone call centres and online services also needs to be examined within the context of prevailing neoliberal economic rationalist policy, where the level of unmet need for health, welfare and housing services has reached crisis level in some parts of Australia and New Zealand (ACOSS, 2008; St John, 2008). The subsequent rationalising of face-to-face service delivery therefore needs to be examined alongside the rise in call centre and online service delivery. Inevitably, within this context, the question is raised about whether these modes of service have been developed in response to best-practice models, or address pragmatic imperatives to squeeze more service out of every dollar spent.

Other limitations of telephone and online counselling are evident in work with people from culturally and linguistically diverse backgrounds, where ready access to interpreters for telephone work is not always available, while online services in both Australia and New Zealand are mostly delivered in English. This being the case, the online environment is reliant upon the client having the capacity to read and write in English, or alternatively have a good understanding of spoken English to receive help over the telephone.

Finally, it is evident that the development of privacy legislation and protocols pertaining to online ethical conduct and ownership of posted material has lagged behind the technical capacity to provide services online. Within this environment, both clients and practitioners may risk compromising their privacy, or being subject to identity scams.

CONCLUSION

The burgeoning development and use of communication technology in all spheres of business and domestic life has had, and will continue to have, a significant impact upon the way services are delivered. Through use of the internet, clients can access information, services and support, and participate in self-advocacy and activism. These developments have impacted upon the traditional client–worker relationship, enabling clients to link into multiple forms of help and information while exercising greater agency in personal problem solving.

While these are the advantages of utilising improving technology for service delivery, there are also significant limitations associated with use of communication technology, and these are outlined in this chapter. We encourage students to explore further the ways in which developing technologies are changing the way social work business is conducted, and to consider how the digital revolution may advance or limit the potential for strengths-based, anti-oppressive practice.

5

PREPARING FOR PRACTICE

Lesley Cooper and Daryle Rigney

There are two stages a social worker goes through in preparing for practice. First, there is the intellectual preparation, which incorporates acquisition and understanding of the intellectual and ethical basis of social work practice. This intellectual preparation then forms the foundation for tuning into and understanding the client's world, whether clients are individuals, groups or communities. Values and ethics continually inform both stages of this preparation. Social workers are obliged to take time to reflect on their practice and on how their values and ethics are expressed in their relationships and demonstrated in their practice. This text uses strengths-based approaches to operationalise an anti-oppressive perspective. Strengths-based approaches use a philosophy aimed at discovering the strengths in, and resilience of, people. Anti-oppressive practice (AOP) acknowledges the multiple oppressions and marginalisations faced by clients, groups and communities. Anti-oppressive practice requires going beyond the empathy of the individual to see the connections between culture and subjective experiences of people.

This chapter details the experience of Indigenous Australians to highlight the impact of colonisation and the use of 'power over' in working with oppressed groups (McCashen, 2005). Refer to Table 3.1 in Chapter 3 for an earlier discussion of this concept.

PREPARING OURSELVES FOR PRACTICE: THE STRENGTHS APPROACH

Strengths are capacities, resources and assets. According to Saleebey (2002, pp. 86–7), strengths include what people have learned through their life struggles, personal qualities, knowledge of the world around them, individual talents, cultural stories and folklore that sustain identity, belonging to families and communities, and pride in small and large achievements. Recognition of strengths and assets brings the possibility of change and empowerment. Empowerment, an important outcome of social work practice, is achieved when individuals, groups and communities discover the resources within and mobilise those resources to make changes to their personal and social world. People gain the strength and aspirations to achieve a better world for themselves. As an example of this, one author of this chapter, Daryle Rigney, is working with his community to build a sustainable future for his traditional land, Ngarrindjeri Ruwe (Country) in South Australia, by working in such areas as educational transformation, water policy and natural resource management, cultural resource management and governance (Hemming et al., 2007).

Accompanying this recognition of the strengths are some core values that traditionally have been associated with the social work profession. These have been captured by McCashen as socially just practice (2005, p. 23). They include:

- a fundamental *respect* for all people, whatever their circumstances, and their capacity to make decisions and choices based on their experiences and that reflect their best interests;
- a commitment to *justice* where justice refers to equity, fairness, sharing of resources and where human rights are respected;
- *inclusion and participation* in decision-making, especially of those who do not participate in community life and may be most directly affected by marginalisation;
- a willingness to provide *ongoing support* to meet the needs of people, organisations and communities;
- being prepared to make our practice and decisions as *transparent* as possible to avoid abuses and excesses;
- the capacity to *collaborate*, recognising the strengths that come from interpersonal relationships, networks, groups and communities.

Saleebey (2002) was a key architect of strengths-based practice. He argues that all social workers preparing to work from this perspective need to undertake consciousness-raising. Consciousness-raising means increasing our self-awareness by understanding ourselves in relation to social work practice and, on the basis of this new awareness, taking action to make personal and professional changes. If we want to see changes in practice, then change must begin with us. Therefore, in preparing for practice, we should reflect on our mindset about people and helping.

Exercise 5.1: Reflecting on your strengths
Identify your existing strengths as a practitioner and consider how to use them in practice. Consider what changes you may be thinking about from an anti-oppressive perspective.

PREPARING FOR PRACTICE: ANTI-OPPRESSIVE PRACTICE

The strengths-based approach had its origins in direct practice with individuals, and acknowledges the value of collaborative practice, inclusion and participation. Anti-oppressive practice is grounded in social justice principles which assert that the origins of individuals' problems lie in social structures. Anti-oppressive practice has multiple theoretical origins, which include radical, anti-racist and structural approaches. Social and structural divisions in society are acknowledged— especially the negative effects of power, hierarchy and status. This framework has an explicitly political view of practice so that every personal problem is seen as both a political and a public issue. The concept of multiple oppressions is at the heart of anti-oppressive practice. When looking at multiple oppressions, it is important to remember that the world is not simply divided into the oppressors and the oppressed. It is not an either/or situation but one where all are simultaneously oppressed and oppressors. Bishop (2002, p. 114) argues that everyone in the oppressed group is an oppressor so that: 'It is ridiculous to claim you are not sexist if you are man or not racist if you are white and so on.' As we all share oppressor and oppressed status, there is much for social workers to learn and understand prior to and during practice.

Oppression can be based on racism, sexism, classism, ageism and heterosexism, as well as disability, national origin or religious beliefs.

Bishop (2002) outlines different ways of thinking about oppression. In thinking about oppression, we need to take account of visible differences such as skin colours, gender and particular types of physical disability, as well as invisible differences such as gay and lesbian orientation or those with hidden physical disabilities and mental illness. The particular histories of cultural and racial groups have also led to oppression. This applies to migrant and refugee groups in Australia and New Zealand. Indigenous people experience oppression because they have been dispossessed and now struggle to maintain their identity, request fulfilment of treaty obligations and seek autonomy in the management of their resources.

Oppression is maintained in multiple ways (Bishop, 2002). First, power and hierarchy play an important role. Oppressors seek to maintain power over the oppressed. This may be as subtle as a social worker being paternalistic and 'knowing' the best way for clients to manage their lives, or it can arise through lack of access to wealth, resources, information or educational opportunities. Stereotyping also maintains oppression by creating separatism between 'them' and 'us'. Whilst stereotyping can be used in positive ways, it is generally used in hurtful and harmful ways. Oppression also occurs through violent acts that can include harassment and tokenism. Anti-oppressive practice requires social workers to consider their own experiences of being oppressed and learn to see how they may oppress others. Our experiences of being oppressed are relatively easy to appreciate as they emerge from our direct experiences, while being an oppressor is hidden from us because we are not aware of the experiences of the oppressed group. In other words, in some areas of oppression we are not able to empathise with the experiences of the oppressed. Part of the beginning stage of practice is learning about ourselves as oppressors.

Exercise 5.2: Reflecting on experiences of oppression
Consider your experiences of being oppressed with people who share the same sort of experiences. For example, if you are a woman, you might consider with other women your particular experiences of oppression. Then, in a larger group, share your particular experiences with other students who have experienced different forms of oppression (for example, ageism or racism). Note the common characteristics shared across groups.

Now put yourself into the shoes of the oppressor:

1   When you were listening to the stories of oppression where you were or may have been the oppressor, what did you learn?
2   How can you use these stories to empathise with your clients?
3   What are the benefits, rights and access to resources you receive by being a member of an oppressor group (being, for example, white, male, young, wealthy or able-bodied)?
4   How does this understanding of privilege impact on your work with people who have been oppressed and marginalised?

TUNING IN: THE PRELIMINARY STAGE OF WORK

As this chapter addresses preparation for practice, the skills recommended for social workers involve learning how to intellectually and emotionally prepare for practice through a process of tuning in. Tuning in occurs in the preliminary phase of helping. It is a period of emotional, ethical and intellectual reflection before the client arrives in your office or before you meet your first community representatives. It is a time for you to contemplate your values, including those coming from both the strengths-based approach and anti-oppressive practice, as well as to collect your thoughts about the work and interactions to come.

This phase of helping was first identified by Shulman (1992) in his research study of social work skills utilised. Shulman used the interactional approach, which demonstrates the reciprocal relationship between people and environments. The four key stages are:

1   the preliminary phase of work;
2   beginning contact and the process of contracting;
3   the work phase;
4   endings and transitions.

Shulman regarded the preliminary stages as a critical part of work with clients, although he did not link this stage to a particular set of relationship or behavioural skills. The skills are mainly cognitive or 'thinking' skills, and are critical for the effectiveness of practice at later stages. Different terms are used for this preparatory work, including 'preliminary planning', 'internal dialogue' or 'tuning in'. The term preferred in this chapter is 'tuning in'. It was first coined by Schwartz (1971), who used the concept to help workers understand the clients or community before they come to the agency or before the workers go to meet community groups. Tuning in enables the worker to become more sensitive to the indirect emotional communication that takes place during the first and subsequent interviews. This indirect emotional communication may arise either from issues that the client brings or from the practitioner's stance about issues such as race, gender, class or sexual preference.

The work with clients, agencies and communities starts well before the first contact and involves:

- thinking about the client and their social situation, especially those structural factors (health, housing, employment or family situation) that have led the client to present at the agency;
- considering the particular client and their social situation, their potential strengths, competencies, and positive and valued experiences that they may have as a result of their experiences;
- informing yourself about the uniqueness and characteristics of the community and its agencies as part of awareness of and empathy with clients and of understanding the social environment;
- imagining the client's feelings and reactions to their social and personal situation that they bring to the first encounter;
- understanding client concerns (fear, ambivalence and distrust) in coming to the agency for assistance with some personal or social difficulty; and
- being aware of the historical traditions of your agency (child protection or probation/corrections), how it has engaged with marginalised people, and the impact of these traditions on the way you work with people and communities.

In addition to thinking *about* clients, practitioners need to prepare for working *with* clients. Shulman (1992) focuses primarily on tuning in skills as part of preparing for practice; awareness of self is also a necessary part of this preparation. It may be as simple as learning how to deal with your anxiety about learning a new skill. Alternatively, it may be more complex, such as working with people who have been involved in a range of anti-social behaviours. Preparation means becoming aware of your attitudes and assumptions and how these are expressed in working with clients. Working with clients also means planning to work with people who are very different from you due to such things as race, culture, ethnicity, gender, sexual preference, ability or religious beliefs.

INDIGENOUS PEOPLE

The purpose of telling the story of Indigenous oppression is to emphasise the historical, political and social foundations of racial ideology which came to our shores with European imperialism and the colonisation of Australian and New Zealand Aotearoa. The reality of these experiences is that they have shaped Indigenous people's values, practices and struggles for justice. They have shaped the lens through which workers view the world. These experiences cannot be denied, and indeed must be accepted as a central premise if workers are to make a positive contribution to Indigenous communities and individuals.

It is a difficult task for any professional to work with Indigenous people who have experienced a history of intercultural relations that have developed around patterns of dominance, subordination and resistance. If practitioners are to work successfully with Indigenous people, tuning in to the political reality of their experiences is an essential component of preparation. The interaction between the personal and the political cannot be ignored. Tuning in and then working successfully involves a consciousness-raising process that includes understanding the history of Indigenous people, their current social and economic circumstances, their experience of oppression and parallel experiences of abuse, and forcible destruction of community and traditions. Tuning in is not only personal and affective; it is also political, dynamic and ongoing.

Building an informed consciousness (critical consciousness) is an important principle for practitioners, and requires both intellectual and affective understanding. This is especially true in working with Indigenous people, where developing a critical consciousness means listening to their voices.

Linda Tuhiwai Smith (1988) and Michael Dodson (1995) are Indigenous leaders from Aotearoa and Australia respectively. They speak of the importance of raising one's consciousness by making connections to the experiences of Indigenous people. Smith discusses the importance of making connection with Indigenous peoples, and argues that:

> Researchers, policy makers, educators and social service providers who work with Indigenous communities or whose work impacts on Indigenous communities need to have a critical conscience about ensuring that their activities connect in humanising ways with Indigenous

communities. It is a very common experience to hear Indigenous communities outline the multiple ways in which agencies and individuals treat them with disrespect and disregard. (Smith, 1988, pp. 17–8)

Michael Dodson, commenting on social justice for Indigenous Australians, states:

> Social Justice is what faces you in the morning. It is awakening in a house with inadequate water supply, cooking facilities and sanitation. It is the ability to nourish your children and send them to school where their education not only equips them for employment but reinforces their knowledge and appreciation of their cultural inheritance. It is the prospect of genuine employment and good health: a life of choices and opportunity, free from discrimination. (Council for Aboriginal Reconciliation, 1995, p. 22)

The dominant Eurocentric culture has oppressed Indigenous people systematically for centuries through the social construction of 'race' to establish difference and to order humans hierarchically. Tuning in to clients who are Indigenous means first tuning in to the history of their respective nations prior to the British landing, and second understanding the Indigenous peoples' experiences of colonisation.

Prior to the British landing, Indigenous people had intact cultures and epistemologies. Colonisation and the racial ordering of society, as informed by the historical, political and social foundations of European racial ideology, fundamentally changed Indigenous peoples' systems of organisation. The colonial racialisation of Australia and New Zealand also led to the exclusion of Indigenous people from the social goods of these colonial societies.

Indigenous colonisation history is littered with accounts of, and testimonies to, the general abuses. These abuses include murder and genocide of Indigenous people, removal of children from their families and cultures, and the forcible destruction of communities and traditions. Indigenous people have been disconnected from their land and in many instances deported to mission settlements, often to be confined by government regulations (see McConnochie et al., 1988; HREOC, 1997; Reynolds, 1987; Walker, 1990). These injustices have occurred over generations and resulted in Indigenous oppression manifesting itself in many ways, such as lower life expectancy; higher infant mortality rates;

higher levels of unemployment; higher levels of arrest and incarceration; alcohol and substance abuse; ill-health—heart disease, respiratory disease, suicide; and poverty and poorer educational outcomes than for the broader population (Council for Aboriginal Reconciliation, 1995). Racial oppression has also led to Australia and New Zealand structuring their respective social systems (e.g. the economy, health, education, political and legal systems) on those of the colonising country (Education for Social Justice Research Group, 1994, p. 17).

TUNING IN TO INDIGENOUS COMMUNITIES

Shulman (1992) recommends that preparation for practice should involve tuning in to the feelings of particular clients. Although it is necessary to empathise with the needs of individuals, this is not sufficient when working with Indigenous clients. Tuning in to Indigenous clients necessitates tuning in to their communities, and identifying their strengths and history of resilience.

Working with Indigenous peoples and communities is complex, but this does not mean it should be avoided. The complexity of the work requires a commitment to a process of becoming a reflective and reflexive practitioner. This stance is more preferable to Indigenous populations than engaging in short-term cross-cultural information sessions. Tuning in to Indigenous communities helps facilitate culturally safe contexts where Indigenous people are able to bring what they know and who they are into the worker–client relationship. The foundation of such contexts premises the sharing of power and a sharing of the space. Culture counts in such an environment. An example of how this work might occur is provided in the work of Cooper and Bowden (2006), who are currently developing an evaluation framework for diabetes self-care and management with an Indigenous self-help organisation in remote Indigenous communities in Western Australia. One of the dangers with this work is labelling Indigenous people as 'diabetic', and blaming Aboriginal communities and individuals for their health problems. Researchers and policy-makers, in commissioning this kind of research tend to focus on what is wrong with communities and ignore the individual and family exceptions. The Indigenous self-help organisation working directly with these remote communities recognises the capacity of individuals to make changes in their lives through better diets and exercise programs. They work from a strengths-based approach.

Students working with Indigenous communities will acquire a new range of skills. It is imperative that practitioners do not assume that world-views held by the general population will also apply to Indigenous communities, as there may be fundamental differences between them. Differences may exist in any of the following areas: child-rearing practices; conception and enactment of behaviour management; relationship to land, spirituality, (extended) family, sharing patterns and obligation among relatives/kin; individual freedoms and autonomy; and communication styles (body language, questioning, non-verbal signs).

The way to acquire or improve skills and knowledge in these areas is to engage with Indigenous communities, organisations and individuals with the focus guided by consultation with Indigenous communities. Before establishing community consultative mechanisms, you need to prepare properly for consultation by becoming informed and conscious of the community, and its organisations and structures at the local level. Proper preparation of this nature will support the development of relationships and enable workers to be more effective when working with Indigenous clients.

There is a range of things of which you should be aware to enable you to build a clear understanding of the world-view, history, dynamics and background of your local Indigenous community against the context of colonisation in Australia and New Zealand. These include:

- the name of the original Indigenous community;
- the profile of the Indigenous people, including the names of elders;
- the nature of the links between the current Indigenous communities in the area and the original community in whose 'country' they are now living;
- places of cultural significance;
- the demographic and geographical profile;
- the history and nature of the occupation and colonisation;
- the names and locations of missions, boarding homes or other institutions that acted as a place of residence for older community members. What links does the Indigenous community have to those places today?
- the social, economic and health issues faced by the Indigenous community;
- the successes and triumphs of the Indigenous community;
- the key people, elders and leaders in the Indigenous community;

- the institutions, organisations and centres that exist within the community (including the leaders of these organisations);
- the support mechanisms that exist to support the Indigenous community (these may not necessarily be only Indigenous organisations);
- the ambitions, expectations and concerns members of the Indigenous community have for the present and the future.

Exercise 5.3: Exploring Indigenous communities
Use the above points to understand Indigenous communities. This can be done using library information, the internet and by talking to people who live in these communities.

TUNING IN TO THE AGENCY

Most new human service workers find themselves employed in a government or non-government agency. Before beginning the process of tuning in to the client, it is essential to understand the agency context, especially the agency's mission, legislative mandate, goals, structures, services and procedures. Effective work with clients depends on this understanding. There are many activities that will help to assist in understanding. It is always useful to go to the agency's website and see how the agency presents itself to the community. Depending on the agency's technological sophistication, you might expect to find a site map indicating what is significant and important to this agency. This may be an illusion—or even an error, or perhaps delusion?

There are some essential tasks in getting to know your agency. The legislative framework, statutory requirements, and your agency policies and procedures should be read and studied carefully, as these guidelines establish the nature of services provided and how these services will be delivered. As you read, note the legal mandate and the non-negotiable requirements for intervention and work with clients. Reading these documents for the first time may be difficult and the language hard to comprehend, but if you engage with these documents they will help you get to know the agency and its services. As part of understanding services, it is useful to read any brochures published for the benefit of clients and other agencies. Another early task is getting to understand the agency's administrative structure, especially the line of control from the chief executive officer to your own supervisor. It is essential for you to know who to go to for assistance if your supervisor is absent or engaged in work outside the agency. The organisational structure also impacts on the ability of workers to provide effective services.

TUNING IN TO INDIGENOUS AGENCIES

As a response to Indigenous political struggles and calls for autonomy, self-determination and sovereignty, governments have established a variety of Indigenous agencies with limited administrative and statutory powers to act as the interface between communities/individuals and the wider Australian and New Zealand community. Most of the agencies are therefore governed by legislation established under the relevant statutes rather than being designed to cater specifically for Indigenous interests. This means that the statutes' legal principles may differ from the values and relationships operating within Indigenous communities, and their social and political interests. For example, the governance model of the legislative requirements of statutory bodies has been developed from non-Indigenous conceptions of governance, both historically and socially. Therefore, the role and legal obligations of an office-bearer in an Indigenous agency may conflict with Indigenous protocols and systems related to kin relationships.

Tuning in to an Indigenous agency in this context means asking a series of questions in order to develop one's awareness of the agency and any factors that may impact on services to clients. Here are some questions in exploring Indigenous agencies:

- Whose interests and agenda is the agency established to promote?
- How were the goals of the agency established and who established them?
- Does the agency build in processes for building representative governance of boards and committees that are also representative of their client base/constituency?
- Whose cultural aspirations and preferences are evident in the agency?
- What are the values and practices of the agency?
- Who are the clients that the agency serves?
- Who will directly benefit from the services the agency provides?
- What is the agency's connection to non-Indigenous organisations?
- What is the nature of the relationships between these agencies?

- How has the agency been able to develop as a distinctly Indigenous agency that is able to facilitate effective engagement with non-Indigenous society?
- To what extent have notions of cultural appropriateness determined the core principles by which the agency operates? How have these principles been enacted in the agency?
- Are Indigenous values and practices operating within the agency? If so, what are they and how are they operating?
- What is the process for ensuring effective and accountable relationships between the agency and the Indigenous community?
- Often the Indigenous membership of an agency's governing body is also part of the agency's client group. How does the agency manage this distinction at the level of policy and practice? Does it need to?
- It is argued that the separation of membership into the governance of an agency and client services assists accountability and reduces factional (family, community) monopoly of agency resources. Is this an issue for the Indigenous agency you have selected in terms of the delivery of their services to the Indigenous community?

Exercise 5.4: Tune in and understand the agency
Select any agency and gather information about its structure and services. When you have completed this exercise, use the above questions to explore an Indigenous organisation.

TUNING IN TO CLIENTS

Tuning in to the client's feelings assists workers to develop preparatory empathy. Being aware of these unspoken feelings contributes to skills in the later work phase of the process, especially the ability to display an understanding of the client's feelings, reaching for feelings and putting feelings into words. There are similar issues in working with individuals as part of either groupwork or family work. Tuning in to clients' feelings is not an intellectual exercise—it is an emotional one. Shulman (1992) expects that workers will try to understand the feelings clients bring to the encounter.

Practitioners come from diverse backgrounds. This is one strength of the profession. Some people have life experiences—for example, experiences of domestic violence—that assist them in understanding the emotions associated with particular social problems or life crises. These people are able to use such experiences to feel with clients and later discuss uncomfortable topics. Other workers have enjoyed a nurturing and protected upbringing with few adverse life experiences to assist the tuning-in process. In this latter circumstance, literature can be of great assistance in the beginning.

Whatever the worker's background, there are dangers in the tuning-in process. It is possible that, in drawing on our own experiences, we may make assumptions about the feelings experienced by the client, tune in to particular assumed or ascribed emotional feelings and get it wrong. On the other hand, our limited life experiences may mean that it is easy to understand the emotional impact of life events *intellectually*, but difficult to understand other people's experiences *emotionally*. Nevertheless, it is important to use emotional imagination and get inside the feelings experienced by people who are about to discuss issues with you as a worker. Remember, tuning in prepares and enables you to respond to the indirect cues presented by the client in the early stages of work.

TUNING IN TO INDIGENOUS CLIENTS

Many Indigenous people carry large emotional stresses and a cynicism about their ability to coherently address the factors causing their stress. There are numerous and varied reasons for these emotional stresses situated within the colonisation politics of Indigenous people's lives. The following list provides some examples of potential factors for causing emotional stress:

- racist harassment—institutional and personal;
- frequent deaths of family and friends (exacerbated by extended family relationships and obligations that are part of Indigenous life), and lower life expectancy;
- high levels of violence, domestic violence and alcoholism;
- detention through the criminal justice system;
- poor health;
- unemployment and poverty;
- the impact of either being forcibly removed from family or having siblings or children forcibly removed.

Alternatively, many Indigenous community members carry within themselves the strength of their resistance to colonising practices. Tuning in here necessitates understanding Indigenous ways for creating space for their knowledge and traditions to govern their lives. In New Zealand, the Maori, in the context of education, have articulated a political discourse termed *Kaupapa Maori* (Maori philosophy and principles) to inform Maori conscientisation, resistance and transformation, and to advance cultural capital and learning outcomes. These principles include but are not limited to: *Tino rangatiratanga* (relative autonomy/self-determination); *Taonga tuku iko* (cultural aspirations); *Ako* (reciprocal learning); *Kia piki ake I nga raruraru o te Kainga* (mediation of socio-economic and home difficulties); *Whanau* (extended family) that hold values (cultural aspirations) and processes (cultural practices); and *Kaupapa* (collective vision, philosophy). Examining and understanding the world from the Maori perspective while acknowledging the limits of one's cultural competence and expertise is important for the worker (Smith, 1998).

Rather than thinking of Indigenous cultural differences as barriers to effective working relationships, culturally skilled and literate practitioners learn to welcome this diversity as positive. They consider specific values, beliefs and actions related to culture, and take responsibility for learning about other cultures and their implications for preparing to work with them. For example, there may be issues of understanding language where English is a second language for the client. Do not assume that the client is literate. Use plain English (or cater for non-English speaking Indigenous people by employing an interpreter) and avoid jargon.

Tuning in to Indigenous clients and recognising Indigenous interests and issues is part of becoming more culturally literate. It is about the acquisition of skills, competencies and sensitivities so that we, as workers, are better positioned to 'read' cultural contexts. While being culturally literate means building awareness, knowledge and skills about other cultures, it also means building awareness, knowledge and skills about one's own culture, and reflecting upon those beliefs and attitudes and their effects, both personally and professionally, as you prepare for client contact.

Exercise 5.5: Using cultural awareness

Assume you work in a correctional services agency where you provide services to people who have been released from prison. Joe Pinkara is 26 and has been in and out of prison many times for a range of misdemeanours. Although he is on parole, he is reluctant to come for regular visits with you, the parole officer. He drinks excessively and takes a range of drugs, usually in a park close to Indigenous services. He now lives in the park with other Aboriginal people but his family lives in an Indigenous community. Recently he attempted suicide through the excessive use of drugs and risky behaviour, and you have been asked to see him.

1   Using your understanding of the history of Aboriginal people, the extent of oppression and your understanding of strengths, tune into Joe's emotional feelings. What might Joe's feelings be?
2   What types of oppression might Joe have experienced?
3   How might you go about having a conversation with Joe about his strengths, in light of his recent suicide attempt?

PART II

Phases of the helping relationship: Engagement

6

DEVELOPING THE HELPING RELATIONSHIP: ENGAGEMENT

Ronnie Egan

This chapter outlines the process of developing the helping relationship. It focuses on several central features of this first phase of client contact. The following two chapters, 7 and 8, will demonstrate specific skills used in engaging clients and illustrate how different practice settings and the voluntary or involuntary status of the client influence the beginning of the helping process. Together, these three chapters examine the use of empathy, respect and authenticity in practice, and focus on the skills of listening, questioning, reflection, paraphrasing and contracting as they are applied to work with clients.

DEVELOPING THE HELPING RELATIONSHIP: ENGAGEMENT DEFINED

Engagement is defined as the beginning phase in the helping relationship. It is variously referred to as setting the scene (Middleman & Goldberg-Wood, 1990), joining (Egan, 2007), beginning (Cournoyer, 2008) and building rapport (Strom-Gottfried, 1999). Engagement is not a discrete event; rather, it is a first step in the helping process. As such, it has both elements of everyday interactions and elements that are unique to the beginning of a professional helping relationship.

The discussion about engagement is founded on the notion of developing a partnership between the client and worker. The aim of such a partnership is to collaboratively work together towards creating positive change for the client. Using a strengths perspective, the client is considered the authority on her or his own life. This way of working is based on a belief that people are resilient, that they have the potential to change and grow, and that they are in fact expert about dealing with the problems they face. In this partnership, the practitioner is not the 'expert', but instead works with the client so that she or he can identify her or his expertise in seeking solutions to the problem. As Saleebey (1997) suggests, this perspective 'is predicated, in some way, on helping to discover and embellish, explore and exploit clients' strengths and resources in the service of assisting them to achieve their goals' (1997, p. 3).

THE MANDATE OF THE AGENCY AND THE IMPACT ON DEVELOPING HELPING RELATIONSHIPS

The relationship between worker and client is tempered by the mandate of the agency in which the worker is employed. Exercise 6.1, below, is designed to help you familiarise yourself with the Integrated Framework used in this text. It demonstrates how the agency mandate will influence engagement in different practice settings (refer back to Figure 1.1 in Chapter 1). In the exercise, you will be using the framework to make the links between the engagement phase, skills, theories and anti-oppressive practice in three different practice settings.

Exercise 6.1

In small groups, develop a case scenario for a client who might attend one of the practice settings (hospital, Centrelink or WINZ, or a sexual assault centre). What is the client's name? Develop a short profile including the client's education, income, work status, religion, age, gender, ethnicity and sexuality. What might the client want or need? How has the client come to the agency? Is the client alone or accompanied? What might the client be wearing? Develop a character and scenario for the presenting client and write this up.

1 Using your case scenario, how might you apply the engagement skills listed in Table 6.1 to engage him/her? Develop six statements you might use to encourage engagement between yourself and the client. Record these statements and identify how each practice setting might influence the engagement process. For example, at an income support agency (such as Centrelink in Australia or WINZ), where might you conduct the interview? Will you have any information before meeting the client?

2 Using the case scenario, identify the potential personal, cultural and structural levels of oppression that the client may have experienced. Brainstorm strategies to address these.

Listed in Table 6.1 are factors related to each dimension of the Integrated Framework that you would need to consider while engaging clients in a hospital, an income support agency—in Australia, Centrelink; in New Zealand, Work and Income Services New Zealand (WINZ)—and a sexual assault centre (see Figure 6.1).

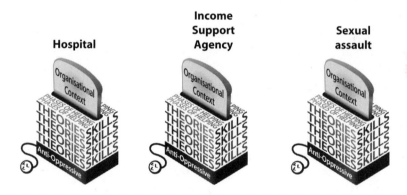

Figure 6.1 Using the Integrated Framework in different practice settings

Table 6.1 Understanding the Integrated Framework and its application to practice settings

		Practice settings		
		Hospital	Centrelink (Aust)/ WINZ* (NZ)	Sexual assault centre
Components of the Integrated Framework	Skills	Demonstrating empathy and respect Interpreting verbal and nonverbal cues Listening Questioning Paraphrasing Contracting	→ → → → → →	→ → → → → →
	Theories	Crisis intervention Ecological/ systems Solution-focused	Problem-solving Solution-focused	Feminist theory Strengths perspective Narrative therapy Solution-focused
	Factors affecting anti-oppressive response	Dominance of the medical model Nature of health policy Secondary status of workers Time constraints for service provision Lack of privacy	Notions of economic rationalism Eligibility criteria for assistance Limitations of service provision Legislation relating to income support	Dominant patriarchal ideology Sensitive nature of presenting issues Addressing safety concerns

* WINZ: Work and Income Services New Zealand

From Table 6.1, you can see that the skills used during engagement are universal across all practice settings, as is the case with the application of some theoretical perspectives. However, the macro issues that require anti-oppressive responses differ significantly between agencies. These macro concerns influence both the mandate of the agency and the practice of the worker.

Chapter 5 discussed the tuning in process. Exercise 6.1 highlights the interface between the lives of clients, and the dimensions of the Integrated Framework. This exercise does not require you to have an in-depth knowledge of the above agencies, or specialist practice knowledge. Rather, it requires you to have an imagination and the ability to consider the life circumstances of different individuals.

The ability to form relationships is central to effective practice. Human service texts consistently emphasise the notion of relationship as a key component to a successful outcome for the client (Compton and Galaway, 2005; Cournoyer, 2008; Harms, 2007). O'Connor et al. (2003) believe the 'foundation of all social work and welfare practice is the process of relationship building and purposeful use of self' (2003, p. 111). This foundation assumes that clients are respected and not pathologised, and that the broader structural impediments impacting on client self-determination are understood.

THE FIRST POINT OF CONTACT

As practitioners, we need to remember that seeking help from a stranger to discuss difficult and often intimate details of one's life might be potentially awkward and embarrassing. To acknowledge this possibility may also provide the opportunity for the worker to address the notion of power in the helping relationship (Mullaly, 2002). An anti-oppressive foundation recognises the inevitable power imbalance between the client and the worker. Such recognition might also highlight the potential for a more collaborative client–worker relationship. This needs to be acknowledged by the worker during the first session in order to demonstrate respect to the client.

In rural areas, where there are limited services and smaller populations, clients may face an additional barrier in seeking help. Access to services may be limited, and the worker may be someone the client personally knows or knows of. The client may have no choice about who or where they seek assistance. Similarly, as a worker, having an initial meeting with someone you know may be potentially disconcerting;

however, it would be expected that practitioners living in rural areas have developed strategies to address such situations. If the client and worker do know each other, then it is the worker's responsibility to initiate a conversation about how they will relate outside the helping context. The case study of Cherise in Chapter 10 (p. 151) provides further considerations when dealing with clients in rural communities.

First contacts between clients and workers can occur in different ways. The first contact with the 'client' may involve meeting an individual, couple, family or group from the community for the first time. Similarly, there will be different ways in which clients first make contact with services. A client may initiate contact with the agency themselves. This is called self-referral. For example, someone may contact a community health centre to discuss parenting concerns about their child. They may have seen a brochure advertising the community health service or been told about the service by another person.

Other clients may be referred to the agency, by telephone or in writing. This is called referral. For example, a family support agency may refer a couple to a mediation service to negotiate child access arrangements.

Mostly, clients will be mandated to attend an agency. There are two types of mandatory attendance: one that is legally required and the other where there is no legal obligation, but nevertheless an obligation to attend because failing to will have negative ramifications. An example of a legal requirement may be where a father is mandated by the Family Court to attend an anger management course before regaining access to his children. An example of the second type of mandated attendance may involve a teenager having to attend counselling for bullying behaviour at school instead of being suspended from the school. In this situation, the adolescent may not want to attend the counselling but recognises that he doesn't want to be suspended either.

The assistance a client can access depends on the range of services available within the agency. This range will provide the parameters of what help is available. It is therefore essential that workers understand the resources and services their agency offers, as well as those it does not. It is the responsibility of the worker to make clear to the client the possibilities and limitations of the services at the time of first contact. In addition, the worker requires a good knowledge of local community services that both complement and provide alternative options for the client. A client given inaccurate or out-of-date information about possible services may not seek assistance again. If a worker is able to effectively connect a client with a suitable service or agency that can provide the service they need, this can be a powerful and positive intervention.

NETWORKING

Workers need up-to-date knowledge of community contacts relevant to the service provided. This includes current information about services offered by other local and regional agencies, including current contact details, names of staff, intake procedures, waiting lists and information service access. Maintaining current community resources is an ongoing challenge for busy practitioners, yet it is essential for accessing appropriate resources for clients. Networking is an integral and ongoing part of the engagement process. Being familiar with current and relevant internet service directories also provides additional resources for clients. For example, a woman requesting assistance about parenting may attend a local parenting group provided at the community health service but she may also ask for information about parenting literature. The agency may have relevant literature or may have access to websites, brochures or information packs. Agencies will have relevant resources and websites that clients can explore before deciding whether or not to approach a service. It is therefore important that agency websites, like agency reception areas, are client-friendly, easily accessed and informative places to go. Whilst undertaking field placement, students will have the opportunity to explore local and regional service networks (Cleak & Wilson, 2007). Visiting these agencies, making contacts with other workers and learning about resources will provide a foundation of community knowledge for your own practice.

CLIENT ELIGIBILITY

The discussion so far has assumed that clients can readily access services and that engagement is the challenge in the initial phases of contact. Tighter restrictions on resources and more stringent client eligibility categories have also meant that client services are harder to access. The current post-welfare environment has led to client filtering systems that provide ways of prioritising limited resources. Greater focus on outcomes in service agreement targets can leave workers feeling pressured in terms of time and resources. These constraints impact on the worker's ability to respond to the needs of clients who do not fit service categories. Identifying client eligibility can potentially enhance or damage the initial engagement between worker and client. Being transparent and clear about eligibility criteria from the beginning of contact between client and worker leads to more satisfactory outcomes for clients (Turnell & Edwards, 1999). Even if the agency is unable to offer the service the client needs, the worker can still assist by engaging them. I am not suggesting this as an excuse, disguise or distraction from the truth that the client has no access to services. Rather, I suggest this as a genuine mechanism to demonstrate a willingness to engage the client rather than leaving them with nowhere to go.

For example, a 74-year-old man may contact an adult clinical mental health service that deals with clients below the age of 65. The worker needs to be clear with the client that the service is available only to people aged below 65. However, it is how the worker conveys this information to the client that will determine the success of the engagement process. It will be demonstrated in the way she speaks with this person, the messages she conveys through verbal and non-verbal communication and the degree of willingness she shows in assisting this person to access the appropriate service. For example, consider the differences in the following two responses to this 74-year-old man.

1   The intake worker is called to the agency counter to speak to the man. There is loud music playing, the day is hot and the worker is tired. The worker discovers the man is not eligible for this service due to his age, so she tells him he is in the wrong place, writes the name and address of the appropriate agency and gives it to him. She is friendly as she does so, wishes him a good day and goes back to her work.

2   The intake worker is called to the agency counter to speak to the man. There is loud music playing, the day is hot and the worker is tired. The worker discovers the man is not eligible for this service due to his age so she tells him he is in the wrong place. Before she explains this to the man she turns down the music and asks him whether he would like to take a seat. Next she offers to telephone the appropriate service, ensures his eligibility with this service and arranges an appointment time with their intake service. Before doing so, she offers the man a glass of water.

While the worker is helpful in the first example, the worker in the second demonstrates the qualities of empathy, respect and authenticity—essential for any engagement process to occur.

WORKER QUALITIES THAT ENHANCE THE ENGAGEMENT PROCESS

Developing the qualities of empathy and respect are central to successful connection with clients in the beginning phases of their work together. It has been well documented that those workers who demonstrate these qualities towards their clients have the best chance of achieving successful practice outcomes (Yalom, 2005; De Jong & Berg, 1998; Hubble et al., 1999). A helping relationship based on these qualities will lay the groundwork for developing trust between worker and client. Without trust, there is less potential for a shared and collaborative and therefore productive relationship and partnership. Not surprisingly, clients feel more valued and able to tell their story to a worker who demonstrates a genuine interest in their situation. Having made this connection, the worker is in a better position to learn about clients' circumstances. The development of helping partnerships therefore requires workers to be aware of and nurture their capacity for empathy and respect. The next section defines respect, empathy and authenticity. Each exercise demonstrates how these qualities can be developed in practice.

Respect

Demonstrating respect involves the worker acknowledging the uniqueness of each client through both verbal and non-verbal means of communication. Approaching practice from this stance enables the worker to see clients as having the potential to make positive changes. Such a belief in the client reflects a hopeful view of the potential work together (De Jong & Berg, 2007). In order to demonstrate this the worker develops their own self-awareness. Self-awareness generates insight, enabling workers to consider both aspects of themselves that enable the development of the helping relationship and those aspects that may create a barrier between the worker and the client (Kondrat, 1999). This self-awareness enables the worker to recognise and contain their own judgment. Exercise 6.2 provides the opportunity to explore your experience of respect.

Exercise 6.2

Consider someone in your life that you respect.

1 Identify what it is about the person that you respect.
2 How do you demonstrate your respect for this person?
3 How does your feeling of respect impact on the way you communicate with this person?

In pairs, discuss the similarities or differences between how each of you demonstrated respect. Now consider someone in your life that you do not respect. Identify what it is about the person that you do not respect.

4 How does this impact on the way you feel about this person?
5 How do you communicate this lack of respect?

In pairs, discuss the similarities or differences between how each of you experienced disrespect.

Empathy

Empathy is the capacity to understand the feelings and experiences of another without losing oneself in the process (Harms, 2007). The starting point of any helping relationship is the client's point of view, along with the client's story and the language they use. Being empathic requires workers to place themselves in the shoes of the client, to distinguish the nuances that make the client's feelings or experiences unique to them and the ability to communicate this understanding back to the client. The worker must listen carefully and openly to the client in order to understand and appreciate what is happening for them, and learn about how the client is responding to the situation. Empathy can be an elusive quality. Nevertheless, it is a quality identified as essential in the engagement process that greatly enhances the worker's ability to engage with clients (Geldard & Geldard, 2005). Exercise 6.3 provides an opportunity to explore the difference between sympathy and empathy. Empathy will be discussed further in Chapters 7 and 8.

Exercise 6.3

In pairs, discuss the difference between empathy and sympathy. How are empathy and sympathy similar, and to what degree are they different? Provide examples of empathic and sympathetic responses.

Authenticity

Authenticity, or genuineness, refers to the capacity to match words with actions. In colloquial terms, it refers to the degree to which workers 'walk the talk'. People are able to assess whether a worker is genuinely interested, honest and motivated to help. Assessing a person's honesty, authenticity and genuineness is something undertaken, unconsciously or consciously, in all human interactions. Authenticity is a quality we can observe in others and others can observe in us. Being authentic is critical to laying the foundation for an honest and transparent relationship between worker and client, and as such it is central to the engagement process. Exercise 6.4 provides practice at using these qualities.

Exercise 6.4

John has been living 'rough' on the streets and seeks emergency accommodation. He has not had access to washing facilities for some time. On first arriving at the agency, both John and the worker will respond to each other initially through a range of non-verbal cues. You have registered shock at the appearance and smell of John; you may even have unconsciously moved away from him. In some way, John will have noticed this. Your first words need, in some way, to match this reaction to demonstrate authenticity. A cheery greeting may not do this as it may convey a lack of genuineness.

Devise some opening responses to begin your conversation with John. How might you demonstrate empathy and authenticity?

Demonstrating empathy, respect and genuineness are common worker qualities for enhancing the helping relationships across all cultures (Lago & Thompson, 1996). These three qualities generally develop and deepen as workers become more experienced in their practice and as they develop further insight into themselves. Exercise 6.5 provides practice at using these qualities in different contexts.

Exercise 6.5

In pairs, discuss how you might convey respect, empathy and authenticity to clients in each of the following scenarios:

- You are a student undertaking a placement in the regional Office of Corrections. You are to meet with a client who is coming to see you as part of a court order to monitor her or his participation in a diversion program.
- You are a student undertaking a placement in a day program for people with intellectual disabilities. You are to meet a young woman who is coming to the program for the first time.

1   What will enhance your capacity to demonstrate empathy, respect and authenticity?
2   What might limit your capacity to do so?

Note the similarities and differences in the way you will convey these qualities to each of the clients.

TASKS FOR BEGINNING THE HELPING RELATIONSHIP

The following tasks and processes occur during the initial phase of engagement with the client or client group:

- conducting greetings and introductions in a culturally appropriate way;
- conveying the mandate of the service;
- making clear parameters of confidentiality;
- outlining the purpose of record-keeping if required.

Greetings and introductions

Building a cooperative partnership is the goal of the helping relationship, so first impressions will significantly influence how the client and worker perceive each other. These impressions will impact on the future success of the work between the client and worker. As discussed, empathy, respect and genuineness form the basis of a successful helping relationship (Geldard & Geldard, 2005). The reason for contact and the physical environment in which the meeting occurs influence how greetings and introductions take place. The worker needs to consider the client's cultural norms in this process. This may include the use of titles and dress code. Such considerations demonstrate a sensitivity to the differing cultural milieu from which clients come. How we dress also conveys a message to our clients. It may impact on the way we engage with clients during the first meeting. Consideration of dress will be affected by the agency dress code, and where and how services are delivered. For example, the worker may have to attend court one day and be involved in an adolescent adventure camp the next. Both activities require consideration of appropriate dress.

In some cultures, it is customary to offer food and refreshments during contact. Chapter 11 provides an example of this in meeting a Samoan family. The refreshments may be a cup of tea or coffee. The importance of sharing food is symbolic in some situations. It may indicate respect, hospitality and collaboration.

A further consideration during first and subsequent meetings with clients will be the arrangement of the interview space. Meetings can occur in formal offices in large organisations or more informal spaces such as a coffee shop. For example, you may share or be with a client while they have a cigarette outside the office (Geldard & Geldard, 2005). In a rural or remote area, you may find yourself helping to set up an electric fence or checking water bores while conducting an interview. Such examples illustrate the diversity of situations in which meetings with clients occur. The case studies throughout this text take us across a range of settings, including a church hall, the emergency department of a hospital, a client's house and other residential settings. The physical surroundings in which the first meeting occurs will influence how you position yourself in relation to the client. Workers need to consider a client's non-verbal communication to gauge the appropriateness of physical closeness and distance. Chapter 13 provides examples of cultural considerations in facilitating a group session with Maori men.

Greetings and introductions in the beginning phase of the helping relationship will vary. Different organisations—particularly statutory agencies—may have specific protocols around how this occurs. A friendly 'hello', a welcome, introduction by name, handshake or informal conversation may be appropriate. Cournoyer (2008, p. 153) rightly cautions against 'exaggerated familiarity' in the early phase of contact because neither party knows the other. Cultural factors also need to be considered before deciding how to greet or introduce one another. At this stage, listening to how clients introduce themselves and ensuring that you understand whether a title is used, and noting the pronunciation of a client's name, are important. Taking the time to clarify this early on in the contact demonstrates both respect for and interest in the client. Exercise 6.6 provides the opportunity to consider how you undertake greetings and introductions in different settings.

Exercise 6.6

You are a student undertaking a placement in a local high school. You are to meet a mother who has sought the school's assistance in dealing with her child's truancy.

Individually reflect on how you might set up the room, and then greet and introduce yourself to this woman. Make notes about what you might actually say in your greeting and introduction.

1   In groups of three, take it in turns to role-play the worker, client and observer using the notes you have made.
2   The observer can take notes about what they observe in the interaction with different greetings.
3   After each role-play, discuss what it was like to be the worker and client, then discuss what the observer noted in this initial interaction.

The purpose of contact and the mandate of the service

Students and new workers often find it difficult to discuss the purpose and parameters of service delivery during the first contact with a client. This difficulty often results from a reluctance to set boundaries in the interview or interrupt clients in this initial meeting. Students must grapple with the contradictory roles of trying to create a positive and comfortable beginning, while at the same time needing to clearly let the client know the parameters of the contact with the organisation. Setting clear boundaries is an integral part of the early dialogue between worker and client. This will occur differently according to the organisational mandate. The helping relationship cannot be separated from the organisational mandate within which the client is making contact. The challenge for the worker is to engage the client regardless of the agency's mandate.

In discussing a solution- and safety-oriented approach to child protection casework, Turnell and Edwards (1999) note the importance of worker honesty and clarity in outlining the legal and ethical parameters of the contact with clients:

> The contact between the statutory agency and the family should be based on honesty, with workers providing clear, straightforward information about who they are, why they have come to talk to family members, what the allegations are, and what actions the agency might or will take at each step of the child protection process. Regular and full exchange of information throughout the life of the case is crucial to service recipients. (1999, p. 34)

As a student on placement, such an approach requires you to:

- understand the role of the organisation;
- consider your opinion about this role;
- discuss your thoughts about the agency mandate, role, resources and services with other colleagues, particularly supervisors;
- learn and develop strategies to enhance the development of a collaborative partnership between yourself and the client;
- practise explaining the role of the agency and the reason for your contact with clients.

Exercise 6.7 provides case scenarios to help you practise how you might have conversations about purpose and deal with different settings.

Exercise 6.7

Using the three scenarios below, discuss in small groups:

- your understanding of the worker's role;
- how comfortable or otherwise you feel about this role;
- what information and knowledge are needed before making contact with the client;
- what strategies could be used to begin building a collaborative relationship with the client; and
- how you might explain the purpose of your contact with the client.

Scenario 1
You are a student on placement at child protection. You are about to meet the family of a fourteen-year-old boy who is currently living out of home. You intend to discuss plans for his impending return to the family home. The family is anxious about the return. This is the first time you have met the family, as your supervisor has been working with them up until this point.

Scenario 2
You are a student on placement at a family crisis accommodation service. You are about to meet a woman seeking housing for herself and her two children. She has been living in her car for the past two nights.

Scenario 3
You are a student on placement at an income support agency (Centrelink or WINZ). You are about to meet a young woman who is wanting to apply for a living-away-from-home benefit.

The Parameters of Confidentiality

Both Australian and New Zealand professional social work and welfare associations have professional codes of ethics and standards of conduct that identify the duty of workers to hold information shared with the client in confidence. The parameters of this confidentiality are qualified. This means that there are limits on the information that a worker can keep confidential. It is therefore incumbent upon the worker to inform the client of these limits early on in the engagement phase (Compton et al., 2005). For example, if clients disclose that they intend to hurt themselves or others in a statutory setting—such as in an in-patient mental health service—the worker must consult with other more senior professionals to make a decision about how to act on such a disclosure and ensure the safety of the client and/or those people around the client. Practitioners are rarely able to offer total confidentiality to clients.

It is therefore necessary to practise having conversations about confidentiality before meeting clients for the first time (Harms, 2007). It may seem like a contradiction in terms to be creating a collaborative client partnership while also simultaneously explaining to clients the limits of the service and parameters of confidentiality. However, managing such contradictions is part of daily practice. Students on placement have the opportunity to observe different worker styles and have conversations with them about how they discuss confidentiality with clients. The supervision process in field education offers time to reflect upon and practise how to handle the confidentility conversations. Subsequent chapters on assessment identify ethical dilemmas about confidentiality. Resolving confidentiality dilemmas provides a challenge for the student or new graduate. However, it is a key task in maintaining the helping relationship. Exercise 6.8 provides different case scenarios that highlight the tensions about confidentiality. Record-keeping also raises similar challenges.

Exercise 6.8

Scenario 1

A fifteen-year-old girl, Tanya, attends a youth drop-in centre where you work. She discloses to you that she has been sexually abused by her step-father. Tanya says the abuse has stopped and she has moved out to live with her friend. Tanya also says that she has younger siblings still at home. Tanya is insistent she does not want the worker to tell anyone.

Scenario 2

An 84-year-old woman, Elsie, who lives in a public housing estate, comes to see you at the emergency relief agency where you work. She has difficulty remembering why she has come. Elsie tells you that she has no other supports in her life and likes to keep to herself. She looks ill and frail, has no money and is very frightened about what will happen to her. Elsie is very clear that she only wants her food voucher and does not want you to do anything else.

In pairs, role-play how you might discuss confidentiality with Tanya and Elsie. Identify the challenges inherent in this role-play.

The purpose of record-keeping

Explaining to clients the purpose of record-keeping and how client files are maintained is another task in the engagement phase. Record-keeping raises similar challenges to discussing confidentiality with clients. There is a tension between trying to engage the client in the first contact, while at the same time explaining note-taking requirements. In the engagement phase of the work, it is important to keep note-taking to a minimum so that your focus can be primarily on the conversation with the client. Note-taking can often be a distraction for the client in this early phase.

The current post-welfare context of service demands increasing public scrutiny, accountability and cost justification (O'Connor et al., 2003). Organisations have record-keeping requirements to ensure worker transparency and accountability in practice. Record-keeping in most organisations is now computerised, and is an integral part of service delivery. It must comply with both agency requirements and standards established in national and state privacy legislation. Privacy legislation provides the parameters for the responsible collection and management of personal information in both New Zealand and Australia. Privacy legislation differs across Australian states and between the two countries. Students need to familiarise themselves with relevant privacy and confidentiality procedures and protocols during the orientation phase of any field placement.

There is no one way to maintain client files, and all agencies will have different requirements for record-keeping that reflect the nature of the work undertaken. Client records include all written documentation that workers complete in relation to their work with individuals, families and groups. For example:

- regular progress notes summarising contacts with clients;
- internal assessments for transferring clients;
- assessment reports for legal or other organisation requirements;
- letters;
- recordings of group sessions.

Ongoing progress notes are made for several reasons. They are used:

- for recording action plans the worker and client have discussed and agreed upon;
- to record factual details on which to base future reports or assessments;
- to provide continuity if another worker becomes involved with the client;
- to facilitate accountability and transparent practice with clients, the agency or professional body;
- to fulfil legal requirements.

The format for progress notes is usually brief and factual, ensuring that the information written is substantiated, while not judgmental or prejudicial. Legal reports, organisational assessments or letters generally require a fuller format based on the organisational mandate. Writing client files or completing assessment reports assumes that others will have access to them. Students find such advice useful because it encourages them to reflect carefully before writing about a client's life. Exercise 6.9 provides a role-play scenario to practise conversations about purpose of contact, confidentiality and record-keeping. Chapter 11 includes further material on record-keeping and identifies potential ethical issues encountered in writing client records.

Exercise 6.9

A court has stipulated that a father, Jeff, is to attend an anger management group before he is able to have access to his child, Nathan. You are the worker meeting Jeff for the first time. You work for a relationship counselling service providing these groups. The courts often use these groups as a condition for a court order. The limit to confidentiality for men who attend these groups is their capacity to refrain from using violence. Explain to Jeff the purpose of the anger management group program, and discuss the parameters of confidentiality and the requirements associated with record-keeping.

1   In groups of three, take turns to role-play being the worker, client and observer in this scenario.
2   Note down which strategies worked in engaging Jeff, and which did not work.

CONCLUSION

This chapter has discussed the engagement process, including an examination of the attributes a worker needs to demonstrate during the beginning phase of the helping relationship. The qualities of respect, empathy and authenticity have been defined and examined in relation to the role of the worker during engagement. The way in which introductions and greetings are facilitated and explanations are given relating to confidentiality, note-taking and the agency purpose and mandate all serve to shape the outcome of the engagement process.

The material and exercises undertaken highlight the dilemmas facing workers in the engagment phase of the work. The following two chapters identify particular skills and approaches to use in engagement. Chapter 7 examines case material from a hospital setting to explore the opportunities and limitations of engaging with clients in this particular context. Chapter 8 focuses on strategies to assist in the engagement of involuntary clients.

7

ENGAGING WITH CLIENTS IN DIFFERENT CONTEXTS

Helen Cleak and Ronnie Egan

This chapter explores how the physical environment can impact on the engagement phase of the helping relationship. The story of Nan, a patient in the Emergency Department of a major hospital, will be used to demonstrate communication skills in engagement and the impact of the hospital setting on the engagement process. The engagement skills examined in this chapter are the use of empathy, interpreting verbal and non-verbal cues, listening and questioning. The chapter also provides an overview of the practice theory of crisis intervention to illustrate strategies consistent with an anti-oppressive perspective in the helping relationship. While the focus in this chapter is on engagement, the use of a particular theory and skills is applicable across all phases of the helping process.

CONTEXT

The agency in which you work sets the mandate for the kind of the work undertaken. Agencies will have different safety, health and other contextual considerations that will impact on the engagement process (Harms, 2007). For example, a family violence or infectious diseases agency requires higher levels of security and confidentiality protocols than other settings.

Engagement occurs within different environments, which provide the context for the conversations between worker and client. The setting offers particular opportunities or challenges in engagement with clients and impacts differently on the skills used. Interviews take place in a variety of settings—for example, an agency office, over the telephone, online, outside a courtroom, in a prison visitor's room, in a client's home, by a bedside in a health-care setting, at a daycare centre, on the street or in a car or coffee shop.

Mostly, workers can plan the setting in which an interview will take place. However, sometimes there may be no choice. Some settings will be more appropriate for facilitating worker–client communication than others. Regardless of the environment, the aim of the initial meeting is to engage and begin to develop the helping relationship. The following section explores some of the considerations involved in engaging clients in different environments.

AGENCY SETTINGS

Workers will meet with clients in different agency settings. These may include over the counter, in office spaces or purpose-built interview rooms, or in a residential or custodial setting. In these environments, the worker may have more control of the physical space in terms of positioning chairs and turning off phones to ensure privacy, confidentiality and lack of interruptions. There is likely to be ready access to paper, pens, relevant information, files, telephones, referral numbers and safety buttons. However, Mulally cautions the worker about the 'comfort of the professional's office', which may be alien to the client (Mullaly, 2002, p. 174). A client may be intimidated by an institutional setting and may not keep appointments in such a setting. People's life experiences of oppressive and threatening regimes or institutions may create a sense of feeling threatened or trapped by formal organisational surroundings. Alternatively, the setting may be culturally alienating—for example, sitting in open-plan offices and speaking about personal matters. During the engagement phase, workers need to attend to client comfort, seating arrangements, and client and worker safety. Even though there may be little choice in terms of how certain settings can be arranged, it is important to maximise the resources or options that do exist. The following section details different contexts and considerations in the engagement of clients.

ENGAGEMENT IN THE CLIENT'S HOME

Interviewing clients in their homes—whether a boarding house, flat or family home—may be more relaxed because the client is in a familiar setting and may have more agency during the interview. There may be more potential for creating a partnership between worker and client. The worker may also have more opportunity to observe informal inter-actions between other people in the client's world. The home setting may also create opportunities for the worker to be part of family rituals or cultural customs, such as sharing food, which may foster a sense of trust between client and worker. Groups of older, frail or isolated people may find it easier to be seen in their homes, and the needs of young chil-dren may also more easily be met in this environment.

If a worker is required to interview the client or family members in the home, then the normal disruptions of home life are to be expected. Workers may need to seek permission for a television or other appli-ances to be turned down, or to access an alternative space inside or outside to provide greater privacy for the conversation. However, in making such suggestions, workers need to be mindful that they are visitors in the client's home. There are also increased risks and safety concerns associated with making home visits. Most agencies require workers to conduct home visits with a colleague or to have a system of formally notifying staff before going ahead with home visits; they are generally also required to carry a mobile telephone. Chapter 14 discusses worker safety issues further.

ON THE STREETS

Outreach work may take place on the street, or in shopping centres, amusement parlours or some other public space which may be the only place where you can meet your client. Clients may include younger people with addictions, people without housing or people experi-encing mental illness. For some clients, the streets are comfortable territory. Meeting the client in this environment has the potential for the interaction with the worker to be less formal and more client led. However, the streets may also pose a risk for both the client and the worker, particularly if the street is isolated. See Chapter 15 for strategies to maximise worker and client safety in such situations.

TELEPHONE AND ONLINE INTERVIEWS

Crisis lines, information lines, 24-hour 'hot' lines and online support groups are increasingly used in human service delivery. Chapter 4 provides an overview of key considerations when engaging clients using different media. These avenues particularly serve people who feel isolated or alone, those who do not have the social supports to share their issues, or people who require total anonymity. Because the worker cannot see the caller, there are only verbal or written cues to guide the conversation. In this regard, Chapter 16 discusses specific skills related to telephone work. The next section will use a case study to demonstrate the impact of the environment on the engagement process and the practice skills used in this phase.

Exercise 7.1 provides an opportunity to role-play how you might begin the interview with someone like Nan, who is confined to a hospital bed.

Exercise 7.1

Nan is a 75-year-old woman who has been living on her own since the death of her husband two years ago. She was admitted to the Emergency Department of an acute hospital last night having taken an overdose of sleeping tablets. Nan has no previous history of mental illness or self-harming behaviour. She has generally been in good health, although she has been speaking to her daughter about loneliness and feeling insecure at home at night. Nan took the tablets at home after a heated discussion with her daughter over the phone. This discussion focused on whether Nan would consider selling her house and moving into an aged care hostel. Nan's daughter realised her mother was upset and rang her back. During this second telephone call, she could sense that her mother was not coherent so she called an ambulance. The ambulance officers found Nan semi-conscious in the bathroom.

Nan is now awake but not fully alert, and appears to be anxious to leave the hospital. She is asking the nurse whether she can get off the hospital trolley in the Emergency Department, get dressed and go home with her daughter. The doctor on duty has asked the worker to assess Nan's social situation and whether she is in danger of further self-harm if she is discharged from hospital.

Think about the impact of meeting clients in different settings during the engagement phase.

1   How might you introduce yourself to Nan in a way that acknowledges the age difference between yourself and her?
2   Brainstorm some opening remarks you might make to Nan, as distinct from introducing yourself.
3   How might interviewing Nan in a hospital bed in the Emergency Department of a hospital impact on a worker's ability to engage Nan?

In groups of three, take it in turns to role-play your opening remarks to Nan. After the role-play, ask 'Nan' what it was like to be interviewed from the bed by a 'young' worker.

4   Discuss from the worker's perspective what it was like role-playing.
5   What did you observe during the role-play?
6   What lessons will you take from this particular role-play?

SKILLS IN DEVELOPING HELPING RELATIONSHIPS

Skills used to engage clients include demonstrating empathy, listening, responding, and interpreting verbal and non-verbal cues.

Empathy

Effective relationship-building between worker and client starts with following the client's lead and seeing the world through another person's eyes (O'Hara, 2006). In order to do this, the worker genuinely attempts 'to understand the thoughts, feelings and experiences from the other person's point of view in order to understand how they might be feeling' (Trevithick, 2000, p. 82). Such connectedness is called empathy. Empathy is needed throughout our interactions with clients, but most importantly in the beginning phase of contact. Chapter 6 refers to empathy and its integral role in the development of building trusting working relationships between client and worker. In the case study, Nan may be suspicious about speaking to a social worker when she is in hospital. She may be reluctant to discuss matters concerning her relationship with her daughter. The challenge for the worker is to establish a respectful, empathic and trusting rapport with Nan to provide the best chance of engaging and assisting Nan to achieve the outcome she wants. The skills that encourage this rapport relate to listening and hearing and looking and seeing both the verbal and non-verbal aspects of the client's communication.

Verbal and non-verbal communication skills

The ability to accurately interpret verbal and non-verbal communication is central to developing an empathic relationship and moving into the client's frame of reference. Careful observation of the client's verbal and non-verbal behaviour should reinforce rather than contradict the messages conveyed by the client, as clients will sometimes give mixed messages or make contradictory statements (O'Hara, 2006). For example, Nan may indicate that she is worried about leaving her home and become agitated when this issue is discussed. Nan's agitation provides clues to the worker that this may be a sensitive topic, which needs careful consideration before proceeding with the conversation. At times Nan may say that she is fine to return home but get distressed about her loneliness when at home alone. There may be an incongruent match between her verbal and non-verbal communication—which is understandable, given her circumstances. Using minimal encouragers, indicate to the client that you are listening to them. For example, verbal minimal encouragers might include expressions such as 'Mmm . . . ', 'Uh huh . . .'. Alternatively, non-verbal signals such as a nod of the head will demonstrate that you have understood what Nan has said.

Questioning

Questions can be categorised as open or closed. The effect of each type of question is different. Open questions are those that give the client an opportunity to provide more comprehensive responses. They allow for the client to have greater control of the information revealed; therefore the interview becomes more client-led. Closed questions are those that lead to a specific short answer. Examples of closed questions you might ask Nan include:

    'Are you feeling better now?'

    'How long have you been here?'

    'Where is your daughter?'

Closed questions are useful for getting certain facts, but if they are used too much may appear like interrogation. They also tend to follow the worker's agenda. Closed questions will produce a different response to ones that require the client to give more information. Examples of open questions are:

'What's been happening to you since you arrived in hospital?'

'What would you like to see happen now?'

'How are things between you and your daughter at the moment?'

Try to avoid beginning a question using 'Why . . .', such as 'Why did you take the pills?' or 'Why were you upset with your daughter?' Questions that begin with 'why' tend to sound judgmental or accusatory in some way.

The use of open questions in the beginning stages of a contact with a client contact provides the opportunity for the client to lead the interview. The worker's choice of questions can encourage or discourage the client's willingness to open up about their situation. Workers need to develop sensitivity in asking questions, particularly when they are communicating with someone from a different cultural background (or ethnicity, age, class, sexuality or ability) from their own. Delving into subjects such as age, money, relationships, sexuality, substance abuse, marital status or violence can be invasive. Sometimes it is useful for the worker to acknowledge this to the client. This demonstrates a willingness on the part of the worker to speak honestly about the difference between the worker and the client. These conversations promote partnerships and provide opportunities to discuss difficult content.

For example you might say to Nan: 'It might seem that it's none of my business to ask you questions about you and your daughter's relationship. I'm wanting to better understand your living situation so that we can work together to achieve what you want . . . [Pause]'. Alternatively, a young student might say: 'You are probably wondering how someone as young as me can be of any assistance . . . [Pause]'.

Other types of questions from a solution-focused approach to practice are coping questions and exception questions (De Jong and Berg, 2007). Coping questions are used to understand how a person had coped to date in their current situation. Exception questions are asked to draw attention to times when the problem is not present. For example, with Nan you might ask about times when she hasn't felt lonely at home. This may provide important insights for both Nan and the worker about the types of supports/resources Nan needs to support her at home. Exercise 7.2 provides the opportunity to develop different types of questions—open, closed, coping and exceptions—and role-play their use.

Exercise 7.2

In groups of three, develop some open and closed questions, including coping and exception questions, that you might ask Nan during this engagement phase.

1   Role-play a conversation with 'Nan' using the closed questions. Then repeat the role-play using the open questions. The observers are to take notes and compare Nan's responses to each of these sets of questions.
2   Get feedback from Nan about the impact of the open and closed questions.
3   Next, develop some questions you will ask Nan about her relationship with her daughter. Try these questions out in a role-play and get feedback about their effect.

The skills discussed above are relevant to all practice settings. It is important, as discussed in Chapter 6, to understand the impact of these settings when engaging clients. The following section uses the health context to explore this further.

PRACTICE SETTINGS

In Chapter 6, the link between the organisation and the nature of the relationship developed between client and worker was highlighted. The mandate of the agency provides the parameters of the relationship between worker and client. As such, this mandate also provides a limit to the length and the type of helping relationship that may be possible, and how and what client information can be obtained. Workers need to understand the distinctive core services that stem from the agency's purpose and goals. Furthermore, workers also need to understand the nature of the practice setting, which can be classified as primary or secondary.

A *primary setting* is where the worker takes responsibility for any decisions made on behalf of the client. This means that the worker has the responsibility for the duty of care requirements. A worker in a state child protection service carries primary responsibility for the care of the client while they are part of that system.

A *secondary practice setting* is where human service workers are not the dominant occupational group (Patford, 2002). In this setting, workers operate in conjunction with other disciplines. Hospitals and schools are two examples of secondary practice settings for social and welfare workers. These contexts offer particular challenges for the worker because clients are referred to the worker as a result of a referral from another discipline. The workers from other disciplines may perceive the presenting issues from a different perspective. The client may not have asked for a service but they may have been referred by someone in a position of authority. For example, in Nan's situation the doctor has referred Nan to the worker. It was not Nan who chose to initiate contact. The following discussion will highlight some of the implications of this, and the skills required to engage with her given these practice variables. The health-care context offers particular challenges because of the secondary status of the worker.

THE CONTEXT OF HEALTH CARE

'Hospitals are primarily concerned with the diagnosis and treatment of illness. Social work within such a health care service is a function described as secondary to medical and nursing care.' (Browne, 2001, p. 99) As discussed earlier, the organisational context will impact on the nature of the work undertaken in all settings. This is apparent in hospitals where the 'medical model' dictates whether and when a referral is made to a worker, as well as the nature of the work being provided for patients. The work in hospitals involves a wide range of specialist professions, such as medical consultants, doctors, nurses and allied health staff. Teamwork and good communication are required between all disciplines to manage the care of the patient. In this model, there is a tendency to focus only on the physical aspects of the client's problems rather than seeing these as only part of the client's situation. This medical orientation tends to focus on care and doing things for people, and not necessarily enough on respect and client self-determination (Healy, 2005). The use of diagnostic labels, such as 'the overdose patient', is a primary form of categorisation which pathologises the client and can be understood as a means of reinterpreting a client's reality. These labels potentially control the client's story. This can lead to a reduction in the client's sense of competence and confidence (Parton & O'Byrne, 2000).

For Nan, the hospital context will largely prescribe the worker's approach. The hospital policy will necessitate an immediate and time-limited intervention with limited opportunity for history-taking or any offer of ongoing contact. Technological and funding changes in the health system have placed pressure on hospitals to reduce the length of stay for inpatients, so there is limited time for staff to engage with patients. Nan's experience in the Emergency Department will impose an urgency to have her situation resolved responsibly but quickly. It is the responsibility of the worker to engage with Nan as effectively as possible to satisfy the hospital requirements, as well as meeting Nan's needs within this context. For the worker to engage the client and understand her needs, there may be a potential conflict of interest between what Nan wants and the hospital duty-of-care responsibilities. For example, the medical team may require the worker to obtain pertinent medical information, such as how many tablets Nan took, and whether she is still at risk of further self-harm. As part of a multidisciplinary team, this information would be shared with the team and the doctor would have the authority to detain Nan if it were thought she was at high risk of further self-harm. Alongside these requirements is the worker's goal to develop a collaborative relationship with Nan, and a duty to safeguard her from unauthorised disclosures of confidential information made in the professional relationship. Nan must be informed of the limits of confidentiality so that she knows and understands what information is required to be shared with the team. Each practice setting will have specific policies related to the parameters of confidentiality. As discussed in the previous chapter, students undertaking field education placements need to familiarise themselves with policies and protocols related to this. Exercise 7.3 provides the opportunity to consider how you might have a conversation with Nan about confidentiality.

Exercise 7.3

Brainstorm what safety concerns you may have for Nan.

1   In pairs, discuss what the boundaries of confidentiality might be in this health care practice setting.
2   How might you speak to Nan about the limits of confidentiality of the material you discuss with her?
3   Role-play your different responses and conversations with Nan about confidentiality.

---

4   Identify which responses you feel are the most appropriate for engaging Nan.
5   Identify the responses that are least appropriate.

In the health-care setting, there are opportunities for working with a range of people—the elderly in particular. Nevertheless, workers will encounter older women such as Nan in many fields of practice. The social stereotype of ageing often suggests an inevitable increase in sickness, disability and problems associated with daily living. These challenges are in fact not an inevitable consequence of ageing. It is therefore important to see each older person and their situation as unique (Healy, 2006). This can limit applying unwarranted negative stereotypes of ageing while at the same time acknowledging the structural barriers older people face. Workers need also to consider that health-related issues may compromise the level and way in which an older person participates in the consultation and decision-making process. In Nan's situation, the worker may want to interview her daughter. This can sometimes raise ethical issues regarding confidentiality and 'who is the client', and whether the family member or carer's opinion can really substitute for the client's wishes. Exercise 7.4 provides the opportunity to practise having a conversation with Nan about speaking with Nan's family.

Exercise 7.4
In groups of three, discuss how a worker might explain to Nan that she or he wanted to speak to her daughter.

1   What sort of issues relating to confidentiality do you think may arise in discussions with family? As a worker, how would you manage these?
2   What are some of the ethical considerations related to consulting with members of the family of an older client?

Different theoretical knowledge will be used in some settings and at different phases of the work. The hospital setting lends itself to the use of crisis intervention theory.

CRISIS INTERVENTION THEORY

As discussed earlier in the chapter, working in an Emergency Department of a hospital will impose an urgency to produce speedy client outcomes. The approach discussed here shifts the focus of the engagement away from the presenting problems to constructing solutions. Crisis intervention theory is not limited to the engagement phase of the work; rather, it can be used across all phases of the helping relationship.

Although Nan is a voluntary patient, the reason she is in hospital is because she has taken an overdose. The context of a medical setting necessitates a speedy assessment and development of a treatment and discharge plan, which may include a transfer to a safe facility and/or the involvement of other health professionals. Crisis intervention is a useful and common approach for working in health-care settings because it allows the worker to engage actively and quickly to assess the client's needs (Cleak, 1995, p. 18). This hospital has a duty of care to protect Nan from further self-harm, and to develop a discharge plan. As discussed earlier, the worker's role is to engage her and assess her needs and the level of risk of further self-harm. Nan's 'crisis' therefore needs to be understood and situated within the context of her current social circumstances and, while to some degree it has been socially constructed, it remains for her a crisis. It is important for the worker and the client to appreciate that 'a crisis occurs when a person faces an obstacle to important life goals and, for a time, the customary repertoire of solutions may fail' (Chenoweth & McAuliffe, 2005, p. 124). This definition infers that crises are normal and that realistic struggles occur throughout a person's life; a crisis is not seen as an illness or pathological. The subjective perception of 'crisis' is defined by the client. Crisis intervention:

- addresses the immediate presenting concerns, often in a practical way (e.g. provision of accommodation for fire victims who have lost their home);
- is brief and time-limited, focusing on addressing specific short-term goals;
- emphasises solutions;
- occurs in circumstances when customary patterns of coping have been unsuccessful;
- acknowledges that all people experience crisis at some point in their lives;

- acknowledges that responses to 'crisis' can follow a predictable series of stages from impact, through turmoil and finally to the resolution stage.

Exercise 7.5 provides an opportunity to consider Nan's experience from a crisis intervention approach to practice.

Exercise 7.5
1   What are the key presenting issues for Nan?
2   What are some of the immediate strategies you might discuss with Nan and her daughter to address this crisis?
3   Write a brief summary of the issues that you would lodge in Nan's hospital file notes. Discuss these file notes with others in the class. What material will you include? Is there material you would leave out and, if so, why?

CONCLUSION

In this chapter, we have covered four main areas. We first discussed the impact of different environments on engaging with clients, and then introduced the skills used in developing helping relationships. Next, using the case study of Nan, we asked students to consider how the environment and context would impact on engagement. We concluded the chapter with a brief overview of crisis intervention theory and its application to the case study presented earlier.

8

ENGAGEMENT WITH FAMILIES INVOLVED IN THE STATUTORY SYSTEM

Robyn Miller

THIS 'SORT OF WORK'

This chapter builds on some of the ideas introduced in Chapters 6 and 7. However, its focus is on the engagement of children, young people and their families who find themselves clients of the statutory child protection and youth justice system, and developing the strengths-based interpersonal skills and values that underpin good practice.

Many families involved with statutory systems have experienced social exclusion, adversity and trauma that is beyond most of our under-standing. The children have often witnessed or experienced violence and fear beyond words, and the shame and stigma of this can be carried for decades—even a lifetime for some—if there is no skilled and com-passionate intervention. Yes, these children need to be made safe, but they also have a deep need to belong, to have stability and, as one young ten-year-old boy in foster care reminded me recently, 'to know that you matter just like any other child'.

What helped him to know that he mattered? I asked him and he was really clear: 'Well my worker made sure I had the new footy boots for training and made sure that someone could pick me up, 'cause my foster mum works on a Thursday night.' When you're ten years old and the only stable thing in your life is your footy, then that connection is vital to having some sense of resilience. Building relationships with children and listening to what they want and need is the basis of a strengths-based approach that will also engage his family.

Children in the statutory system need to have the same developmental opportunities as 'any other child' in our community, and to access supports to catch up on their learning and development—often impacted by the trauma they have endured. Their recovery process is so dependent on the strengths and commitment of their family that practitioners forming strong partnerships and engaging with the family are *critical* to good practice. Even if the child cannot or should not go home because it is unsafe, physical separation rarely equates with emotional separation. The child may have been hurt within the family context, but fantasises and aches for family to provide the comfort. Families are complex, and children's identity needs are real. Practitioners shouldn't be seduced by simplistic polarised notions of 'goodies and baddies', nor should they allow unsafe contact that is not in the child's best interests. Careful assessment should take place to discern the level of safety that would enable safe contact to take place.

Family work in a statutory context is not 'soft'; it is intellectually rigorous and interpersonally challenging, as there are multiple agendas and multiple layers of experience and 'truth'. The expectations are high, while initially the family's hopes are often low. It requires practitioners to have 'grounded hopefulness'—where you 'keep it real', but also positive. It requires flexible engagement with a range of family members who are often locked in a battle, or overwhelmed with their own issues and the range of expectations and stakeholders in 'the system'. Focusing practice with the child's best interests at the centre of the family ensures that the voice of the child does not get lost.

Despite the involuntary nature of statutory work, there is compelling evidence that empathic and effective engagement can and does occur. Furlong's (1991) research into the successful engagement of statutory clients in a family therapy agency found that this was not dependent on or constrained by their involuntary status, but rather by the skill and respectful approach taken by the therapist. Schorr (1993), in an evaluation of maltreatment intervention programs, found that those with skilled workers who could build relationships of trust and respect with the families were the most successful. The widely acclaimed UK review of research on child abuse was unequivocal in its finding that: 'No single strategy is of itself effective in protecting children. However, the most important factor contributing to success was the quality of the relationship between the child's family and the responsible professional' (Dartington, 1995). Strong engagement in purposeful change is possible, and a strengths-based approach informed by a multi-theoretical knowledge base has been embraced in many statutory services.

This chapter highlights that, while the work can be complex, the essence of good practice is simple: it is about relationships—relationships that engage people in change, that build on strengths and look creatively with families for solutions that will make a difference; relationships that have warmth, and are non-judgmental, curious about the experience of each member of the family, and honest. Good strengths-based practice means speaking respectfully about difficult things, the wise use of authority and being transparent; it also means 'hanging in there' through stormy times, sensitively responding to need, and celebrating and enjoying the steps forward. One young woman who had endured years of horrific sexual and physical abuse, and had been a 'high-risk adolescent' in both the child protection and juvenile justice systems, was later asked about which intervention was most useful. We imagined she might choose one of the more sophisticated, creative interventions we had engaged in. However, like many other young people have told us since, she was adamant that the most useful thing we did was: 'You didn't give up on me even when I had given up on myself . . . and you didn't give up on my mum, even when she couldn't believe me at first.'

This young woman was a great character. Memorably, she also wryly commented that the other important things for her were that we could have a laugh, that we walked sometimes while we talked, that we sat outside when she smoked, that she could bring her pet rat to sessions, 'even though you were a wuss and you wouldn't pat him', and that: 'You were interested in all parts of my life not just the shit from the past . . . Plus, you look normal.'

'What do you mean?' I inquired, unsure about whether to be relieved or nervous.

'Well, if you were on a train, people would just think you were normal . . . like, you know they wouldn't know what sort of work you did.'

This still makes me smile all these years later, as I reflect that this 'sort of work' is the most deeply rewarding area of professional practice I know.

ENGAGEMENT AROUND THE BEST INTERESTS OF THE CHILD

Engagement is the process of purposeful change occurring within the family, as a result of a shared agenda that has developed between the family and the practitioner. Engagement occurs as a consequence of the practitioner's skilled relationship-building with the family that eventually develops shared goals. This relies on there being some agreement and enough trust to begin to work together. It is constantly renegotiated throughout the life of the case.

Figure 8.1 reflects the Best Interests Case Planning Model that has been developed to integrate practice across sectors in Victoria. The emphasis in Victoria is on early intervention with vulnerable families and an integrated service system that is based on the rights of children to be safe and have stability in their lives, and to promote their development. Children, young people and their families need to be empowered to connect with their communities and cultures in ways that are meaningful to them. Culturally competent practice is essential in a statutory system that has in past generations inflicted so much pain and trauma by the policies of the forced removal of Aboriginal children from their families and communities and from their land.

Figure 8.1 Best Practice Model diagram

Initial engagement is often fragile, and practitioners need to 'earn their stripes' before families will believe they can be trusted. The practice model in Victoria is strengths-based and trauma informed, and is built on a culture of reflective practice.

The process of engagement is dependent on building relationships with children and families, and this is helped by the practitioner being respectful and courteous at all times. In the writer's experience, the essence of a successful engagement is to be genuinely committed to being a helpful resource for the client and to be down to earth, avoiding jargon or an officious tone. Endeavour to find something you like about the person and give yourself permission to enjoy the process of getting to know them, even if it is because they are stretching you and challenging your professional skills and self-image. Deliver what you said you would whenever humanly possible. If it is not possible, or you make a mistake, apologise and endeavour to fix it or to make reparation.

Professionals and the court might have a long list of conditions or goals to be achieved, but from the mother's perspective initially, what may be most engaging is to address her need here and now and get the fridge fixed, buy some disposable nappies and negotiate an extra day at the child-care centre. What may be most useful for the father is to 'get the welfare off our backs'. You might respond with: 'Yeah, that sounds pretty normal—what do you think it would take to convince them to get out of your life?' This discussion, in my experience, has often led to the engagement of the family in setting some goals, which we could then brainstorm ways to achieve.

In the 'signs of safety approach' (Turnell & Edwards, 1999), the focus of strengths is reframed into how they can be used by the family to increase safety for children. The level of danger and risk of harm to a child is compared with the strengths and protective factors, and the safety of the children is the key focus. Turnell now refers to this as 'safety organised practice' (Turnell, 2006).

SUSPEND BLAME: REFLECT ON WHAT YOU BRING TO THE INTERACTION

The research is clear that the most healing thing for victims of child abuse is the belief and support of non-offending family members or significant others in the child's life (Miller & Dwyer, 1997). Strengths-based practice is interested in the constraints to parents providing that belief and support—that is, it is concerned with unpacking the layers of what is preventing this relationship from being a nurturing one. People who are hurting and stressed or traumatised are exquisitely sensitive to blame. If you, as a practitioner, are angry or blaming of the client, get some good supervision and explore the process issues. You may be intuitively picking up on a sadistic offender, or you may have unresolved issues in your own life that have been triggered by what you have witnessed in this family; many other possibilities exist. A culture of reflective practice is critical to embedding good practice in any organisation. Your tone of voice, your manner, your facial expression, your general presence and way of being will give it away even if you're mouthing the 'professional question'. Nothing replaces an attitude of genuine openness to listening to the client's experience and learning from them how you might be helpful.

When parents feel blamed by professionals, they can respond defensively, and their hurt and despair can often be projected into angry blame and at times rejection of the child for being so difficult, and at the professionals for being so 'hopeless'. This in turn can engage a defensive and more critical response from the professionals, and the family is often labelled 'resistant' or 'non-compliant', or worse. A strengths-based approach sidesteps blame, instead focusing on seeking to understand the constraints for the parents and for the child, empathising with their difficult journey and being curious about how this relationship might be helpful in finding a way forward that works for everybody. Purposeful engagement takes skill, empathy and emotional intelligence to manage often-conflicting agendas. The complexity of families presenting to services can feel overwhelming for practitioners, and this is generally paralleled in the way the family is feeling. Reflecting about your emotional responses and your beliefs about the family, and then integrating these with the relevant literature and research, will engage you in lifelong learning. Good supervision, a supportive and positive team culture, a personal commitment to self-care (including the self-discipline to exercise) and ongoing professional development are healthy habits to start early in your career.

As outlined in Chapters 6 and 7, engagement requires the use of self, providing sensitive and empathic attunement to the experience of others. This process requires exquisite attention to the use of power and authority that is based on values of social justice and respect for the human rights of each person, regardless of their behaviour. This requires that you develop your capacity for empathy and compassion for the experiences of others, which may or may not be foreign to your own life experiences. Rich learning can take place when you reflect on your own life experience. Exercises 8.1 and 8.2 are intended to connect the theory with your own affective and lived experience. The aim is to strengthen your emotional intelligence and ability to connect with others, especially children.

Exercise 8.1

In this exercise, practise the art of deep 'listening'—that is listening for content and feeling. Make direct eye contact and make sure you're at the same level as the client.

Paraphrase what the client is saying—in other words, reflect back in your own words what you think they are saying, feeling or meaning. Make sure you allow space and silence for them to respond. Ask questions that explore and add meaning, to open up another layer of experience. Allow yourself to relax and enjoy learning about the other person.

In the shoes of the child

1 In pairs, interview one another about your recollections of a time during kindergarten/early primary school where you were distressed, and experienced an adult as helpful or unhelpful. What did that adult do or not do that made a difference?

2 Note down the verbal and non-verbal actions and process issues that can be shared with the bigger group, rather than the content of the stories. (Remember that this is a training context, so protect yourself from discussing issues that are too raw or distressing.)

3 Repeat this process for recollections of a time when you were around eleven years of age.

4 Repeat this process for when you were an older adolescent. Come back together as a big group and share your reflections. What are the key learnings for you as a social worker in relation to working with children and young people? What are the recurring themes that emerge?

Exercise 8.2

In silence, think about a time in your life where you felt excluded from the group.

1　What feelings did this experience provoke in you?
2　What meaning did you make of it?
3　How did this impact on how you thought about yourself?
4　How did this lead you to behave?
5　In groups of three, discuss what you have written. Do any common patterns emerge?

TRUST AND TRANSPARENCY

As a practitioner, I often raise the issue of trust and caution people not to trust me until they get to know me. Exploring the 'good, bad and ugly' of talking about painful things before you do so with victims of trauma is good practice. *Talking about the talking about* helps to create safety as the family members are able to have some sense of control over the process and timing of the session. I sometimes slow down the disclosure of abuse so there is a clear plan of support organised in advance to manage any distress or self-harming impulses that may erupt after the session. The implicit and explicit message is that process needs to be safe and that you as a practitioner must take responsibility for facilitating the process while the family member takes responsibility for honouring the contract to stay safe.

Issues around confidentiality need to be explicit and clear about the detail and the process of how you will share information.

SETTING GOALS

Clarifying a detailed safety plan that is individually tailored and practical is critical when working with victims of trauma. Clarification of *who will do what, to whom, by when* is grounding, and provides structure and a sense of purpose and control when internal feelings and external life circumstances seem chaotic and out of control.

Engage families in solution-focused thinking. Ask families the miracle question:

> If you woke up in the morning and a miracle had happened and all your problems were fixed, what would be different? What would there be more or less of in your life? How would we know? Who would notice? (De Shazer, 1984)

Alternatively, you could ask families the nightmare question:

> How will you know when the nightmare is over? What would be different? What would help you to wake up from the nightmare? What are your dreams for your child? What gets in the way of these becoming real?

Frequently, when I am joining with a family in an effort to engage them and I am hearing about their experience, I will often hear such difficult things that the nightmare question seems to fit more than the miracle question. I ask their permission to be challenging and to talk out loud about what they are thinking. I ask: 'If us meeting together was good use of your time, what would you want to get out of it? What do you want to walk away with today?'

NO-BULLSHIT THERAPY: WHAT IS IT?

In working for ten years in a Ministry of Housing high-rise estate in inner Melbourne, my role was to provide family counselling to vulnerable families, most of whom were involved in the statutory system. I learnt very quickly the importance of being able to engage families by showing them I was genuinely there to help, that I was interested in what they wanted, and that I would be upfront about what I could or couldn't do. There is often a small window of opportunity when you are first meeting a family whose members are sceptical or openly hostile about previous experiences with social workers or counsellors, to capture their interest that you might be relevant and worth 'giving a go'. This is particularly important where they have been mandated to see you. Most people respond positively to an upfront but friendly approach which is not defensive when they get heated, but which quickly attunes to their need to be listened to. It was in this context that the nightmare question (outlined above) usually fitted. I would only ask it after I had empathised with them and listened to their story enough to be genuinely able to reflect back how hard things must have been. If combined with warmth and care, honesty and directness can enhance connection and trust.

One man taught me a lot about effective engagement, as he was adamant that it was 'all bullshit': 'All you wankers are the same—it's all bullshit—you're just wanting us to break up—s'pose you'll send the cops around for the kids—it's just bullshit.' As the decibels and the tension rose, all I could manage to get out verbally was something like 'Fair enough . . . I don't like bullshit either . . . fair enough that you don't like bullshit—any normal person doesn't.' He then calmed down slightly with a tirade of all the 'bullshit' he had copped over the past year since he had lost his job: he couldn't sleep, his wife had tried to leave him, he couldn't trust anybody anymore . . . His partner was silent with large eyes and the kids looked frozen. After a lot of listening, and showing genuine interest by clarifying what he was saying and empathising, we found agreement that I would only work with his family in a 'no bullshit way' and I would be totally upfront. This actually gave me permission to talk about the difficult issues in a way that was acceptable, usually prefixed by the question, 'Is it OK then if I'm upfront?' I'd say 'I know you don't want me to bullshit you, but it might be hard stuff to talk about and I know it's been a tough time, and I can see you're passionate about your kids . . . sounds like it's been a nightmare.' 'You're not wrong there,' he'd reply.

At this point we were at the half-hour mark. He offered me a coffee and we sat at the kitchen table and talked for another hour. Asking him whether he could ever imagine getting out of the nightmare, and what that would look like, was only appropriate after I had listened hard and long enough for him to have a sense that I had 'got it'. By this stage, he was close to tears. He had calmed right down and I could be upfront about what I could and couldn't do. The most important thing for his wife and children was that the process did not escalate and that this man could get some help. That began a very fruitful engagement over a period of seven months where we 'didn't bullshit' and we did the work. He kept in touch every few months for a few years, and the family was great to work with.

Jeff Young, a colleague at the Bouverie Family Therapy Centre, developed the 'no bullshit therapy' (NBT) approach into a framework for working with individuals and families who are not comfortable users of therapeutic services (Findlay, 2007). It has been very successful in the drought counselling work undertaken in rural Victoria in recent times. NBT has five basic clinical guidelines:

- striving for mutual honesty and directness in working relationships;
- overtly negotiating levels of honesty and directness;
- marrying honesty and directness with warmth and care;
- being upfront about constraints;
- avoiding jargon.

Alan Jenkins (1990), a narrative therapist, has also developed an excellent model for the engagement of men who are violent and abusive, which is highly useful in practice.

ENGAGE WITH THE SERVICE SYSTEM

Work in the statutory field requires collaboration across sectors and engagement of professionals from diverse settings to achieve good outcomes for children and families. Historically, services have been at odds regarding their role and mandate, often with Family Violence and Family Services providing more support and advocacy for the parents (usually mothers), and Child Protection advocating for the focus to be on the child's needs. Increasingly, advocates have promoted the voice of the child being heard and the child's rights being privileged. This is clearly not without its inherent contradictions between the rights of the family and the rights of the child.

This unavoidable contradiction and the highly emotive response within the media and the community to the plight of abused and neglected children, or to the practitioner's perceived trespassing on the sanctity of the family and the rights of parents, is reflected in the polarised views that are often presented in regard to child protection and family services work:

> Child Protection Services workers are criticized either for intruding too much into the integrity and sacred privacy of a family or for not doing enough to 'pull' children from abusive and neglectful adults who do not deserve to be parents. (Berg, in Turnell & Edwards, 1999)

A strengths-based approach acknowledges the positive aspects of family life and looks for exceptions to the problem-saturated view of the family. A strengths-based approach looks for what people do despite problems, how they have tried to overcome their problems and what they do well. It also explores their dreams and hopes for their children. A strengths-based approach is transparent and does not avoid difficult conversations about discrepancies in family member's accounts of events. Exercise 8.3 extends your exploration of your experience of respect from Exercise 8.2.

Exercise 8.3

In groups of three reflect on positive and negative experiences where you or members of your family were in need and in a disempowered position, requiring the services provided by an organisation. Reflect on the culture.

What did staff within the organisation do that made a difference to the way you or your family experienced the situation? List the attitudes and behaviours that were experienced under the headings of:

Oppressive/'power over'   Anti-oppressive/'power with'

Try to be specific—for example, if you experienced someone as respectful, deconstruct what it was about their manner or behaviour that conveyed respect.

ENGAGEMENT INFORMED BY A MULTI-THEORETICAL PERSPECTIVE

Information is power, and it is helpful for practitioners to become familiar with key messages from the research and literature so that there can be appropriate sharing with families in ways that are non-blaming and empowering. There has been an explosion of knowledge over the past ten years in regard to the detrimental impact of neglect and child abuse trauma on the developing child, and particularly on the neurological development of infants. It is critical to have a good working knowledge of this growing evidence base so that we can be more helpful to families and more child focused.

TRAUMA AND CHILD DEVELOPMENT

The child's experience of traumatic events is influenced by many factors, including their individual characteristics and the subsequent level of stability and support, offering an explanation as to why the impact of adversity differs between children. However, the effects of trauma in early developmental stages negatively impact upon the maturation of the child's stress coping systems and the architecture of the brain, significantly increasing their vulnerability to a range of behavioural and emotional disturbances and learning difficulties, which can overwhelm the most resilient child. These effects are now quantifiable, recognisable and well documented in scientific research and literature (Schore, 2002; Perry, 2001; Shonkoff, 2006).

When threatened by overwhelming events, the child's 'freeze, flight, fight' response is activated; biochemical changes then occur and they can remain stuck in this dysregulated and hypervigilant state, which in turn impacts on their brain development and future behaviour. Experienced practitioners have observed the 'frozen watchfulness' of the traumatised infant, the irritable hyperactive child, the self-harming and dissociative high-risk adolescent and the depressed or volatile parent. An understanding of trauma theory helps to make sense of these distressing behaviours and to engage the children and their parents in understanding that they are not 'mad or bad', but rather they are having normal and predictable responses to trauma that is abnormal and overwhelming. In the writer's practice experience, it is an incredible relief and very engaging for families to be told by a professional that they are normal, in the context of the adversity and social exclusion they have experienced, and that recovery and change are entirely possible.

Externalising the behaviour from the child's personality allows for a more hopeful and positive engagement of the family, without condoning or minimising the risks. White & Epston (1990) describe the narrative therapy technique of externalising the problem behaviour from the person, which is a very helpful process when working with families. To externalise the problematic behaviours from the person and to create space for new meanings and stories to emerge can free people to think, feel and choose to behave differently, without minimising issues of responsibility.

In the pre-verbal child, cumulatively harmful and traumatic experiences such as abuse, experiencing or witnessing family violence, neglect and unpredictable attachments are stored in a child's pre-verbal memory. Similarly for older children and adults, traumatic memories are stored differently in the brain compared with everyday memories. They are encoded in vivid images and sensations, and lack a verbal narrative and context. As they are unprocessed and more primitive, they are likely to flood the child or adult when triggers like smells, sights, sounds or internal or external reminders present at a later stage. These intrusive and deeply distressing experiences or flashbacks can be overwhelming, and can pull the sufferer towards avoidant behaviours, the most common one being alcohol and substance abuse. It can be useful for practitioners to reframe addictions as a form of self-medication to anesthetise deeply confusing, often shameful emotional and psychic pain. There is considerable literature that documents the frequent comorbidity of depression, personality disorders and a history of trauma (Van der Kolk, 2005; Herman, 1992). We should not be surprised, then, that the most frequently presenting problems when working in a statutory context are family violence, parental substance abuse and mental health disorders. Strengths-based practice explores the way that these issues get in the way of these adults being the nurturing parents they want to be.

ENGAGE THE YOUNG PERSON IN CONNECTING WITH OTHERS

Clark (2000) found that workers who were able to engage the young person and their family and/or significant others achieved better outcomes. The enhancement of resilience in the young person requires the practitioner to be skilled, well supported, flexible, timely and inclusive of the young person and their family in any decision-making. Clarke also notes the importance of well-organised program management that supports, mentors and creates a coherent culture based on trust and respect.

The findings from this study of exceptional practice indicate that a central focus of direct care and casework practice is the search for that caring, consistent relationship for the young person, and the ongoing support of that relationship. In some cases, the exceptional practitioner built bridges between the young person and a parent; in other cases, a lot of time and effort was put into finding the right person amongst the caring staff to establish connectedness with the young person (Clark, 2000, p. 40).

Dwyer and Miller (1997) have described the role of parents, carers, workers and teachers bearing witness to the child's grief and suffering in the context of their strength and survival, and the healing that takes place when this occurs. Connection builds resilience and attachment mediates the impact of trauma. This requires a care-team approach with the child and family at the centre, and Child Protection, family service workers, teachers, therapists and significant others providing consistent support, respite and leadership when needed. Recovery is rarely neat; it is usually messy, circular and multi-layered, and often needs to be revisited at anniversary times. While working with or caring for young people who have suffered severe cumulative harm is not for the faint-hearted, witnessing and participating in their recovery is a wonderful experience. Exercise 8.4 provides the opportunity to role-play a case conference about the family situation of Mia.

Exercise 8.4: Mia's story

Mia was born chemically dependent to parents with a long history of drug abuse and family violence. They lived in a rooming house at the time of Mia's birth, and had not engaged with antenatal care. Her father, John, was described by the extended family as a violent, unpredictable man who had repeatedly assaulted her mother during pregnancy and after Mia's birth. Her mother, Sally, was frightened, frightening and overwhelmed. Her behaviour was unpredictable, she had a long history of heroin use and she had mostly severed ties with her family of origin, who despaired of her lifestyle. Years later, Mia's mother disclosed that, as a child, she had been repeatedly sexually abused by a trusted uncle and had never been able to tell her parents. After Mia's birth, her mother appeared to be trapped in a series of crises and despair.

Mia had been admitted to hospital as a 'failure to thrive baby' at the age of nine months, and her hospital records state that she was irritable and easily startled. Child Protection was notified by the hospital, which described Sally as 'trying hard to connect with her baby'. The hospital informed Child Protection that the parents had reunited since Mia had been in hospital.

Role-play

1   Participants need to be in the role of Mother, Father, Mia and two Child Protection practitioners. Reflect on the different things each of you wants from the interview. As the practitioners, given the history, how might you respond differently to engage Mia's parents? What sort of position would you take with them? How can you be respectful and direct about the issues of concern about Mia? Be creative.

2   After ten to fifteen minutes, someone else interviews the participants regarding their experience of the process. Focus on the
style of questioning: how it felt, the non-verbal responses,
the use of silence, the attempts at paraphrasing or reframing,
and the general feeling in the room.

The relationships between engagement and authority, or change and
coercion, are not simple. Rather than seeing anger and hostility as resistance, the wise use of authority entails acknowledging these emotions
and working with the client through the different perspectives that are
at the heart of the matter. Establish a process with the client that allows
you to:

- acknowledge the position of the client. This does not necessarily
  mean agreeing with the client; it means making sure the client feels
  heard and understood: collaborate with the person, not the abuse.
- be clear about your professional assessment; communicate the
  reasons for your concerns and what needs to happen to resolve
  these worries. Feedback from Child Protection Service users
  indicates that clients did not understand what Child Protection saw
  as the problem, or what they were meant to do to change it. Clearly
  explaining your risk-assessment and gaining agreement on what
  needs to change to ensure their child's safety can be very empowering. A focus on safety moves us away from a focus on blame.
- establish and maintain clear *bottom lines* based on what is required
  to best ensure the child's safety and well-being. Allow options
  and choice about different courses of action and about how to
  negotiate different positions.
- ensure the client is aware of the different review processes to
  pursue justice if he or she feels unheard.

Young people who have been victimised repeatedly can become
stuck on the classic triangle of victim, perpetrator and rescuer. It is
critical to not view them in these fragmented polarised ways, as 'victims'
or 'offenders'. They need to be called by their name and we need to
understand the unique individual they are. *They possess enormous
strengths and potential and should not be defined by the abuse they
have suffered or re-enacted.* They can be engaged in facing up to and
taking responsibility for their offensive behaviours once they are

129

engaged in a relationship that is compassionate, hopeful and that reliably means something.

To heal, interventions need to be thoughtful, purposeful and integrated, rather than reactive, episodic attempts to 'rescue':

> Remember: It is important to understand that the brain altered in destructive ways by trauma and neglect can also be altered in reparative, healing ways. Exposing the child, over and over again, to developmentally appropriate experiences is the key. With adequate repetition, this therapeutic healing process will influence those parts of the brain altered by developmental trauma. (Perry, 2005, p. 3).

When children, young people and their families trust workers enough to reflect, discuss and plan ways to improve their children's lives, or trust them enough to 'have a go' at a new parenting strategy (or a new school, counsellor, detox program, new mothers' group or men's behaviour change group), or speak out about secrets and shameful events, then genuine engagement in a change process has occurred. Practitioners engaging with families in statutory settings have the opportunity to make a real difference with anti-oppressive, strengths-based practice that focuses on safety and well-being.

Exercise 8.5

1 From a strengths-based perspective, how would you describe your engagement in the learning process?

2 What practice skills have you learnt in this chapter that you can apply on placement or in everyday interactions with family and friends?

3 Think about three key ideas that you have learnt that you want to remember. Write them down and think about the values and attitudes that underpin the strengths-based approach.

PART III

Phases of the
helping relationship:
Assessment

9

INTRODUCTION TO COLLABORATIVE ASSESSMENT

Jim Anglem and Jane Maidment

In this chapter, we outline the central components of assessment. We are particularly mindful of discussing assessment from a strengths perspective that is embedded within an understanding of the social, environmental, economic and cultural influences that impact on individual, family and community functioning. From this perspective, we do not accept—and in fact challenge—traditional processes of assessment that have focused on problem identification, pathologising the lives of clients and viewing clients in a way that highlights deficits rather than personal resources. Rather, the focus is on collaborating with clients to develop assessments about their lives.

The chapter is divided into three sections. In the first, we provide a definition and overview of a contemporary assessment framework that takes particular account of structural influences on functioning. This section will also include a critique of more traditional social work assessment protocols. In the second part of the chapter, we focus specifically on understanding cultural dimensions and considerations when conducting an assessment. The final section of the chapter discusses principles inherent in anti-oppressive social work practice, while demonstrating how these can be integrated into the collaborative assessment process.

DEFINITION

To inform our approach in writing this chapter, we have drawn from the work of Lum (2000) who defines assessment as the:

> in-depth investigation of the psychosocial dynamics that affect the client and the client's environment. This approach analyses the forces between the client and the situational configuration, with particular focus on the environmental impact on the client and the resources available for responding to the problem. In multicultural practice, assessment identifies positive cultural strengths in the client's ethnic background. It moves away from the pathological investigation that tends to evaluate internal and external liabilities. (2000, p. 210)

From this definition, it is clear that we are concerned with approaching the assessment from a strengths perspective, which includes working with the client and accounting for the cultural and environmental context within which the assessment occurs. Understanding the social, economic and political influences that impact on the daily lives of the client group is central to this process. In both Chapters 2 and 5, discussions focused on how critical it is for the worker to engage with both the community and diverse groups within the community to gain an appreciation of the differing perspectives that can be used in formulating strategies to resolve issues. This is particularly necessary when undertaking an assessment.

FRAMEWORK FOR ASSESSMENT

In this chapter, we advocate for a process of collaborative assessment that acknowledges and seeks to redress the impact of the socio-economic context from which current problems arise, while at the same time endeavouring to mobilise client resources, both internal and external. Internal resources are those related to coping, motivation, intellectual functioning, decision-making, hope, faith and self-esteem. External resources are those found in the environment around the client and client system. These include relationships with friends, family, community and cultural networks, formal support services and spiritual associates. In earlier literature, it has been noted that the relationship and degree of congruence and 'fit' between an individual's mind, body and environment determine social functioning (Gittermam, 2001). To this analysis we would also like to add three further dimensions.

These are accounting for the notion of 'spirit' in terms of influencing personal well-being, and recognising the impact of both social and economic determinants on functioning. The scope of assessment is illustrated diagrammatically in Figure 9.1.

Agency and worker mandate

Worker system   Client system

Figure 9.1 The strengths perspective

Figure 9.1 illustrates the six dimensions to consider when making an assessment. These include the client's internal and external resources. The internal resources of mind, body and spirit form the inner core of Figure 9.1, with the external economic, environmental and social resources surrounding these. The two-way arrows between the inner and outer circles indicate the transactions and interconnectedness between the client's internal and external worlds. Both internal and external resources are in turn embedded within a broader cultural context. This suggests two things. First, our understandings of each of the six dimensions will be influenced by the cultural context in which the assessment is taking place. Second, the cultural context will have a direct influence on how the six dimensions of the whole system interact. We are, however, reminded by Dean (2001) that no cultural context remains static, and in fact contexts are ever-changing, emerging, transforming and political. She strongly challenges the notion of becoming a 'culturally competent' practitioner, and instead suggests we learn to sit with the paradox of being 'informed' and 'not knowing' simultaneously (Dean, 2001, p. 625). From this position, we acknowledge our lack of cultural competence, yet continue to seek better understanding and build trusting relationships across cultural divides, through respectful, deeply interested, non-judgmental exchange of beliefs and ideas. It is from this perspective that we need to consider the interrelatedness of the internal and external dimensions embedded within any given culture. You will notice that the internal, external and cultural contexts of both the worker and client interact, and that the scope of this interaction is influenced to a large extent by the agency and worker mandate.

The internal and external resources include specific factors to consider during an assessment. These are listed in Table 9.1.

Table 9.1 Internal and external dimensions for assessment

INTERNAL RESOURCES			EXTERNAL RESOURCES		
Mind	Body	Spirit	Environment	Social	Economic
Mental health	Physical health	Aspirations Faith	Housing Transport	Relationships with	Employment Income
Mental ability	Physical ability	Hope Values	Climate Electricity	friends and family	support
Self-esteem	Senses Nutrition	Religious and	Sanitation and	Education Leisure	
Self-concept	Genetic and	church links	hygiene Rural/urban	activities Cultural	
Judgment	chemical		Crime	links	
Coping	bias		Means of	Language	
Motivation	Gender		communication	Legal issues	
			Pollution	Formal services	
			and	Political	
			toxins	regime	
			Climate		

Source: Adapted from Germaine (1991).

These six dimensions located within a cultural context illustrate a configuration for collaborative assessment. Nevertheless, the lens through which the worker views the configuration will influence both the manner in which the assessment is conducted and the outcome of the assessment. In Figure 9.1, the assessment is conducted from a strengths perspective, and the connecting lines between the client and worker systems highlight the principles inherent in using this approach. You will note that the worker view originates from alongside the client system, not from above or below. This positioning emphasises that the relationship of the worker to the client is one of partnership and collaboration.

Exercise 9.1: Case scenario

You are the housing worker for your local council. A fire officer from the local station has contacted you saying he is concerned about the safety of Miss Flowers (aged 87) and Miss Thompson (aged 86). The fire officer noted they were called to a small kitchen fire last night that could easily have got out of hand. He said both women seemed to be very forgetful.

On visiting the women, you note that both show signs of short-term memory loss and you can see where there have been several small fires in the kitchen, on the bench, up the wall and on the floor. Both women present as being happy in their flat, and neither of them could remember the fire from the day before. They are very pleased to have a visitor and spend quite some time telling you about themselves. They have lived together for over 60 years, having first met while working in the same haberdashery shop in the city. Both are accomplished dressmakers. Neither woman has children, but Miss Flowers has a surviving brother.

Using the six dimensions of assessment discussed earlier in the chapter (mind, body, spirit, social, economic and environment), complete the following tasks:

1 Role-play your discussion with Miss Flowers and Miss Thompson where you discuss the report you have received from the fire officer. The two women are keen to talk, and tell you a lot about their lives. The role-play should run for at least fifteen minutes. (Different students may take turns at being the worker during this time.)

2 Next, role-play a brief impromptu discussion you have with the women's neighbour, Mr Green (aged 80), as you are about to leave their property. Mr Green is keen to tell you that he has concerns about the way Miss Flowers and Miss Thompson always leave their windows and front door open at night.

3 Write a summary of what you have noted in your conversations with these people. When writing the summary, bear in mind the concepts used in strengths-based assessment.

4 Finally, note down factors that you believe could contribute to the structural oppression of these two women.

5 As a class, discuss your perceptions of the role-play and what you believe would need to be recorded about this encounter.

A CRITIQUE OF TRADITIONAL ASSESSMENT MODELS

Many texts have been written that focus on how to carry out a social work assessment. Even though social and welfare work has historically stressed the importance of promoting client dignity and self-determination, Cowger (1992) notes that human service workers have been big on philosophies and theories but unforthcoming with practice guidelines to bear witness to these ideologies (1992, p. 139). Problem typologies, protocols, checklists and copious warnings about safeguarding the client, yourself as a worker and any significant others in the client's world are included in earlier publications on assessment (Compton & Galaway, 1999; Cournoyer, 2000). While these protocols and procedures include important material that we will also cover in this and the following three chapters, the discourse in traditional social work literature has focused on identifying deficits in behaviour, ensuring risk management by the practitioner with an implicit emphasis on the 'control' function of the worker.

The following summaries demonstrate different ways we can view and work with clients. Think about the distinctions between the summaries of the following scenario:

Summary 1: Aysha is a 33-year-old single parent who has immigrated from Egypt. She is a qualified dentist but has not been able to find work in this field. Currently, Aysha is working full time in a hosiery factory where she earns just enough to cover the cost of her rent, living expenses and child-care fees. Aysha has a three-year-old son who attends day care while she is at work. Aysha presents as being lonely, depressed and barely able to cope with her energetic three-year-old.

Summary 2: Aysha is a 33-year-old single parent who has immigrated to New Zealand from Egypt. She arrived in New Zealand six months ago, after having left her marriage of ten years which had been fraught with domestic violence. New Zealand is to be a 'new start' for Aysha and her son. She is a qualified dentist but has not been able to find work in this field. Currently Aysha is working full time in a hosiery factory where she is able to earn just enough to cover the cost of her rent, living expenses and child-care fees. Aysha wishes to supplement this income with a second job. Her three-year-old son attends daycare while she is at work and Aysha notes he is learning to speak English very quickly. Aysha says she feels lonely and depressed, but has begun to make connections with two sets of neighbours. She gets on well with other staff from the factory and the daycare centre.

138

You will recognise the difference in tone between Summaries 1 and 2. In Summary 1, all the facts are correct but some pieces of information to suggest strengths in Aysha's character and environment are missing. In Summary 2, while the facts remain the same, the worker has included information that highlights features of resilience, future expectations and Aysha's beginning connectedness with community. Identification of and further building upon these factors are integral to working with people from a strengths perspective.

Table 9.2 contrasts traditional assessment approaches and assessment from a strengths perspective.

Table 9.2 Contrasting traditional and strengths models of assessment

	TRADITIONAL ORIENTATION	STRENGTHS ORIENTATION
Theoretical framework	Psychodynamic Behavioural	Strengths perspective situated within an ecological/ systems framework
Assessment discourse	Problem identification Diagnosis Psycho-pathology Focus on historical antecedents	Resilience and optimism Enhancement of expectation, hope and opportunities Acknowledgment of systemic oppression
Assessment dimensions	Emphasis on physical and psychological components	Incorporates physical, psychological, social, environmental and spiritual dimensions The impact of oppression on the client acknowledged Focus on client agency
Client–worker relationship	Characterised by a focus on boundaries and marked differences in status Power rests implicitly with worker	Client and worker in partnership Issues of power acknowledged. Power shared between worker and client in explicit ways Client is expert in presenting issues
Process	Focus on problem-solving, task-focused orientation	Identifies and builds upon client solutions, options, possibilities and achievements Identifies exceptions Includes consciousness-raising

In this chapter, we are not arguing for the 'wholesale abandonment' of traditional models of assessment (Graybeal, 2001), but wish to endorse recent calls for additional items to be included in assessment schedules, along with changes being made to the process of conducting and reporting assessment outcomes. Integral to this approach is understanding and building upon client cultural links and resources. As noted in Chapter 2, our definition of culture includes acknowledgment of diverse cultural beliefs and practices that may occur on the basis of ethnicity, gender, class, sexuality, ability or age.

UNDERSTANDING CULTURAL DIMENSIONS IN CONDUCTING ASSESSMENTS

In all formal assessments where the client is not of the same culture as the social worker, there is likely to be some miscommunication and/or misunderstanding. The seriousness and consequences of such miscommunication is determined by the level of competence of the social worker. It is this cross-cultural competence that lies at the heart of good social work and welfare practice, and obviously informs the sound assessments fundamental to appropriate and effective client outcomes. In this chapter we focus on Maori culture; however, there are parallels in this material for all different cultural groups.

The following Maori *whakatauki* (proverb) refers to the need to be sensitive when dealing with people because not all matters pertaining to feelings are obvious:

He kokonga whare e kitea he kokonga nga ekore e kitea

The corners of the house may be seen, but not the corners of the heart.

Similar sentiments are expressed by several writers when considering relationships between workers and clients of different cultures. We need to remember that, due to exploitation and discrimination, many First Nations people and other minority ethnic groups may not be trusting of white workers. Indeed, 'it is futile to expect people of colour, given their contravening history with the Caucasian world, to immediately trust the intentions of Caucasian workers or to honestly disclose deeply personal and threatening information about themselves or their families' (McPhatter, 1997, p. 272). Additionally, particular difficulties may arise regarding communication when problems of child abuse, domestic violence and other morally unpalatable allegations occur. Such matters may not be revealed easily to strangers of a different ethnicity, who may also be seen as judging the client to be inferior (Lum & Lu, 2003).

With Maori and Pacific Island people, for instance, specific phenomena such as *whakamaa* (acute embarrassment, shame, feeling of injustice) and *musu* (similar to *whakamaa*) may arise. They highlight an aspect of behaviour that may cause the worker to worry over the withdrawn, stony silence or even outrageous anger or irrationality of a client. The worker's ability to understand or deal with this behaviour is likely to be limited, as the intervention might well be part of the client's problem.

Both *whakamaa* and *musu* manifest themselves in a range of ways, but often the associated behaviours will be misdiagnosed. 'Rude', 'aggressive' and 'uncooperative' are terms that are often used to describe clients acting on such feelings. These behaviours are not uncommon at the initial meeting, where serious allegations may have been made against either a Maori or Pacific Island person.

A range of emotions is likely to have arisen for such behaviours to have emerged, but central to the issue will probably be the perceived damage done to the *mana* (personal standing) of the individual as well as the individual's family. If the worker is not Maori or of Pacific Island descent, there is a strong chance that such behaviour on the part of clients will impair the worker's ability to proceed effectively. This theory is reinforced by Kaplan et al. (1994), who suggest that all psychiatric syndromes are, to some extent, influenced by culture. Like many Western psychiatrists, human service workers are often inclined to the view that welfare interventions are culture free.

Hospitals provide an interesting example of an institutional model which (like banks, courts and mainstream educational institutions) is quite monocultural. Hospitals are representative of a white, or Western, ethos in terms of the way they are administered. For example, many Maori people feel extremely uncomfortable about entering a hospital. This discomfort can be likened to *whakamaa*. There is usually an obvious lack of Maori staff to tend to them so the perception of vulnerability on the part of the patient is increased, particularly if they are requested to disrobe, asked personal questions about their lives, or are prodded by strangers of a different ethnicity in places considered *tapu* (private and sacred). For Pacific Island cultures, similar reactions are not uncommon.

A consideration that a Maori might have in mind when entering hospital is the probability that the bed that they might be asked to lie in may have been one in which a previous patient had died. Such an idea may cause extreme upset to a Maori patient who has a strong sense of *tikanga* (traditional values and beliefs). These concerns can lead to a patient feeling so overcome with shame and acute embarrassment (*whakamaa/musu*) that this element may add to their original illness. If not recognised and treated appropriately for an illness affecting mind and body, such a person may not heal. 'Snapping out of' *whakamaa* or *musu* is not possible.

In some cases, Maori or Pacific Island people can be overwhelmed by *whakamaa* or *musu* after having what might be called 'normal treatment' for 'minor' illnesses. They can feel that their bodies have been so violated that they have refused to return to hospital even though they may need simple procedures to deal with non-complex but life-threatening health issues. The seriousness of *whakamaa* and *musu* is not widely appreciated by non-Maori or non-Pacific Island professionals.

Whakapapa (genealogy) forms the single most important element in Maori society, as it links an individual with their family and their tribal history. Offending or insulting someone sometimes has the effect of casting a slur against not only the individual but their family and ulti-mately their ancestors. In many Maori people's eyes, such an insult may be worse than, for example, a physical assault. This view is also shared by many Pacific Island people. Thus, flippant or ironic comments may not be understood in the way they are meant by a well-intentioned worker and could have unfortunate repercussions (refer to the *whakatauki* noted above).

The significance of familial and tribal histories can be illustrated by the often-stated Maori proverb that says, 'Our past lies before us'. Another variation says, 'Our future lies behind us'. Both indicate the view that many Indigenous cultures have, which is that they see their future tied inexorably to the past. Thus, if one has little knowledge of one's family or tribe, one will have no knowledge of self. Without this knowledge, an accurate diagnosis of one's mental health is probably not possible (see Figure 9.1).

In the context of assessment, McPhatter reminds us, 'the very ques-tions we pursue are determined by worldview and practice theory' (1997, p. 273). If there is little understanding of a client's culture, it is likely that the information obtained from an interview may be inaccurate and possibly quite unhelpful (McPhatter, 1997). It is therefore critical for the worker to create an atmosphere which is collaborative and consultative, and where assumptions are tested in the initial meeting with the client.

Appreciating the differences between the views, values and histories not only of different ethnic groups, but within them, is a vital component of the worker's knowledge bank. Indeed, the competence of a worker to engage effectively with people of different cultures depends largely on the acquisition of knowledge.

When a worker first moves into the particular area where they will be employed, it is suggested that they consider the following points:

- They realistically cannot be expected to know everything about every culture.
- The development of community networks ensures that the social worker has a bank of cultural experts to whom they can turn when confronted with cultural questions that have no obvious answers.
- When meeting with clients, be guided by them. Clients will be able to provide a lead into giving information about their lives. They, after all, are the experts on the culture which affects their lives. The worker's role is one of the 'gentle inquirer', not necessarily the informed expert.
- Within cultures, there are likely to be significant variations in knowledge and understanding of issues, and these variations may be present between and amongst families.
- Being of the same ethnicity as the client may allow a relationship based on a perceived shared understanding of values to be initiated; however, there is a risk of collusion if workers 'over-identify with the client' (Lum & Lu, 2003, p. 129). Workers may also make assumptions and not treat each situation as unique.
- Workers need to recognise and understand their own values, and have access to high-quality supervision in order to develop good practice when working across cultural boundaries.

In summary, it is possible to present these additional considerations within the context of a bicultural model of welfare delivery, as shown in Table 9.3, which refers specifically to Maori culture.

Table 9.3 Considerations of some key elements within a bicultural model

MAIN ELEMENTS	SPECIFIC ELEMENTS	MAORI COMPONENTS	TRANSLATION
Knowledge	Qualifications Experience	Whakapapa Te reo Maori Tikanga Maori	Maori genealogy Maori language Maori history and customs
Professionalism	Code of ethics Code of practice	Matauranga Maori Mana	Maori knowledge and wisdom, status, pride, influence and strength
Compassion	Sense of caring Sense of valuing	Aroha Wairua	Caring and valuing spirituality related to emotional connectedness
		Manaakitanga	Process of helping

ASSESSMENT FROM AN ANTI-OPPRESSIVE PERSPECTIVE

In Figure 9.1, you will notice that our approach to assessment includes situating the client issues within a context that takes account of environmental, social and economic influences. This approach therefore involves the worker in a process that includes a critical analysis of structural inequities that impact upon the client and adds an overt political component to the tasks carried out by the worker. In a critique of anti-oppressive practice, Maori authors have warned practitioners about the risk of reproducing dominant power relations under the guise of anti-oppressive practice (Matahaere-Atariki et al., 2001). They go on to say that effective practice strategies can only occur on the basis of understanding the severe sociopolitical consequences of colonisation for Indigenous people. Taking account of the historical context from which current social relations emanate is central to understanding how an anti-oppressive approach to practice may be instigated.

In Chapter 1, we introduced the Integrated Framework as a means of conceptualising the connection between practice skills, theory and the phases of the helping relationship. You will recall that this matrix is underpinned by an anti-oppressive foundation. Burke and Harrison (1998) outline five principles that underpin anti-oppressive practice. These include:

- exploring notions of social difference;
- linking the personal with the political;
- overtly acknowledging power differentials;
- locating presenting issues within a historical and geographical context;
- highlighting elements of reflexivity/mutual involvement (1998, p. 231).

Exercise 9.2

Go back to the case study in Exercise 9.1 where you role-played the work with Miss Flowers and Miss Thompson. Focus particularly on how the worker might have addressed these five principles of anti-oppressive practice in both the role-play and the written recording of the home visit made by the worker.

In Chapter 2, there was a discussion about the scope of oppression and marginalisation, which noted that people can be oppressed on the basis of a range of factors. The next case study and exercises are designed to attempt to identify how our assessment may be influenced by some of these factors.

Exercise 9.3: Case study

You are a school social worker. The Smith family has come to your attention after reports from a teacher concerned about one of the children and a phone call to the school from the Smith family's neighbours. The neighbours had reported a number of late-night gatherings at which loud music was played and shouting occurred.

The two children in the house are William, aged six, and Victoria, aged four. The next-door neighbour, Mary Brown, an older *pakeha* (white New Zealand) woman, has many concerns about the frequency of these late-night sessions and the impact that they may be having on the children.

The following information has been gathered from one home visit by the worker and information from the family's neighbours.

The mother, Rena, is Maori and the father, Harry, is *pakeha*. They are aged 22 and 24 respectively and moved into these rented premises recently from Western Australia where they had been living. Harry had been employed in a highly paid position in a mine north of Perth in Western Australia but Rena wanted to return to New Zealand as she missed her family members.

Rena Smith is Tainui (a tribal area south of Auckland). Harry is not interested in Rena's culture and has been most unhappy being back in New Zealand, as the jobs he has been able to get are not nearly so well paid. The children have been isolated from their wider family (*whanau*), but as they now are living in South Auckland and Rena's family live near Hamilton, only about an hour away, they should be able to see more of each other.

The neighbour suspects that 'there is considerable drug trafficking occurring from the Smith house and the children appear to be poorly dressed and cared for'. She also reports that 'they are mostly barefoot, untidily dressed, unkempt and often have running noses and incessant coughs'. She also says that 'occasionally Rena is seen pegging washing out on the line but most often neither parent is visible'. It is 'rumoured' from the neighbours that Harry has been 'rough with the children and even his wife but Rena's brothers once visited and the roughness seemed to lessen'. Harry is known to the be a hard worker but with relatively little education and very strong views about the place of Maori in New Zealand. During the social worker's visit, Harry said that he thought that 'the Australian attitude towards their black people should be adopted here' (in New Zealand) but did not explain what he meant. Rena said nothing about Harry's comment.

The teacher of the older boy, William, has reported that he seems to have health problems and attends school on an irregular basis. The neighbour reports that Victoria, the younger child, 'appears often to be quite miserable'. Rena reports that her own family is unhappy with her and rarely visits. Despite returning to be near her family, Rena admits she has made few efforts to contact them.

1   Identify the main issues, explicit and implicit, in this case study and consider the following:

- cross-cultural matters—Australia/New Zealand, Maori/*pakeha*;
- racism;
- health and safety;
- sociological issues—the effect of leaving high-paid employment unwillingly;
- parenting knowledge and skills and developmental age;
- the role of the wider family (*whanau*), both Rena's and Harry's.

2 What is your opinion about whether the children are safe in both the short and long term?

3 How do you weigh up the strengths and validity of the sources of the information you have about this family to date—for example, the neighbour, the school and the family?

4 What is your assesment of this situation?

CONCLUSION

In this chapter, we have outlined our approach to conducting a generic assessment that is informed by an anti-oppressive analysis where the worker collaborates with clients using a strengths perspective. The material in the chapter also highlights the importance of gaining competence in understanding the impact of cultural factors. We have attempted to demonstrate that assessment has many complex and intriguing aspects to it but that, as in all areas of human service work, there are some principles and frameworks that can be used to guide this process. More specialist frameworks for assessment, such as suicide risk, mental health assessment protocols and models for assessment of domestic violence, are examined in the following chapters.

10

CONDUCTING RISK ASSESSMENTS

Christine Morley

Increasingly, the language and assessment of risk are featuring dominantly in social work and welfare practice (Bessant, 2003; Webb, 2006). This chapter explores the social and political contexts in which the concept of risk has been constructed, and the practice of risk assessment has emerged. The limitations of risk-assessment instruments will be acknowledged. Risk-assessment tools will be explored, using anti-oppressive and strengths-based approaches to guide practice. A case scenario will demonstrate the use of domestic violence screening and suicide prevention risk-assessment tools when working with victims/survivors of domestic violence in a rural setting. The skills of universalising, validating, contextualising, consciousness-raising and affirmation will be defined and demonstrated within the context of this case scenario.

SO WHAT IS RISK ASSESSMENT?

Risk assessment is the process of categorising and recording particular information about clients to make predictions about the likelihood of future hazardous events occurring (Webb, 2006). Risk-assessment tools assist practitioners in organising and classifying information related to risk so that decision-making about the prioritisation and allocation of resources is enhanced. Risk-assessment tools aim to:

- ensure that workers consider a wide range of variables as risk factors;
- improve the transparency and consistency of practitioner decision-making;
- provide a way of documenting the decision-making process;
- enhance agency and practitioner accountability; and
- prioritise services and target resources. (DePanifilis, 1996; Wald & Woolverton, 1990; Camusso & Jagannathan, 1995; Stanley & Manthorpe, 1996).

Despite these aims, critiques of risk-assessment models suggest they fall short of their intended purposes (Bessant, 2003; Webb, 2006; McDonald et al., 2003). In this chapter, caution is expressed about the uncritical adoption of risk-assessment tools in practice. However, this chapter examines how to use these tools in conjuction with anti-oppressive and strengths-based perspectives.

ANTI-OPPRESSIVE AND STRENGTHS-BASED PRACTICE

An anti-oppressive perspective has a particular commitment to social justice and challenging oppression (Burke & Harrison, 1998) through acknowledging the inextricable links between the personal and the political, and critiquing dominant ideologies and power relations. Central to this is a structural analysis that locates people's private experiences within broader social and political contexts (Thompson, 2001; Mullaly, 2002; Dominelli, 2002).

Combining anti-oppressive and strengths-based approaches provides a focus on the structural, cultural and personal levels of oppression and client strengths. This includes people's intellectual, physical and interpersonal skills, capacities, interests and motivations (Maluccio, 1979). The resources and supports that people may be able to access in their own environments, and their aspirations which enhance motivation, are also considered important resources from a strengths perspective (McCashen, 2005). A strengths philosophy contends that everyone has strengths and capabilities, to which the problem (separate from the person) may blind people; that, given the right supports and resources, people can make positive changes; and that clients are the experts on their own situation (McCashen, 2005).

WHY A SHIFT TO EMPHASISING RISK ASSESSMENT?

Many fields of practice in the human services have increasingly shifted their emphasis to the language and assessment of risk (Bessant, 2003). Within a globalised context (globalised markets and technologies), market relations have commodified social work services, and new technologies such as risk assessments have thrived. Professional legitimacy and competence in this context are seen to be linked with scientific, 'objective' knowledge and the quest for certainty. It is argued that some discourses in social work have also complicitly embraced this 'technocratic managerialism . . . by claiming to be a science-based profession with an important role in the monitoring and control of problematic populations at risk' (Davies & Leonard, 2004, p. 10).

Paralleling global conditions, the local context has also experienced changes, which have resulted in an emphasis on risk assessment. The dominance of economic rationalist policies has meant that community resources to provide services to marginalised groups are inadequate. In addition, changes to legislation, such as the introduction of mandatory reporting in child protection, have meant services in Australia and elsewhere have been dramatically overwhelmed with service demands, without the comparable increase in adequate resourcing (Goddard et al., 1999). It is within this social and political environment that risk assessment has been adopted to cope with and respond to these service demands, perhaps in the absence of lobbying political systems for more resources (Goddard et al., 1999). This has led to a rise in the development and implementation of a plethora of risk-assessment tools (Dutton & Kropp, 2000; Walsh & Weeks, 2004; Webb, 2006).

RISK ASSESSMENT IN DOMESTIC VIOLENCE

While risk assessment models are now used broadly in the human services, their use in the community and voluntary sectors of practice, such as domestic violence, has been far less prominent (Waterson, 1999; Parton, 1996). 'Domestic violence is a term used to cover any violence in the home when one partner abuses the other in a way that wounds, belittles or threatens the other. It may take the form of physical, sexual, emotional or social abuse' (Smallgood, 1996, p. 129). Traditionally, policy and practice in this area have largely been informed by anti-oppressive and strengths-based approaches. Practice has therefore placed emphasis on people's rights in relation to empowerment, rather than explicitly focusing on risk (Stevenson & Parsloe, 1993, cited in Parton, 1996). Practitioners working with intimate partner violence advocate practice that supports clients' choices, self-determination and control. Practitioners that operate from anti-oppressive and strengths perspectives also tend to have more of an emphasis on social change, rather than the social control and surveillance imbued in the assessment of risk (Bessant, 2003; Webb, 2006).

Despite this, some domestic violence practitioners and researchers have embraced risk-assessment tools as a means of improving practice. While the broader global context has influenced this, within this field specifically, this move has also been prompted by the recognition that many professional responses to disclosures of domestic violence are inappropriate and inadequate (Walsh & Weeks, 2004). Common responses by professionals to disclosures of domestic violence reflect the conservative assumptions that 'marriage was made to last forever. If the woman expresses a desire to leave, it was quashed' (Scutt, 1990, cited in Walsh, 1999, p. 129). Thus, many practitioners have uncritically contributed to women and children remaining in abusive relationships, often by minimising the violence and ultimately failing to act appropriately to support the woman. The consequences of this are extremely serious, and in some cases may be fatal. 'It is estimated that between 30–40 women and children are murdered each year in Victoria alone' (Women's Coalition Against Family Violence, 1994, p. 1, cited in Walsh, 1999, p. 140). Similarly, other Australian research indicates that 60 per cent of all women who are murdered are murdered by their partners (Bonner et al., 2002).

Compounding inadequate professional responses, many social myths surround the issue of domestic violence. These myths operate to blame the victim/survivor, by examining her behaviour to see if it has caused the perpetrator to react to her violently, and protect the perpetrator by trivialising, denying or justifying violent behaviour. These myths also conceal that most perpetrators are known to the victim/ survivor, to instead convey that violence is mostly perpetrated by strangers. Myths also obscure the power dynamics of domestic violence, and ultimately act to perpetuate the patriarchal (male-dominated) structures that create family violence and allow it to continue (CASA House, 1992).

As human service workers, we have a professional and ethical responsibility to challenge social myths and their consequences. It is thought that risk assessment may be one way of raising consciousness about the incidence and prevalence of domestic violence, and the factors that indicate potential harm. In New South Wales, for example, the introduction of routine screening for domestic violence has been proposed in response to both local and international research indicating high incidence of domestic violence experienced by clients and poor detection by health services (Bonner et al., 2002, p. 1). Using risk-assessment tools to routinely screen women, particularly during antenatal care, is also gaining considerable popularity among health-care providers. Some researchers argue that this is an intervention in itself through conveying the unacceptability of violence (Stratigos, 2000; Lawler, 1998; Walsh, 1999).

SOME RESERVATIONS ABOUT RISK ASSESSMENT

Other research, however, indicates that women may only choose to disclose violence to professionals once a trusted and supportive relationship has been established (Walsh & Weeks, 2003). Conducting risk assessments may actually be more about covering agency accountability requirements rather than enhancing services for clients (Morley, 2003). As Walsh and Weeks (2004, p. 139) argue, '"[R]outine screening" will perhaps absolve health care professionals from guilt, but may or may not create the trusting and safe environment that will enable women to talk freely about their lived experience.'

In addition, given that risk assessments aim to locate clients' experiences within a 'predetermined agenda of categories' (Webb, 2006, p. 76), they have also been critiqued for objectifying and blaming clients for complex structural issues (McDonald et al., 2003), over-simplifying the complexity of issues with which clients sometimes present, and reducing practitioner discretion and autonomy by limiting the parameters of our work (Bessant, 2003; Morley, 2003). It has therefore been argued that 'a small number of open-ended questions would reveal much more about a client's life-world and relations than a closed tick-box method' (Webb, 2006, p. 75).

Other concerns relate to the knowledge that risk assessments are based on the assumption that risk can be quantified and empirically measured (Bessant, 2003; Webb, 2006). This is consistent with the belief that scientific methods can eliminate uncertainty by objectively predicting risk. Attempting to objectively define risk, however, assumes a rational, linear, singular and fixed reality. Given that the problems clients experience are often complex, messy, changing and unpredictable, it would appear that risk assessments are based on a number of 'flawed assumptions' (Webb, 2006, p. 74).

Related to this point, the pursuit of objective 'facts' assumes that risk assessment can be a value-free exercise. Yet all interpretations are mediated by our own social, political, cultural and gendered biography and social positioning (Fook, 1999). Risk assessment, therefore, 'is coloured by subjective judgments at every stage of the process—from the initial structuring of the risk problem, to the process of what is considered relevant information, to deciding . . . the kind of outcomes that experts are seeking' (Webb, 2006, p. 76 citing Slovic, 1999). This is oppositional to an anti-oppressive and strengths perspective contention that clients are the experts on their own experiences (McCashen, 2005). The absence of a clear theoretical or philosophical framework within risk-assessment tools relates to other difficulties in which practitioners make assessments about risk based on their own unarticulated values and assumptions, under the mistaken guise of objectivity (Parton, 1996; Morley, 2003; Webb, 2006).

Given these critiques, it would seem that conducting risk assessments may be fundamentally at odds with anti-oppressive and strengths-based practice. As Stanley and Manthorpe (1997, p. 34) comment: 'For social workers trained in the theory of empowering users through involving them in decision making, risk assessment may appear to offer little in the way of choice or autonomy to users, while placing heavy responsibilities on these professionals undertaking risk assessment.' Bessant (2003, p. 32) extends this critique further by situating risk assessment as 'unethical' and 'antithetical to building and sustaining relationships with clients'. However, many agencies require that we use risk-assessment models as a core part of daily practice. How can we practise from an anti-oppressive and strengths-based perspective when the organisation within which we work demands that we conduct risk assessments? The remainder of this chapter will explore how the use of an anti-oppressive and strengths-based practice may address some of these dilemmas.

CASE STUDY OF CHERISE

You are working at a rural community centre in Australia. Cherise, a 27-year-old woman from Malaysia, has come to see you. Cherise tells you that she moved to Australia eighteen months ago with her husband John, aged 46, who was originally from Australia, but lived in Malaysia for business opportunities. Cherise tells you about how they met, fell in love and married about six months before John needed to return. Cherise joined her husband and plans to make a life in Australia. Despite this, Cherise misses her family and friends terribly and tells you she has found it difficult to meet people, given that she lives in such an isolated area.

Cherise tells you of an incident last week with her husband that has made her question their relationship. On the way home from an outing in town, she tells you that John didn't say anything, but glared at her and silently walked out of the club. He waited until they were in the car, and then started yelling. She said John 'drove like a maniac' on the way home, at high speeds and taking risks on dangerous sections of the road. Cherise was terrified, screaming and pleading for him to take more care, but this only seemed to make him worse. When they arrived home, she tried to talk to him and he yelled and swore at her, repeatedly saying she was useless and hopeless. He then grabbed her and pushed her to the floor. Shaken, she stayed there sobbing while he continued to rage and smash things up. John kicked the door in, said he would kill her if she told anyone or thought about leaving him, and then went out.

Cherise said she felt very afraid for her safety. Cherise described herself as 'walking around on eggshells at home', trying not to upset him. She said this was not the first time an incident like this had occurred. Cherise tells you she blames herself for these incidents and has also thought about harming herself. She is sad, uncertain and tearful as she explains to you that she has given up everything to move to Australia to be with John. She feels like she and her marriage are a failure. She tells you that John is acting 'normal' again this week, but nothing has been discussed or resolved, and she is still fearful that he might 'lose it' again. Cherise tells you she doesn't want the violence, but she does not want to leave her husband because she loves him.

Exercise 10.1 provides the opportunity to consider Cherise's situation from an anti-oppressive perspective.

Exercise 10.1: Brainstorm

1 From an anti-oppressive perspective, how do you understand Cherise's situation and experience of violence?
2 What might be some important cultural factors to consider?
3 From an anti-oppressive perspective, what might be some of the skills you use to work with Cherise?

> 4 What roles or purposes might risk assessment have in working with Cherise?

Theorising practice with Cherise

From an anti-oppressive perspective, working with Cherise may involve working in partnership with, or referring her to, a culturally appropriate service if available. The dominant community in Australia may not always value people from culturally and linguistically diverse groups. It is important to reflect on our cultural assumptions and values that we bring to the interaction, and deconstruct the position of white power and privilege in order to challenge our own unconscious racism (Dominelli, 2002). Working in conjunction with a cultural consultant will assist in making our work more culturally sensitive and relevant; however, it may be unlikely that such services will be available in rural areas, where services are generally limited and under-resourced.

Given that an anti-oppressive perspective draws on a structural analysis, which connects people's personal experiences with the broader social, cultural, economic, historical and political context, gender is also acknowledged as a key social structure (Fook, 1993). Anti-oppressive practice aims to challenge patriarchal (male-dominated) structures and power relations because these are implicated in domestic violence (Dominelli, 2002; Marchant & Wearing, 1986). These perspectives situate domestic violence as a community responsibility, rather than as an individual problem. It is a criminal act directly related to gender, reflecting the power disparities that operate between men and women, in which the victims are never to blame. The philosophical position of this analysis has direct implications for how we would work with Cherise.

Some of the practice skills to emerge from a feminist perspective are:

- *Universalising*—This may involve letting Cherise know that she is not alone in experiencing domestic violence by drawing out the links between her experience and that of others in similar situations. This involves not only personal empathy, but social empathy.
- *Normalising/affirming/deguilting*—These skills involve recognising and conveying to Cherise that her feelings, thoughts, responses and actions are legitimate and understandable given the situation she is in and the experiences she has endured. This may also involve

letting Cherise clearly know that she is not to blame for what has happened to her.

- *Contextualising*—This involves locating an understanding of Cherise's situation and experience in the broader societal context—for example, exploring domestic violence in the context of social, political, economic, historical and cultural structures.
- *Consciousness-raising*—This entails providing information about the causes and consequences of domestic violence to facilitate Cherise in identifying the connections between her own private experience of oppression and the structural context in which women are situated.
- *Affirmation*—This may involve acknowledging the courage it has taken for Cherise to speak out against the violence she is experiencing, and affirming her decision to do this, reminding her that the violence in not her fault, and reminding her of her strengths and capacities (Moreau, 1979; Fook, 1993; Hurst, 1995; McCashen, 2005).

Using risk assessment in anti-oppressive and strengths-based practice with Cherise

Domestic violence risk-assessment tools are part of some service technologies. One example of such a tool is the *Rural Family Violence Indicator Tool* (Parfitt, n.d.). Consistent with anti-oppressive and strengths-based approaches, this model can be used collaboratively with Cherise to minimise risk and increase safety and support options in relation to her needs and rights. While risk assessment generally seems to be orientated towards identifying dangers and hazards, this tool also aims to identify client strengths and capacities to reduce potential harm and risk, and is useful because it acknowledges some of the rural location issues that compound the experience of domestic violence. People living in a rural area often have significantly fewer options available to them than people based in urban areas. The availability of transport, for example, is one factor that can compound rural isolation and restrict options. Other considerations are summed up by Baxter (1992, p. 193), who acknowledges that, 'issues of choice and anonymity need to be specifically addressed in services provision'. Privacy and confidentiality may be more difficult to maintain in rural communities, where there may be a higher likelihood that people know each other.

In working with Cherise, risk-assessment templates such as the Rural Domestic Violence Indicator Tool can be used to clarify the supports she can draw on should a crisis arise. The assessment might highlight Cherise's particular vulnerabilities and might assist in identifying strategies to address these and maximise Cherise's options for safety. For example, the tool might assist in clarifying the level of Cherise's isolation, her capacity to access escape transport and the levels of violence she is experiencing, and may identify a clear route to safety and a plan to facilitate this (Parfitt, n.d.).

Additionally, Walsh (1999) has developed a domestic violence risk assessment which aims to 'provide the practitioner with a guide as to what area to target questioning, based on an interview with a woman without contact with the violent partner' (Walsh, 1991, p. 141).

Risk assessments informed and underpinned by anti-oppressive, feminist and strengths-based perspective principles have several implications for use in practice. Walsh (1999), in outlining the risk-assessment tool developed, outlines several key issues to consider. These include:

- that 'Risk can be determined by seeing the woman as the expert in her own situation' (Walsh, 1999, p. 142);
- that risk assessments in domestic violence must include an understanding of the level of powerlessness and loss of control that the woman experiences;
- that conducting a risk assessment for the issue of domestic violence needs to be a collaborative exercise with the woman. As Walsh (1999, p. 142) explains: 'The ultimate assessment must be a shared one between the woman and the worker. The woman must be invited to see her safety needs as an issue and participate in the direction of the intervention for it to be meaningful to her and her situation.' This emerges from a feminist philosophy which respects the input of the woman, and allows her to have control over the working process, which has been denied to her in the context of an abusive relationship;
- that the risk of violence increases when the perpetrator knows the woman has disclosed his actions to others, if she decides to leave him, and at or shortly after separation;
- that the risk may not simply cease to exist if she does leave him, as some male perpetrators may continue to harass and stalk their partners years after a relationship has ended;
- that this risk of violence may also extend to the women's friends and family, as well as to her worker.

These issues emphasise collaboration, valuing the client's input and reducing the client's powerlessness—all of which resonates with anti-oppressive and strengths-based frameworks. Chapter 3 considers the impact of power imbalance between service users and providers. It details McCashen's (2005) comparison between power over and power within the helping relationship.

Walsh (1999) outlines several factors that need to be explored when assessing the risk in domestic violence situation. We will explore these by looking at Cherise's situation.

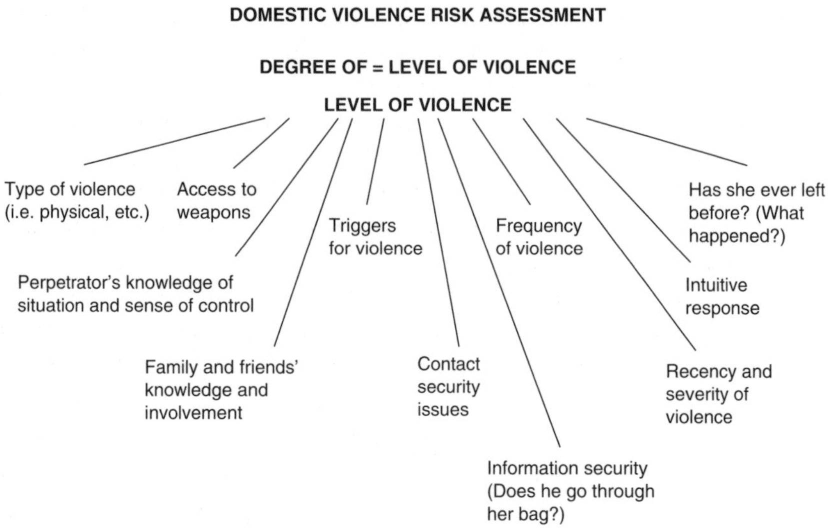

DOMESTIC VIOLENCE RISK ASSESSMENT

DEGREE OF = LEVEL OF VIOLENCE

LEVEL OF VIOLENCE

Type of violence (i.e. physical, etc.)

Access to weapons

Triggers for violence

Frequency of violence

Has she ever left before? (What happened?)

Perpetrator's knowledge of situation and sense of control

Intuitive response

Family and friends' knowledge and involvement

Contact security issues

Recency and severity of violence

Information security (Does he go through her bag?)

Figure 10.1 Domestic violence risk-assessment tool
Source: Reprinted with the kind permission of D. Walsh.

The domestic violence risk-assessment tool in Figure 10.1 directs us to gain an understanding of the types of violence experienced. It is important to establish the types of violence being perpetrated because it assists workers to determine what support options may be available to her. We know, for example, that Cherise is fearful of her partner, socially isolated, and emotionally and physically abused. Escaping to a women's refuge and/or reporting the assaults to the police may be some of her available options. However, other social and cultural factors may impact on Cherise's decision to avail herself of supports, such as the reluctance of police to become involved in supporting women who are being assaulted by their partners, particularly in rural areas. Any domestic violence risk assessment needs to include this sort of information to ensure the prioritising that emerges from this process is appropriate.

Additionally, as part of the assessment, we need to ask about the perpetrator's access to weapons. Walsh (1999) stresses that we should not assume that women will volunteer this information, and that we need to remember that weapons do not only include guns, but may also include vicious animals and martial arts equipment and/or training.

Risk assessment also needs to include an exploration of what triggers the perpetrator's violence. This will provide us with some information about the level of control John has over Cherise. Walsh (1999, p. 145) asserts that 'identification of triggers can assist in determining the safest option', which helps us prioritise what needs to happen in terms of intervention. When exploring what triggers the perpetrator's violence, it is important from an anti-oppressive perspective to challenge and reframe any beliefs that Cherise has about being responsible for his actions. This may involve skills of deguilting, as women who have been victimised by violence often experience a sense of guilt, blame, shame and responsibility. It is important to contextualise and universalise this response, while consciousness-raising about the structural conditions and myths that result in woman unfairly blaming themselves. When working with Cherise, we need to consider the possibility that this may even be magnified due to cultural factors and her socially isolated position. The common responses of guilt, shame and self-blame, however, raise important issues in relation to recording. While a contentious practice, many practitioners avoid documenting such responses in case notes because, if a legal process is initiated, case notes can be subpoenaed and used to support the defendant's case. This means that any record of self-blame can be taken out of context, manipulated and used to exonerate the perpetrator.

The frequency, recency and severity of the violence are also factors to incorporate into a domestic violence risk assessment. Collecting information about the recency and severity provides an indication of the potential danger that the woman is in. For Cherise, the violence would be considered serious. From an anti-oppressive and strengths perspective, looking at the frequency of Cherise's partner's violence with her can also be an opportunity to validate her fears, and affirm her courage in disclosing the violence to you.

Exploring with Cherise whether she has ever left before, and what happened if she has, is also important information for the risk assessment. This will give us, as workers, insight into what may happen if she decides to leave again. Leaving, however, may not necessarily resonate with Cherise's experience as a woman from Malaysia. Feminists from culturally diverse backgrounds have criticised mainstream feminism for being culturally unaware and making inappropriate assumptions about family structure, and the importance to identity of gender over ethnicity (Pine, 1996).

Another factor to consider involves establishing whether John knows about Cherise's contact with the service. We know that Cherise has not disclosed this information to him because of his threats. The fact that he has also directly threatened her about leaving is vital information for us as workers because it indicates the level and sense of his control over her (Walsh, 1999). Considering his knowledge of her accessing the service may also involve discussing whether she has told friends and family. Sometimes these people may be threatened by the perpetrator, or alternatively recruited against her. As Walsh (1999, p. 147) warns: 'On some occasions well meaning family and friends have told the perpetrator what is happening and placed the women at risk.'

Central to risk assessment from an anti-oppressive and strengths perspective is the perception of the woman. Cherise's intuitive response will provide us with much valuable information about her level of risk (Weisz et al., 2000). However, it is also important to challenge and reframe any minimising of violence that she might be inadvertently participating in (Walsh, 1999). We need to encourage Cherise to see her own safety risks and needs as significant.

In addition to formal risk assessment, your own intuition as a practitioner should also be included, as a way of incorporating other information that may not be captured by risk-assessment tools, and as a means of critically reflecting on your assumptions and subjective interpretations, which will unavoidably have impacted on how you have conducted the risk assessment (Fook, 1999). Using domestic violence risk assessments may clarify potential hazards and supports available to the woman. However, it would be remiss not to caution that: 'The use of "screening" and "screening tools" [in isolation] are problematic strategies with which to respond to complex psychosocial issues including intimate partner violence and abuse. Any mistakes in our implementation of offering help to victimized women in health care settings could be very costly to the women and children we seek to support' (Taft, 2001, p. 45).

Hence, anti-oppressive and strengths perspectives are crucial in addressing some of the concerns regarding the implementation of risk-assessment tools in practice. Other difficulties with using these tools to assess risk in violent intimate partner relationships include inconsistencies in how violence is defined, controversy over what is measured by the risk-assessment tools, and what is regarded as constituting abuse (Yllo, 1990), which could result in ineffective responses and further harm (Taft, 2001). Exercise 10.2 provides the opportunity to role-play a conversation with Cherise using the domestic violence risk-assessment tool in Figure 10.1.

Exercise 10.2: Role-play

Use the domestic violence risk-assessment tool (Walsh, 1999) to collaboratively assess Cherise's level of risk.

1 Did this approach to assessing domestic violence risk add to anti-oppressive and strengths-based approaches to practice?
2 What cultural and rural factors were relevant to conducting this risk assessment?
3 Practise recording what you would document from conducting this risk assessment.
4 On the basis on the risk assessment, what needs to be prioritised?
5 Have you included any information which could jeopardise potential future legal proceedings (e.g. omit any comments about Cherise feeling responsible for the violence)?

SUICIDE RISK ASSESSMENT

Domestic violence risk assessment is not the only risk-assessment tool applicable to Cherise's experience. Given what we know about Cherise's present situation, a suicide prevention risk assessment may also be relevant. However, in conducting suicide risk assessments, there are some important ethical dilemmas to consider when working from an anti-oppressive perspective.

Perhaps the most telling indicator about needing to conduct a suicide risk assessment with Cherise is the fact that she has disclosed that she has thought about harming herself. However, even if she had not disclosed this information, research indicates that self-harming behaviours, suicide ideation and/or attempts are common to victims/survivors of violence (Anthony et al., 2000).

Conducting suicide risk assessments involves collecting and analysing information about clients to determine a person's suicidal ideation and intent—in other words, the desire and capacity to end his or her life (O'Donnell, 1998). Research has identified five components of risk assessment in suicide prevention. These are:

- being aware of potentially dangerous circumstances;
- identifying the hazards and the people who may be affected by these;
- evaluating what the current safeguards are;
- documenting what is agreed to by both the worker and the client in terms of a suicide prevention contract; and
- conducting regular reviews of this process (Blom-Copper et al., 1995, cited in Stanley & Manthorpe, 1997).

Additionally, O'Donnell (1998) states that suicide risk assessments analyse information related to: the demographic characteristics of a client—for example, age, gender, marital and employment status, sexual orientation, the client's history of previous self-harm; the client's medical and social history; and the level of suicidal ideation and intent he or she is experiencing. Other suicide risk-assessment tools emphasise the need to identify previous attempts, regarding this as the highest risk factor (Sederer, 1994, cited in O'Donnell, 1998).

The suicide risk-assessment tool used by our local mental health services in Geelong is shown in Figure 10.2. Geelong is a large regional city in Victoria, Australia. This tool is called the Barwon Health Suicide Risk-Assessment Tool. It assesses a broad range of risk factors, including suicide ideation, prior attempts, clarity of suicide plan and access to means according to the plan. It also looks at the person's state of mental health in relation to feeling angry, hostile, impulsive, depressed, anxious, and so on. It assesses the client's sense of hope or hopelessness, medical status, whether there are symptoms of psychosis present, substance abuse issues, their current social supports, coping strategies, current role functioning, their history of psychiatric treatment, and other social factors such as access to resources and lifestyle stability (Hantz, 1999).

Figure 10.2 Barwon Health Suicide Risk-Assessment Tool

Barwon Health assessment template

Suicide risk-assessment Patient name/UR/date etc. (attach label)

Assessing suicide risk is not an easily accomplished task. Asking another about his or her intention to live or die is not part of normal conversation; nevertheless the inquiry must be made of someone suspected of being suicidal. Risk assessment requires not only an understanding of the risk factors but also a knowledge of the symptoms or behaviours which a suicidal person may display. This assessment is to be completed for every new assessment and subsequently depending on level of risk assessed.

Please rate each issue by circling the appropriate risk level

ISSUE	LOW RISK	MODERATE RISK	HIGH RISK
Suicidal ideation	None, or some vague	Frequent	Continual/ specific
Suicide plan	None, or ideation but no plan	Vague plan	Specific and lethal
Access to means (according to suicide plan)	Not applicable or no access	Access to means of low lethality only	Ready access to means of high lethality
Prior attempts	None	One, low lethality	Multiple, or one with high lethality
Anger/hostility/ impulsivity	None/mild	Moderate	Severe
Depression (current level)	None/mild	Moderate	Severe
Anxiety	None/mild	Moderate	Severe

Figure 10.2 Barwon Health Suicide Risk-Assessment Tool *(continued)*

ISSUE	LOW RISK	MODERATE RISK	HIGH RISK
Disorientation/ disorganisation	None	Mild/moderate	Severe
Hopelessness	Feels hopeful about the future	Some feelings of hopelessness	Preoccupied with hopelessness, can't see any future
Substance abuse	Nil or infrequent	Moderate/ frequent	Frequent/ excessive/ intoxicated
Psychosis	Asymptomatic	Some symptoms	Command hallucinations to suicide
Medical status	No significant problem	Acute but short-term illness	Chronic illness/pain or catastrophic acute illness
Withdrawal from family/friends	None/mild	Moderate	Withdrawn and isolated
Expressed communication	Wishes for help	Ambivalent	Wishes to die
Psychiatric service history	None, or good outcome	Yes, some reservations	Yes, viewed as negative
Coping strategies	Constructive	Marginal— some deliberate self-harm	Destructive— self-harm and risk-taking
Current role functioning	Good	Some difficulties	Poor

Figure 10.2 Barwon Health Suicide Risk-Assessment Tool *(continued)*

ISSUE	LOW RISK	MODERATE RISK	HIGH RISK
Lifestyle stability	Stable	Marginal	Unstable/chaotic
Resources, e.g. home, money, job	Adequate	Marginal	Inadequate
Supportive others (connectedness)	Highly connected, good relationships exist	Moderate connectedness, few relationships	Poor connectedness, lack of supportive relationship/only hostile relationships

OVERALL LEVEL OF RISK: (*please tick*)
None: No risk factors identified
Low: Majority of risk factors given low rating, with suicidal intent factors rated as low
Moderate: Majority of factors rated moderate, suicide intent factors rated no higher than moderate
High: Some factors rated high, some suicide intent factors rated high
Extreme: Majority of factors rated high, all suicide intent factors rated high

Source: Reprinted with the kind permission of P. Hantz, Barwon Health Division of Psychiatry, Geelong, Victoria.

To use this tool in working with Cherise, we may conduct a semi-structured interview to ask her about each of these risk factors. We would then record this information, which would assist us to prioritise what (if any) preventative measures need to be put in place. For example, Cherise's comments about feeling like she wanted to harm herself need to be explored more fully regarding the meaning she attaches to this. If we use the Barwon Health Suicide Risk-Assessment Tool, we may ask Cherise some direct questions to assess her level of suicidal ideation such as 'Do you ever think about ending it all/killing yourself?' or 'How strongly do you have thoughts of suicide?' (Hantz, 1999). We may also ask Cherise whether she has actually constructed a suicide plan, and try to ascertain how specific this is. If Cherise does indicate that she has a concrete and detailed plan, we would need to ask about her access to the means to carry out this plan. For example, if she is planning to take an overdose, we need to find out whether she actually has access to the medication to do this. Additionally, we would need to ask Cherise whether she has attempted suicide in the past, because this is considered to be an important risk factor (Hantz, 1999).

The Barwon Health Suicide Risk-Assessment Tool ultimately aims to assess whether people are at low risk, in that suicidal intent factors have been rated low; at moderate risk, which is when the majority of factors are rated moderate; at high risk, when some factors are rated high; or at extreme risk, when the majority of factors are rated high. Depending on the rating, the tool prescribes an appropriate level of intervention according to the risk. For example, if most of Cherise's responses indicated that she was not at risk, she would just continue to receive routine clinical care. If, however, Cherise's responses indicated a high risk, as social workers we would have a legal and ethical responsibility to make a referral to psychiatric services. Further risk assessments would be conducted at this point, and possible recommendations made for hospitalisation if she were assessed as being at risk of self-harm or of harm to others (Hantz, 1999).

While the domestic violence risk-assessment tool may be used in an anti-oppressive way—through, for example, uncovering and maximising Cherise's strengths—using a suicide risk-assessment tool may also be problematic. Practice dilemmas that may potentially emerge from this combination relate to the contradiction between social change and social control functions simultaneously. For example, using a suicide risk assessment in this scenario may prioritise Cherise in gaining access to needed resources if Cherise is admitted to hospital. This intervention could also be perceived as sending Cherise a clear message that we value her safety and her need for protection, either from herself or her husband. However, through an analysis of power, anti-oppressive perspectives would also recognise the irony, and perhaps injustice, of Cherise losing her freedom, while the perpetrator remains free. This loss of freedom may also be culturally significant and experienced by Cherise as traumatic and invasive. Such intervention is also potentially in conflict with anti-oppressive and strengths-based principles about service users having choice, autonomy, control over decision-making processes and contact with a worker (McCashen, 2005). Additionally, defining Cherise as being at 'high risk' of suicide may be experienced as pathologising, which focuses on deficits rather than being strengths-based (McCashen, 2005). This is in contrast to the skills of universalising, normalising and affirming her experience, in terms of seeing her responses as legitimate in the context of the violence she has suffered. The focus on deficits to assess risk may also make it challenging to work collaboratively with clients to produce positive changes (McCashen, 2005). Chapters 6 and 7 also highlight these tensions in different practice settings.

Other dilemmas raised in classifying Cherise as being at 'high risk' of suicide result from disclosing sensitive information to psychiatric services. Cherise may have trusted that this would remain private. As Stanley and Manthorpe (1997, p. 20) state, the sharing of information 'may compromise principles of confidentiality and may appear unfair or oppressive to service users'. This highlights the importance of boundary-setting in relation to confidentiality in terms of making it clear to Cherise the limits attached to confidentiality regarding information which may put either her or someone else at harm. During the initial stages of meeting with Cherise, it would be important to set these boundaries and outline our legal and ethical requirements to disclose such information. Exercise 6.7 in Chapter 6 provides the opportunity to practise these conversations with clients.

Additionally, while risk-assessment tools are inherently individual-istic, Cherise's responses are separated from the broader structural context that anti-oppressive and strengths-based theories emphasise (McCashen, 2005). As Kempshall and Pritchard (1996, p. 1, cited in Stanley & Manthorpe, 1997) explain, 'many risk decisions are made in a context where philosophies and policies on risk minimization on the one hand and normalisation of service users on the other, are often in conflict' (cited in Stanley & Manthorpe, 1997, p. 35). Risk-assessment tools, used in isolation, may therefore act to compound Cherise's guilt and shame about feeling responsible for the violence she has experienced, which undermines the anti-oppressive and strengths approaches' intention of empowerment. The use of anti-oppressive and strengths frameworks in this context helps to prevent risk-assessment tools from devoting inadequate attention to power, and the social constructions of responsibility (Goddard et al., 1999).

Another tension, or paradox, in relation to empowerment is that often, by facilitating greater service user autonomy and choice, we are also facilitating increased exposure to risk. With Cherise, for example, encouraging her to make her own decisions may mean that she chooses to stay in an abusive relationship where the perpetrator may continue to harm her. It is her right to make this decision for herself, and as workers we must respect this; however, conflict remains between the demands to value the expertise that clients bring and to empower them to make their own decisions, while also trying to reduce harm. Exercise 10.3 provides the opportunity to role-play the experience of undertaking the risk assessment with Cherise.

Exercise 10.3: Role-play

If a client returns to live with a violent partner, where they will almost certainly experience harm, as social workers we have no legal mandate to intervene. However, if we suspect someone might engage in self-harm, we have both a legal and ethical responsibility to respond. At what point do you think that, as a worker, you have the right to make a judgment that a client is not in a state to make competent decisions for themselves? How could you use risk-assessment tools to assist with your decision-making?

Use the Barwon Health Suicide Risk-Assessment Tool in conjunction with an anti-oppressive perspective to role-play conducting a suicide risk assessment with Cherise.

1   How did you feel about administering this assessment? How did the person role-playing Cherise feel?
2   Were there any ethical dilemmas? If so, how did you resolve these?
3   What were some of the cultural issues that arose, and how were these responded to?
4   What would be some of the benefits of using a structured risk-assessment tool?
5   What might be some of the limitations?
6   How might you use anti-oppressive and strengths-based practice to address some of the limitations of risk-assessment tools?

CONCLUSION

Risk-assessment tools are increasingly being used in social work and welfare practice. In this chapter, I have overviewed some of the models being used in the field of domestic violence, and explored the relative benefits and ethical dilemmas of using domestic violence and suicide-prevention risk-assessment models in conjunction with anti-oppressive and strengths-based practice. While risk-assessment frameworks can be conducted in ways that are consistent with anti-oppressive approaches, and through maximising clients' strengths, there are tensions that exist between practising with these commitments, and focusing practice on the assessment of risk. It is perhaps necessary to draw on the positive elements that risk assessment offers, while also being critically reflective about how we apply risk-assessment frameworks to anti-oppressive and strengths-based practice.

Exercise 10.4: Reflective questions

1 How comfortable are you with using risk-assessment tools in social work practice?
2 Do you think risk assessment is replacing rights-based practice? Or can it provide a vehicle to enhance these practice goals?
3 How can anti-oppressive and strengths-based theories be used to inform how we conduct risk assessments?

11

COLLABORATIVE ASSESSMENT FROM A CROSS-CULTURAL PERSPECTIVE

Lynne Briggs

Throughout Australia and New Zealand, social workers practise in a range of settings, including non-government-funded agencies and private practice as well as government-funded general health and crisis emergency services, specialist services, acute inpatient and rehabilitation services, and mental health services. Although state laws in Australia may dictate different agency policies, in general, practice in mental health services tends to occur in much the same way as it does in New Zealand. That is, social work practice in traditional mental health services has a clinical focus.

Clinical social work practice shares with all human services work the goal of enhancement and maintenance of psycho-social functioning of individuals, families and small groups. The main focus is on mental health assessment, diagnosis, treatment (including therapy), client-centred advocacy, consultation and evaluation.

Culture also plays an important part in mental health, as different ethnic groups have different ways of expressing health and illness. Social workers in mental health services will engage with clients from a variety of different cultures. Thus, as well as requiring clinical knowledge, social work with culturally diverse clients must be based on a foundation of culturally competent and anti-oppressive practice. You will find further discussion about cultural competence in Chapter 2.

Similarly, alongside enhancing cultural competencies, the strengths-based perspective in clinical social work practice continues to develop conceptually. While most social workers are comfortable working from a strengths perspective, it may seem difficult to imagine actually practising in traditional mental health primarily from this perspective (Weick et al., 2001, p. 353).

The focus of this chapter is on how strengths-based social work practice can be achieved in mental health settings while working with people from a diverse range of cultures. In doing so, the following elements are considered:

- strengths-based and anti-oppressive practice skills relating to mental health intervention;
- skills for working with culturally diverse mental health clients; and
- a case study highlighting how a strengths-based approach can assist resolution of some of the complex mental health issues that emerge when working cross-culturally.

STRENGTHS-BASED PRACTICE

The idea that people can resolve serious social and emotional problems by focusing on the strengths in their lives is, as Glicken (2004) points out, an elegant concept, but one at odds with many current notions of psychotherapy that focus on what is wrong with people rather than what is right. Chapter 3 canvasses the limitations of a strengths-based approach.

Despite these inherent difficulties, a strengths perspective has been included as part of case management in many services working with people with mental illness. The strengths perspective shows us how the day-to-day work that most of us do to keep ourselves going, even in the midst of crisis, is the basis for a more effective way of helping people.

The strengths perspective suggests that, even without the help of trained professionals, many people in deep despair show resilience and actually resolve their problems by using the positive influences of family, community, support networks, religious and spiritual beliefs, and a philosophy of life that not only guides them through moments of deep sorrow, but actually enhances and improves their social and emotional lives.

STRENGTHS-BASED SKILLS

As McCashen (2005, p. 52) notes, the single most important challenge in strengths-based practice is ensuring that each and every part of the change process is owned and directed by the people accessing the services. Workers therefore become facilitators rather than drivers of change. This is achieved by the use of a variety of skills that are particular to strengths-based approaches, and are gained over time through practice and reflection. They include:

- acknowledging and validating people as we listen to identify the problem and understand its context and impact;
- developing concrete descriptions;
- identifying and mobilising strengths, resources and exceptions;
- reframing;
- developing a picture of the future and establishing goals for noticing and measuring change;
- identifying strengths and strategies;
- externalising.

In making assessments, the strengths perspective demands that professionals view individuals, families and communities differently— that is, that the capacities, talents, competencies, possibilities, visions, values and hopes (however dashed and distorted these may have become through circumstance, oppression and trauma) are acknowledged (Saleebey, 1996, p. 297). Working from this perspective requires composing a roster of resources within, and around, the individual, family and community.

Strengths-based practice also involves being very aware of the language we use as professionals, as certain words are the key to the strengths perspective. As Saleebey (1996, p. 298) explains, *empowerment* means both increasing the awareness of people to the tensions and conflicts that oppress and limit them and helping them free themselves from such constraints. *Resilience* refers to the skills, abilities, knowledge and insight that accumulate over time as people struggle to surmount adversity and meet challenges. *Membership* relates to being respon-sible and valued members of a group or community. People without membership can feel alienated, and are at risk of marginalisation and oppression.

Particularly important strengths for people of other cultures are their cultural and personal stories, narratives and folklore. Cultural approaches to healing may provide a source for the revival and renewal of energies and possibilities. Cultural accounts of origins, development, migrations and survival may provide inspiration and meaning. Personal and familial stories of falls from grace and redemption, failure and resurrection, and struggle and resilience may also provide diction, symbols, metaphors and tools for rebound (Lifton, 1993).

CULTURALLY COMPETENT PRACTICE

Migration, particularly forced migration, is an area that social work is just starting to address, and social work practice now includes resettlement of immigrants (Valtonen, 2001). Refugees are a particular category of migrants who flee from their homeland for humanitarian reasons. That is, they leave families and friends behind, knowing it is very unlikely they can ever return. In contrast to this scenario, economic migrants choose to leave their homeland and can settle in a country of their choice; they know they can return to their country if they wish to, and they often bring family members with them.

Although the vast majority of refugees flee to neighbouring countries, recent history has seen the mass displacement of people seeking entry to Australia and New Zealand. This means social work practitioners are more likely than ever before to encounter people from a variety of different ethnic groups and from non-English speaking backgrounds presenting at mental health services. With the increasing numbers of refugees entering Australasia, the need to become culturally competent in practice also increases. Thus, social workers need to understand both the plight of refugees and migrants as well as some of the salient oppressive practices that directly impact on their lives following arrival to their host countries.

In providing intervention with refugee and migrant people, issues of language, cultural differences, the use of medications and empirical knowledge about effective treatments need to be considered. Therefore, it is essential that practitioners working with refugees and migrants are skilled in a range of treatment interventions that can diminish anxiety and assist the client to regain their equilibrium.

During the past decade, much has been said about the need to include cultural issues as a factor in the helping process (Weaver, 1999). This message has not gone unnoticed, and increasing expectations for cultural competency can be found in emerging guidelines and standards in the New Zealand health and disability sector (New Zealand

Mental Health Commission, 2001). However, while the expectation may be there, the notion of cultural competence in health care remains a sensitive issue. For example, while international recognition is given to the need for and benefits of representation from diverse ethnic groups, in reality workers from mainstream culture will routinely provide care for mental health clients from diverse cultural backgrounds (Jackson & Lopez, 1999, p. 4). Probably one of the most important barriers to culturally competent health care is the dominant ethnicity of the workforce.

EXPLORING CROSS-CULTURAL WAYS OF HELPING

From both a strengths-based approach and a clinical point of view, understanding the client's view of their problems is important as different cultures express their symptoms differently. In human services work, the term 'cultural competency' refers to knowledge and a set of skills that a worker must develop in order to be effective with culturally diverse clients. As Weaver (1999, p. 221) suggests, skills for culturally competent social work practice are not radically different from those generally required for practice. However, given cultural differences, some skills are of particular importance when working with different ethnic populations—for example, the ability to sit, listen and respect silence rather than talking.

Knowledge acquisition provides the practitioner with a set of principles that serve as boundary guidelines. Skill development applies knowledge acquisition to actual practice with clients from a culturally competent perspective. As Potocky-Tripodi (2002) warns, though, such practice cannot be learnt overnight (2002, p. 181). It involves an ongoing process in which a practitioner is continually developing, learning and improving attitudes and beliefs, knowledge and skills in order to work effectively.

While resettlement in a different country with a totally different culture is in itself traumatic and stressful, many refugee groups may not understand or accept a concept of mental illness. It may not be within the understanding of their culture to do so. If they are familiar with the concept of mental illness at all, they may tend to associate it with the more severe forms of psychopathology that require institutional care. This means all conditions are highly stigmatised and interventions are shunned (Gong-Guy et al., 1991).

Other factors that contribute to this understanding includes the belief that mental illness is familial or inheritable, with serious implications for marriageable family members. That is, information about illness in one family member may be spread throughout the ethnic community, and be damaging to family reputation. Thus, knowing a family member had to attend an interview at a mental health service may be confusing and frightening for some.

You will recall from Chapter 5 the exercises focused on learning about a cultural context that is different from your own. Exercise 11.1 provides a further opportunity to reflect upon your experiences in this regard.

Exercise 11.1

Culture plays an important part in any practice setting. People from one culture may go into an assessment with very different understandings and expectations to people from another culture. In small groups, consider the following questions:

1 How much personal/social time do I spend with people who are culturally similar or culturally different to me?
2 When I am with culturally different people, do I reflect my own cultural preferences or do I spend the time openly learning about the unique aspects of another person's culture? (McPhatter, 1997)

WORKING WITH INTERPRETERS

Different cultures express their symptoms of illness in their own ways, and without a shared language it can be difficult to form a working relationship. This makes the involvement of interpreters in the assessment process, the negotiation of therapeutic goals and ongoing treatment crucial when neither the worker nor the client speaks the same language with a degree of fluency. As such, interpreters are the voice of the client and play an important role by ensuring the client's view of their mental health problem is understood. For example, somatic complaints are common among some refugee populations. However, it is important for interpreters to have had appropriate training in interpretation for mental health services. Untrained interpreters or family members should not be used if possible, though in emergencies there may be no choice.

Exercise 11.2

In class, discuss the following questions:

1   What social work skills do you think are important for working with an interpreter?
2   How would you prepare an interpreter for an assessment?

ASSESSMENT

Refugee and migrant clients do present, or are referred, to mental health services with mental health problems that need to be addressed. During the assessment process, the worker needs to obtain a clear understanding of what the client and their family expect will happen as a result of the assessment. We need also to remember that any mental health assessment takes into account the context of the client's total situation. While poverty, racism and oppression are important issues to be considered for all clients, for the culturally diverse client this is particularly so.

The case study in Exercise 11.3 discusses a referral made by the client's general practitioner (GP) to a Refugee and Migrant Mental Health Service (RMHS). The referral was the only information provided to the mental health team.

Exercise 11.3: Case study

The referral to the RMHS stated that Samia, an eighteen-year-old Afghani woman, had been complaining of ongoing tiredness alongside an inability to sleep, lack of appetite and associated weight loss, constant weeping, poor concentration, headaches and dizzy spells since her arrival in the country 22 months ago. Her mother and sister had gone to the GP because, despite many investigations, no physical explanation could be offered for Samia's ongoing loss of appetite and weight, headaches and constant dizzy spells.

Additionally, they were concerned about her lack of interest in family and community activities. Her sister was further concerned that Samia was missing many of her classes at the local polytechnic/ TAFE college they both attended and that she isolated herself from other students during the day. Furthermore, on several occasions

Samia had been found weeping in the corridor outside the classroom. On the basis of this information, a referral was given for a mental health assessment to rule out an anxiety or mood disorder.

Samia duly arrived at the RMHS with her mother, sister and interpreter for the initial assessment. It quickly became apparent to the social worker undertaking the assessment that Samia thought she was there for her mother and was unaware that the referral had been made for her.

The GP had made the referral on the basis of the results of the previous tests and the information provided by Samia's mother and sister. In small groups, discuss:

1 Why do you suppose the GP did this?
2 How does this fit with anti-oppressive practice?
3 Do you see this as an ethical dilemma?

Assessment interviews with migrant and refugee clients tend to take longer than assessments for non-migrant clients. Gathering information about pre-migration and departure, transit and resettlement experiences is additional to the presenting problem. Therefore, time is an important factor that practitioners need to take into account when arranging assessment appointments with culturally diverse clients.

It also needs to be noted that mental health assessments are usually carried out in the worker's agency. Culturally diverse clients may not know what is expected of them in such an environment. This leaves them feeling anxious, threatened and frightened. In order to avoid these efforts, both physical and psychological needs should be anticipated and attended to before the assessment begins—such as giving clear directions to get to the agency and including multicultural literature in the waiting room.

The assessment process, the reason they are attending the agency and possible outcomes also need to be fully explained to clients. Interview questions need to be open ended, stated very clearly, and should focus on facilitation and clarification. Statements that require considerable interpretation may need to asked and restated if the worker does not understand the response. This makes summarising and feedback of the information gained by the worker to the client essential to ensure the client's views have been accurately captured. The assessment can also take other collateral information into account, thus it is not totally reliant on the client and family responses to questions.

NON-WESTERN VALUES, TRADITIONS, USE OF THE DSM AND THE STRENGTHS PERSPECTIVE

Although its usefulness as a diagnostic tool has prompted an ongoing debate over the past two decades, both Australia and New Zealand use the *Diagnostic and Statistical Manual of Mental Disorders*, fourth edition (DSM-IV) for diagnostic purposes in mental health services. Generally speaking, signs and symptoms are unique expressions or indicators of underlying health or mental health problems. As such, they are subjective experiences reported by individuals that are universal across cultures, meaning people of any culture can experience certain signs and symptoms of mental illness.

On the other hand, diagnoses are medical constructs based on the presentations and patterns of such signs and symptoms. As Potocky-Tripodi (2002) says in regard to mental health, it is important to distinguish between the concepts of *universality* and *cultural relativity*, as diagnoses are culture-bound. This includes the diagnostic categories developed by the APA (1994). That is, these diagnostic categories have been developed in a certain time and place.

Potocky-Tripodi (2002, p. 262) also argues that while 'seemingly universal psychiatric disorders found commonly in the West are absent from other cultures this does not mean that people from other cultures do not suffer symptoms associated with mental illness but that the presentation and patterns of those symptoms do not necessarily correspond with the APA diagnostic categories'. Thus, most cultures have cultural-bound syndromes or *idioms of distress* that refer to characteristic modes of expressing suffering. The point Potocky-Tripodi (2002) makes is that practitioners must keep both concepts of universality and cultural relativity in mind when conducting assessments in order to avoid misdiagnosis.

With the help of an interpreter, Samia was given a clear understanding of the process for this session. After consenting to the assessment, the reasons identified in the referral from the GP were summarised and fully explained to Samia. Her mother and sister were also invited to voice their concerns about her health and well-being, and to explain why they had gone to the GP without inviting Samia to accompany them.

Open-ended questions were then used in order to clarify each concern separately. For example, Samia's mother was concerned that her daughter would not join in family activities, that she was shutting herself in her room and that she spent a lot of time weeping. Her sister was concerned that she left the classroom and isolated herself from other students, and at times had been found weeping outside the classroom. The dizzy spells were also of concern, as was her obvious weight loss.

The assessment process provided an opportunity for Samia to respond to their concerns while expressing her own pain about the loneliness and isolation she felt living in a strange country without friends of her choosing; how she felt about not being able to work as a teacher, even though she had a teaching diploma; and how she felt about undertaking a course of study in which she had no interest. Overall, she had lost her sense of purpose in life. Samia stated that at times she was so overwhelmed by these thoughts that she felt dizzy and faint. She explained that, when this happened, all she wanted to do was be alone. This meant going to her room at home, leaving the classroom or just not going to class. Samia also reported that she did not want to socialise with the other students as there was no one of her age in the class—they were either much older or younger than her. She knew no one of her own age.

Samia's situation demonstrates the need for culturally competent practice. From a Western perspective, some of the symptoms with which she presented (e.g. weeping, feeling sad a lot of the time, poor concentration, sleep disturbance, loss of appetite and weight, lack of enjoyment in life in general) may have been indicative of a mood disorder. However, they could also be indicative of many other issues. As such, this challenges health professionals to look beyond the presenting symptoms.

Samia's case is no exception: as a young adult, she was expressing her suffering through physical complaints of headaches and dizziness. Thus, mental well-being is, as Brown (2001, p. 36) notes, the result of a dynamic and interactive process involving social, environmental and life circumstances as well as biological factors. Although greater recognition is now given to cultural understandings of behaviour that could be perceived as being the result of mental disorder, if the mental health social worker involved had not acted in a culturally appropriate way, this case may indeed have had a different outcome. For example, Samia may have been assigned a diagnosis of clinical depression and could have been offered a trial of anti-depressants with some one-to-one counselling. This course of action may, or may not, have been helpful.

Instead, the assessment enabled Samia's mother and sister to better understand her behaviour. While the social worker had to complete the psychiatric assessment in a way that met the requirements of a mental health service, an alternative explanation for some of the concerns expressed by Samia and the observations reported by others was able to be taken into account. By using a strengths perspective, the social worker was able to focus on Samia's aspirations in life. The questions asked were not about what kind of a life she had lost, but what kind of a life she now wanted. It also provided an opportunity for Samia and her family to propose ways they could make personal and social resources available to accomplish this goal.

Exercise 11.4

In pairs, address the following two questions:

1 How does this assessment process differ from that outlined in other chapters?
2 How do you account for these similarities and differences?

SUMMARY

This chapter has discussed some of the issues involved in undertaking a mental health assessment with a person who was unaware of the referral. While the social worker was obliged to make a DSM-IV diagnosis and formulation as a culturally competent practitioner, she was aware of the cultural biases contained in the DSM-IV, and used it as just one tool for assessment purposes. The knowledge and skills of the worker in Samia's case allowed for problematic behavior/symptoms/ concerns to be redefined as loneliness and loss. This exploration assisted diagnostically, but also allowed for the family to find ways in which it could assist in resolution of the issues. Thus, it is important to remember when assessing culturally diverse clients to take other matters such as different cultural expressions of emotional distress into account.

Exercise 11.5: Reflective questions

1 What is my commitment to becoming culturally competent?
2 How much work have I actually done to increase my knowledge and understanding of culturally and ethnically distinct groups?
3 What are my gaps in cultural competence?

12

WORKING WITH FAMILIES
Yvonne Crichton-Hill

Everybody knows a lot about families . . .

Yet the more one knows, the less one seems to know. The family is a wonderful institution that is the source of so much pride and yet so much shame; so strengthening and yet so draining; so nurturing, yet so demanding; so easy to understand yet so confusing.
(Berg, 1994, p. ix)

Work with families differs from work with individuals in that many different perspectives may confront the worker at one time. Each family member may have differing perceptions of the issue at hand, and of the family strengths and resources available to deal with that issue. Family meetings, in particular, can foster rich opportunities to pull all minds in one room together to produce exciting and creative family outcomes. However, meetings can also be a time when tension and family conflict is at the fore, and where family discussions move in many different directions.

Responsibility for effective assessment work with families lies with human service workers in the first instance. It is the human service worker who is responsible for engaging with the family system in a way that is culturally responsive and focused on family strengths. The responsibility for working towards, and achieving, successful family outcomes is a shared process between worker and family.

The objectives of this chapter are to:

- identify the perspectives that inform family work; and
- identify and explore skills central to assessment processes with families, including conducting family meetings, managing conflict and negotiating goals.

FAMILIES

Families have been described as the 'nexus of almost all people's social, economic, political and cultural lives' (Crothers et al., 2006, p. 6). The structure, membership and roles of families vary over time, within and between families, and within and between cultures. Therefore, there can be structural membership and role differences within families of the same culture; between families of the same culture; and between families of different cultures. Furthermore, multiple diverse cultures, with varying ideas about role, membership and structure, can exist in one family system. Recognition that not all families are organised in the same way, or have the same members with the same part to play, is a crucial component of effective family work.

Saleeby (2001, pp. 265–83) describes many different ways in which families are structured—including nuclear, single-parent, extended, dual-earner, remarried, gay and lesbian families. There is no one definition of family that fits for all, nor is there one family 'type'. Increasing diversity in family structures has been accompanied by an increase in inter-ethnic partnerships (Connolly et al., 2005). The change in family structures over the last few decades has been attributed to a number of factors, which include changing views of the role of marriage, greater social acceptance of divorce and same-sex relationships, and the growing economic independence of women (Archard, 2003; Carling, 2002; Cherlin, 1992). The diversity in family structures makes family work demanding and complex, yet exciting.

FAMILY WORK INFLUENCES

To enhance our understanding of the nature of family work, and the skills that are necessary for effective family work, it is necessary to briefly examine the approaches that have contributed to the development of family work. These include systems, structural, social constructionist and strengths approaches. Arising from these key family

182

work influences are a number of common concepts that workers should consider in their interactions with families.

Systems theory

Systems theory has its roots in biology, where it was used to describe how living systems function. Since then, it has been adapted to a variety of other fields, including family therapy and family-based social work. You will find further discussion about the ecological-systems approach in Chapter 15.

In systems theory, the family is described as a system, a set of related components that work together in a particular environment to perform whatever functions are required to achieve the maintenance of the system. In order to do this, the family system is self regulating and held together by unspoken rules. In the systems approach, attention is drawn away from the individual and individual problems. Instead, the focus of attention is on the relationships and relationship issues between individuals in the family (Becvar & Becvar, 2000). Rather than focusing on cause and effect explanations, the systems approach encourages a more holistic examination of the multiple factors within a family system that interact to produce problems.

Structural approach

The structural approach to family work was initially developed by Salvador Minuchin (1974). It is important at this point to make the distinction between the structural approach to family work that Minuchin has developed and the structural analysis of society as outlined in Chapter 1. The former relates to a model of practice, while the latter is referring to the major source of social problems being located in the structures of society.

Minuchin saw families as complex entities, which adapt to continually changing internal and external conditions. Families, therefore, are perceived as never static, but as ever-changing in response to internal and external influences. In addition, family members are interconnected and interdependent, so what happens to one family member affects all others. Families are also described as having a structure or a way of being organised, and within this a pattern of interacting with each other. According to Minuchin's structural approach, some family systems are dysfunctional in that they produce and perpetuate suffering on members of the family. The structural solution is to restore functioning through the encouragement of hierarchical structure, which includes sub-systems, and boundaries.

Sub-systems are described as supporting family functioning. Underpinning the structural approach are three key family sub-systems: the spouse sub-system (the primary concern is each person's role as part of a couple); the parental sub-system (the focus is on the leadership role, which is child focused); and the sibling sub-system (the focus is on the children's private system where they learn to relate to one another and experiment without parental interference).

Boundaries are the invisible barriers which surround individuals and sub-systems, regulating the amount of contact with others. Essentially, boundaries refer to rules that define how family members should interact with one another.

Social constructionism

Social constructionism is a postmodern theory. It is concerned with the nature of knowledge and how knowledge is developed. Therefore, it 'seeks to understand the processes by which people describe, explain, and ultimately view the world and themselves' (Freeman & Couchonnal, 2006).

Mailick and Vigilante (1997, p. 362) suggest that social constructionism 'fosters the expression of unique family cultural perspectives'. Importantly, an individual's cultural background (including family background) does strongly influence interactions with others.

The social constructionist approach has at its core a focus on the family's perspective of the situation at hand. Just as individuals within a family system hold unique perspectives of the family situation, it is expected the worker's cultural values will influence his or her perception of the family problem and possible solutions. According to constructionism, the role of the worker is to share his or her perceptions with the family in order to enhance family knowledge and extend identification of possible solutions. In this sense, the worker is not the expert with the answers, but a collaborative partner with the family system. It is this telling and revising of experience, both by family and by the worker, that intersects to create new meanings and understandings of experience. This ability of families to 'reshape and shift their perceptions and definitions of reality is a critically important resource in their efforts to deal with the problems. Clients' capacity to change is connected to their ability to see things differently' (De Jong & Berg, 2002, p. 284).

184

Strengths approach

Dennis Saleebey (1997) has written widely on the strengths perspective. He states:

> practicing from a strengths orientation means this—everything you do as a social worker will be predicated, in some way, on helping to discover and embellish, explore and exploit clients' strengths and resources in the service of assisting them to achieve their goals, realise their dreams, and shed the irons of their own inhibitions and misgivings. (Saleebey, 1997, p. 3)

The strengths perspective has at its core a belief that humans have the potential for change and growth, and are resilient. Families are the experts on their own lives, on how they are structured, how roles are defined, and on what resources—individual, collective, internal or external—exist. The worker's role, therefore, is to encourage families to give meaning to their own situation. The family's collective voice is valued. Rather than spending time trying to understand the cause of the problem, the worker must facilitate concentration by all on seeking exceptions to patterns of problem behaviour. The strengths approach is solution focused. It promotes collaboration between worker and family members.

The strengths perspective advocates for the development of creative solutions. This way of working often requires an attitudinal shift on behalf of practitioners away from seeing families as lacking to seeing families as systems with untapped strengths and resources. The attitudinal shift may also need to occur for families who may have become familiar with, or been encouraged by workers to become skilled at, recognising their own deficits in favour of recognising their strengths and potential.

CONCEPTS TO CONSIDER

While there are a range of approaches to family work, there are a number of concepts for work with families that are familiar across approaches. Craft-Rosenberg et al. (2006) examined the family work literature and isolated a number of conceptual themes that inform work in the area. These may be thought of as concepts that workers should consider when engaging with families and include the following:

185

- *Mutual trust*—This concept highlights the importance of establishing and maintaining respectful relationships with all family members. It includes the reciprocal sharing of information between worker and family members.
- *Shared decision-making*—Highlighted here is the commitment to collaborative decision-making and planning with the family.
- *Reciprocal relationships*—Here the focus is on recognising that workers must respect the dignity of families. It includes recognition of the diversity and uniqueness of each family structure, and the inherent values and beliefs that exist.
- *Family participation*—This concept places family members as collective partners with the worker in identifying and solving the presenting issues.
- *Strengths-based practice*—In working to this concept, workers recognise the often-untapped strengths and resources that exist within family systems.
- *Interdisciplinary teamwork*—This concept acknowledges the need for workers to provide services for families that are comprehensive and integrated across a range of professional fields.
- *Cultural responsiveness*—Here the worker respects that family culture is informed by multiple cultural identities, including age, gender, sexuality, class, ethnicity and ability.

Exercise 12.1

Divide into groups of four. Each group is assigned one of the models for working with families (systems/ecological; structural; social constructionism; strengths). During the following week, research and critique the assigned model and prepare a brief (fifteen-minute) presentation on your model. All groups will present to the class. After the group presentations, discuss and justify the preference of model you have for working with families.

ASSESSMENT WITH FAMILIES

It can be argued that social work with individuals directly or indirectly involves family systems. When a worker meets for the first time with the client, they may have some details of the client's family background—that is, information that may contribute to understanding the issues at hand for the client. In order to work effectively, workers need to enhance understanding of the client in context. This context should include the client's family and cultural background. Here, culture relates not only to ethnicity, but also to other cultural elements that inform individual and social identity—ethnicity, disability, sexuality and social culture. The worker must be guided by the internalised or unique culture of the client, as suggested by the assessment model presented in Figure 9.1 in Chapter 9.

Ultimately, the client is not an individual who stands alone in the world, but a person within a social and political context. Involvement of family members potentially enhances our understanding of this context, which in turn can add to the overall assessment. It is important to stress that 'family' must be who the client identifies as family, not those the worker perceives as family.

Meeting with families as a group is a useful way to gain understanding of clients in context. The worker is privileged in family meetings to enter the rich and complex tapestry of the family world in order to develop appreciation of the family system and its strengths.

Conducting family meetings

The success of any family meeting is dependent not only on the competent facilitation of the process during the meeting, but on the preparation undertaken before the meeting. Preparation should include some consideration of the following questions:

- What is the purpose of the meeting? Is the family clear about the purpose of the meeting?
- What is the timeframe for the meeting?
- How does the family define 'family'? Has everyone who is part of the family group been invited?
- What is the structure of this family? What roles do people play? Which members of the family do family members perceive as holding positions of status?
- How will the meeting begin and end? Is there a particular way in which the family would like to do this—for example, by prayer? Is the family clear about what will happen at the meeting?
- What is the internalised culture of the family? Are there any cultural protocols regarding the process of the family meeting that the worker should know about? Does the worker have a cultural adviser from whom she/he can seek guidance? Will it be necessary for the cultural adviser to play any role in the meeting process?

- How will conflict be managed?
- How will goals be negotiated and set?
- What picture does the worker have of this family? What attitudes does the worker hold towards this family? Will either the picture or attitude the worker possesses inhibit her/his ability to facilitate a meeting where the family's strengths and resources are expanded and enhanced, in order to work towards resolution?

As noted in Chapter 1, an important component of effective practice with both individuals and families is a worker's ability to critically reflect, both personally and professionally. Each of us has certain values, beliefs and attitudes about the world within which we operate. These influence our perceptions of others and ourselves, and of the issues we face and others face. Competent work with families is more achievable when a worker has the ability to reflect on these personal and professional values and beliefs, and to consider the impact they may have on work with a particular family.

Fundamentally, the purpose of a process of critical reflection is to ensure workers give life to a belief in human dignity and human diversity. Critical reflection assists workers in ensuring their values and beliefs do not get in the way of effective practice. Workers with families need to embrace and demonstrate a commitment to accepting families as they are, 'warts and all'. This does not mean accepting that whatever families do is right or appropriate; it means accepting the reality of family life. This notion of critical reflection is noted above in the final question about attitudes towards family and the impact these may have on practice.

There is a natural progression from considering how one will work with a family and the influence of cultural values and beliefs, to implementing this in practice with families.

SKILLS

Ka Tat Tsang and Usha George (1998, p. 87) define skills as 'specific courses of action taken by practitioners to achieve positive changes needed by their clients'. To recognise and acknowledge the impact of values and beliefs on worker interaction with families is important, yet a worker's ability to translate this learning into meaningful and appropriate professional behaviour is of equal importance. As Ka Tat Tsang and George go on to say, 'valued attitudes and knowledge in cross cultural practice like self-awareness, understanding, and respecting the differences between practitioner and client have to be translated into actual professional behaviour to be meaningful' (1998, p. 87).

It is with this in mind that we turn to examine the skills important in family work. In order to do this, a case study is presented, followed by descriptions of the meeting process, and appropriate skills to be utilised.

The following case study details further the skills associated with conducting an assessment where a whole family are involved in the process.

Exercise 12.1: Case Study

Louana and Joseph have three children—twins who are four years old, and a boy aged seven. Also living with the family is Louana's son, David, from a previous relationship. (The father of this child lives in Samoa and has occasional contact with his son by phone.) David is twelve years of age. Louana is a New Zealand-born Samoan, while Joseph—also Samoan—was born in Samoa. They have been married for nine years. More recently, there has been a deterioration of the relationship between David and Joseph. Louana believes that Joseph has started treating David more harshly than he has always treated the other children. Joseph disputes this, and states that Louana is now more protective of David than she is of the children they share together.

The school reports that lately David has been disruptive in class and aggressive in the playground. He is now known as the school bully, and other children appear to be fearful of him. The school suspects that David is being physically punished at home. Joseph has admitted to slapping David from time to time.

Ana, a Samoan worker with Pacific Social Services, has been involved with the family for the past two weeks. She has met on a number of occasions with Louana and Joseph, both separately and together as a couple. She has also spent some time with David, and with extended family—Louana's mother Sina, and Sina's sister Mona and husband Tai. Joseph's younger brother John and his wife Moana have also spent some time with Ana.

It was decided that it would be useful to hold a family meeting. Ana's primary goal for the meeting was to ensure that physical punishment of David was halted. Joseph and Louana decided they wanted all family members mentioned above to attend. They also

---

decided that at this point it was inappropriate for the children to attend the meeting.

Before the meeting, Ana met with Manu, the Samoan cultural adviser attached to the child and family agency with which she is employed. Manu is held in high regard within the Samoan community, values confidentiality, and is known by the community as someone who commits considerable time to the support of Samoan families. Manu is aware of this family and has been able to offer insight as to the family context. It was then decided that it would be useful for Manu to attend the family meeting, if the family was agreeable. The intention was that having male and female facilitators would be useful in work with a Samoan family. In addition, the presence of Manu allowed discussions to occur in Samoan if desired by the family. As Ana is not a speaker of Samoan, Manu could act as interpreter. This would ensure clear understanding by both professionals and the family of the discussions within the meeting. The family was agreeable to the joint facilitators. This highlights how help-seeking behaviours differ within and between cultures. The Samoan community can be defined as collectivist, in that group norms are likely to have a powerful influence on family decision-making and behaviour. This Samoan family, as part of a collectivist community, has a help-seeking preference first to a Pacific Social Service Agency, and second to a member of their cultural and social community (Manu). It is important to recognise that help-seeking behaviour in one culture may be classified as inappropriate in another.

The meeting was held in a church hall. It began with a prayer conducted by Tai, followed by the singing of a hymn by everyone in the room. Ana clarified that the purpose of the family meeting was to find a way of smoothing the relationship between David and Joseph, and Joseph and Louana. Ana went on to say that her basic goal was to ensure that David was not hit. Ana also stated that the family members could have time alone during the meeting if they wished—all they had to do was let Ana and Manu know. In addition, Ana stated that if anyone felt they needed time to themselves, they could excuse themselves from the meeting, but they should return so the rest of the meeting knew they were alright.

The meeting proceeded. At first family members were a little reluctant to talk, but as the meeting moved along some family members became more than a little animated. Ana and Manu used strengths-based questions in a culturally respectful manner as a way of encouraging a meeting focused on the family's capacity, resilience and potential.

During the meeting, it became clear that in recent times Louana and Joseph had been fighting frequently. Most often the arguments were about who should have the authority over the children—who should be the disciplinarian. Joseph sees himself as the disciplinarian of all the children whereas Louana sees Joseph as the main disciplinarian over the children they share together. Louana believes she should have more of a role to play in David's discipline. Joseph perceives Louana as being disrespectful of his role as head of the family, and believes David is noticing this disrespect and behaving in the same way towards Joseph.

At one point, tension became apparent. Joseph appeared stuck in his belief that his method of disciplining David was appropriate. He suggested he should leave the meeting—he'd had enough, and wanted to 'wash his hands of everyone'. Ana and Manu used careful courteous questioning, which affirmed Joseph's care and feeling of responsibility for David, and led to Joseph being able to admit he was unsure of what to do next. Joseph's brother Tai, and Manu, the cultural adviser, supported this line of questioning. Both affirmed Joseph as head of his family, but were clear that slapping David was not appropriate.

Eventually, the family made goals and plans which focused on ensuring the safety of David and on supporting the relationship between Joseph and Louana. The goals were specific, reasonable, achievable, and based on previous successes the family had experienced. One goal was that Joseph and Louana would learn some additional disciplining options. The plan was that they would attend a Pacific Parenting Course run by the Pacific Social Service Agency. The meeting ended with prayer, and then food was shared.

Question
Devise six strengths-based questions you might use in this family meeting.

FAMILY MEETINGS

This section of the chapter examines the process of conducting family meetings, including beginning meetings, facilitating family strengths, managing conflict and setting goals.

Beginning the meeting

The worker should begin the meeting in a way that fits with the cultural values, beliefs and protocols of the family. There needs to be consideration given to the venue, the seating arrangements and the way in which family members are welcomed into a process of family discussion. In the case study, the church hall was chosen, as it was a familiar and comfortable place for the family. In addition, it was a large space, which meant people could be seated comfortably without any risk of encroaching upon each other's personal space. The family decided it was important to begin with prayer, and they chose an appropriate family member to begin the process. As is customary with many Samoan families, the prayer was followed by song. These two acts are described as religious rituals, used by 'some Pacific agencies as part of their social work practice with Pacific clients' (Mulitalo-Lauta, 2001, p. 252).

The worker's role was then to thank the family for coming, welcome them and begin the process of clarifying the purpose of the meeting. Even though family members may have been spoken to individually about the purpose of the meeting, it is necessary to have that purpose stated 'out loud' at the beginning of the meeting process. A possible beginning by the worker could be:

> I want to begin by thanking you, Tai, for opening our meeting today. I would also like to thank all of you for being so willing to come and talk with each other and with Manu and I today. Your willingness to attend shows how much you must care about your family. I would like to begin by hearing from each of you your expectations for the time we spend together today—what you hope will be achieved.

Family members' responses to this question ranged from 'I want to leave here knowing Louana, Joseph and the kids are going to be alright', to 'Children should be treated fairly so they can learn'. The meeting agreed that initially discussion would take place for 60 minutes and, if not finished at this point, a review of progress made would occur. All participants would then decide whether to continue with the meeting, or set another meeting time to continue discussions.

A strengths approach to family work recognises that all families have the capacity and potential to effect change for themselves. It is the worker's role to assist families to identify and cultivate this capacity and potential as outlined previously in Chapters 4 and 7. In order to do this, it is the role of the worker to ask the family questions at appropriate times in the meeting process.

Listening actively to the family's answers casts 'light on how they view themselves, how they define their challenges and solutions, and their attitudes towards change' (Freeman & Couchonnal, 2006). This understanding can then be put to use in assisting the family to identify goals and strategies of action that fit with the family culture.

The worker in the case study began by asking purposeful questions of the family, intended to encourage the family to think of times when:

- the family group was peaceful;
- Joseph disciplined David in a non-physical way;
- Joseph and Louana were composed in their relationship with each other.

Traditionally, in work with families, workers have tended to focus on a families' challenges and weaknesses, thereby reinforcing the issues at hand (Freeman & Couchonnal, 2006). It is much more useful to work with the family to develop 'exceptions' to the issue or problem behaviour. Strengths approaches to social work stress that this process enables the family to consider times in their family life together when they successfully negotiated an issue or difficulty. This is often a difficult undertaking for families; however, it may help families to first identify how someone else they know has overcome similar challenges (Norman, 2000). Some examples of exception questions are:

- *Can you think of families you know who have faced a similar challenge to yours—how did they manage?* Louanna stated that she knew of a family that had recently 'got together'. They had two children each and were finding it hard to get along as a new family. They gained support from family and the church, and had attended a Pacific Parenting course. In addition, they had decided the children should continue to attend their separate schools so that the children didn't feel isolated from their own friends. Over time, with a lot of support, things had improved.

- *How have you managed so far?* Louana pointed out that their extended family was a tremendous support. The children often spent time staying overnight with other family members, and this gave Louana and Joseph an opportunity to spend time alone. Joseph mentioned that the church they attended was a source of spiritual and emotional support. The church reminded them of what is important in life—family and love for one another.
- *Louana, when things were going well in your life, what was different?* Louana replied that it was only in the last year that David had started to behave badly, both at school and at home. Before this, David had been achieving well at school and had appeared happy. Joseph had not needed to use any physical force to discipline David. The family had felt proud of David's sporting and academic achievements and had often celebrated these achievements with extended family.

As the family identifies exceptions, the worker should acknowledge these—no matter how small or seemingly insignificant they may appear to be. Additionally, the family may find it difficult to identify their strengths and so the worker should look for past successes. These exceptions to unwanted behaviour need to be understood clearly by all, as they will be influential in goal development. Therefore, it is useful to encourage families to be specific about their exceptions by finding out how the exception happened, who was there, and who was central in making the exception happen.

The family may wish to have the opportunity to spend time alone during the meeting. If this is the case, the worker should leave the meeting and wait until called back in. In the case study, Ana raised the possibility of family time alone at the beginning of the meeting. This gives the family support to make the choice for family time should they wish. Family time alone supports the notion that families are experts about themselves, while also recognising that workers are not the experts and their presence is not always required—in fact, it may inhibit family decision-making.

Conflict management

Conflict is a natural and very typical phenomenon in every type of human relationship, and has already been referred to in Chapter 8 regarding work with families involved with the statutory system. In

Chapter 15, there will be further discussion about managing conflict with individuals. Optimistically, conflict allows people to learn about a problem from different sides, and often the most creative ideas and solutions emerge from conflict. Even though conflict is natural and typical, families do not have homogenous responses to coping with conflict. Workers should consider the patterns of dealing with conflict that have developed for families over time. For example, there may be varying roles that each player in the family system takes when conflict occurs. Some family members may withdraw when tension arises, others may become louder and more authoritarian, some may become supportive of the person they perceive as being most vulnerable. It is as important to consider how families have resolved conflict in the past as it is to uncover new ways of resolving conflict.

One way of thinking about patterns of conflict resolution, as a worker, is to consider your own family experience. The questions in Exercise 12.2 may be useful.

Exercise 12.2

1 Can you think of a time when conflict occurred in your family system?
2 What role did you play in the conflict?
3 How did your response to the conflict escalate or de-escalate the situation?
4 What role did others play in the conflict?
5 How did each of their responses to the conflict escalate or de-escalate the situation?
6 How does this knowledge and understanding enhance or inhibit your ability to work with families at times when conflict may be at the fore?

In the case study, Ana had planned for possible strategies should conflict arise. She spent time with Manu, the cultural adviser, and wisely decided it may be useful for him to attend the meeting. Questioning was employed once strain became evident in the meeting. What follows is an example of this process in the meeting:

Joseph: (raised voice) This boy is in my house, in my family. He will obey my rules. Whatever I say he has to do, he has to do. Nobody can tell me what to do. This is my family and my business. The boy just has to listen to me. That's it. What's so hard about this? Children are supposed to obey their parents!! I have had enough of this, I should leave and forget about this.

Ana: So, Joseph, it sounds as though you really care about David and that things have been difficult with him lately?

Joseph: (a little quieter) Yes, the boy has been disrespectful. He's been getting into trouble at school. He won't listen to his mother, or to me. The boy has got to *learn*.

Ana: It sounds like you want David to learn, and you want him to be respectful?

Joseph: Yes, it is my job as his father to teach him right from wrong, to teach him to behave so he doesn't bring shame on our family.

Ana: So you believe it's your job to teach David. How do you do that?

Joseph: I tell him, and tell him to show respect. Sometimes he's so rude I have to slap him.

Ana: And how do you find this works?

Joseph: It doesn't work so much and the boy won't listen. It's getting worse.

As this conversation shows, Joseph moves through to the point of admitting that slapping David is not working. This admission was possible as Ana's approach was respectful, non-judgmental and gently inquiring. She expressed respect by not interrupting Joseph as he yelled angrily; rather, she allowed him to find expression for his feelings. When Ana did speak, she used her voice quietly but firmly. At no point did Ana become consumed in the struggle that was occurring for Joseph. This is consistent with traditional Samoan approaches to conflict that focus on maintaining group harmony through respectful interactions with one another.

Angry clients

Sometimes the pressure of a situation becomes so much that people will become very angry and frustrated. Perhaps family members begin to scream at each other in the meeting. The worker should not get into a situation of having a screaming competition with the family. The worker may stand up to gain the attention of family members. Another option is to whisper to the person next to them. Often a whisper catches others by surprise, and is enough of an attention-grabber to prevent the screaming match from continuing any further. On other occasions, the worker may allow the conflict to continue for some time before intervening. At a minimum, workers should be aware of a range of options available for dealing with angry clients. Chapters 8 and 15 discuss further strategies for dealing with angry clients.

Of prime importance is making sure that methods employed to deal with angry clients are culturally appropriate. For example, in the case study Ana does not employ the technique of standing up to gain the family's attention amidst an escalating situation. Standing up in the middle of a meeting with a Samoan family is deemed both offensive and disrespectful. Selecting an unsuitable response to situations of conflict can result in escalating the situation. The primary focus for the worker is de-escalation of conflict. It is, however, crucial that dangerous conflict (violent, physical or increasing verbal and emotional abuse) is halted straight away. This may mean moving all family members who are not involved in the screaming match out of the room, which on occasion can be enough of a change in the environment to put a stop to the conflict. The potential for violent outbreaks during family meetings should be considered before the meeting, and strategies for dealing with potential violence developed.

Negotiating goals

At this stage of the process, there is an overlap between the assessment and intervention stages of the helping process.

Goals define what the family is striving for and how they are going to get there. In strengths-based practice, there is a focus on families developing their own goals. Families are more committed to solutions they are able to develop for themselves, because they usually develop solutions that are within their range of resources and are achievable. Ideally, workers collaborate with families to develop goals that relate to the expected direction of events.

This idea of collaboration implies equitable power relations. There is, however, an inherent power that workers hold because of their role (*role power*). This may be especially the case when a worker is employed by a statutory agency. Power is also inherent in any discussion about anti-oppressive practice. Burke and Harrison (1998) suggest that a number of principles inform anti-oppressive practice—these were outlined in Chapter 1. They advocate that these principles 'provide an approach that begins to match the complex issues of power, oppression and powerlessness that determine the lives of the people who are recipients of social care services' (1998, p. 232). To work in an anti-oppressive way therefore requires an understanding of issues of power, and how power may corrupt or inhibit working in collaboration. For some, the thought of encouraging families to take time on their own—for example, during a family meeting—is degrading to the role of social work. Workers can feel threatened in being 'left out of the loop' of decision-making. This is more likely to occur if workers see their role as central to the process; if this is the case, a worker is more likely to use his or her role power to impose assessment outcomes, thereby developing goals that do not match the family culture. The opposite of this is the worker who acknowledges their role power and how use of this power may inhibit working in collaboration with the family, and recognises how such role power may further oppress the family. This worker is able to use role power to empower the family.

Often practitioners will enter into work with families with clear goals, such as in the case study where Ana's fundamental goal is to ensure the discontinuation of physical punishment of David. Joseph may be more concerned with improving David's behaviour. Negotiation, then, is central to any goal-setting with the family.

Negotiation

The first step to negotiation is preparation. Where possible, the worker should consider in advance their fundamental goal and the goals that the family may have. Additionally, workers—in the spirit of collaboration—need to be committed to a win–win approach; therefore, the skill required in negotiating with families is that of steering negotiations in a positive direction. In order to do this, the worker needs to be open about his or her fundamental goal. Sometimes, family goals may appear to be different from the worker's goals. It may be that:

> even if your goals appear different from those of the client, frequently what the client wants and what you want are the same, only they are expressed differently and with varying degrees of emphasis. For example, the client reluctantly meets with you in order to keep the children with her. Your goal is to insure that the children are safe and reasonably well taken care of, by the biological parent, if possible. The client's goal may be to 'stop the social service from coming around', and

in order to do that, she must do certain things to meet the minimum standard of adequate child care. (Berg, 1994, pp. 78–80)

Goal-setting

Goal setting is the process of setting and working towards specific, defined client goals. Workers should be mindful that goals should be:

- the family's goals;
- recorded in the language of the family—in the case study, family goals were recorded in both Samoan and English;
- written down and a copy given to all;
- simple; however, goals should not be so simple that no sense of success will be perceived by the family once goals have been achieved;
- broken down into short-term and long-term goals;
- measurable—that is, the family has to be able to identify how it will know when the goal has been achieved.

Goals are not merely statements about an achievement in the future; they represent action. Discussion of goals should therefore focus on *behavioural tasks*. The worker can focus on helping families identify how they want their family to be in the future in terms of how they communicate and behave with each other. It may be useful, depending on the preference of the family, to have a tool for goal-setting, or the family may develop its own tool. The table in Example 12.3 is an example.

Exercise 12.3

Using the following table, identify three goals that Louana and Joseph have for their family. Complete the table using the information we have about this family and the worker's agency.

Name	Goal	Tasks	Resources	Measure	Date

The goal is stated along with any tasks required to be undertaken by each person to reach it. Resources refers to the people and other resources required to assist with achievement of the goal. The measure relates to how the family will know when the goal has been achieved, and the date refers to the period of time the family gives itself to achieve the goal.

As previously stated in Chapters 3 and 8, the development of goals with families is directly related to the identification of exceptions to behaviour. Another way of encouraging clients to identify goals is to ask what is known as a 'miracle question':

> 'Miracle' questions are useful as they give family members insight to a range of possibilities, and they give clients a view in to the future, thereby moving away from 'their current and past problems and toward a more satisfying life'. (De Jong & Berg, 2002, p. 85)

Examples of miracle questions asked in the case study are:

- What if all of you went to sleep tonight and a miracle happened, and when you woke tomorrow the issues we have been exploring were solved? What would you notice that was different?
- Imagine that we are six months in the future: what do you see as being different in your life?

Of course, the worker needs to be mindful of the culture of the family, and whether the family would understand the concept of miracle questions.

Closing the meeting

Just before closing the meeting, the worker should provide the family with a summary of the discussion, with particular emphasis on the goals that have been formulated. At this point, affirmation is given to the family for the work its members have done. The meeting is then closed according to whatever protocols are appropriate to the family. In the case study, as is consistent with Samoan protocol, the meeting was closed with prayer followed by sharing of food provided by the agency and family together.

CONCLUSION

Work with families places practitioners at the centre of a system which has rules, boundaries and protocols regarding ways of behaving and being. Many of these will be unspoken by the family, meaning the worker will have to be guided by family members as to what is appropriate and what is offensive to the family system. Strengths and anti-oppressive perspectives provide the opportunity for workers to be involved with families in ways that are considerate of family systems, and around which the process of family work can be built.

Although the skills identified in this chapter are used in strengths-based and anti-oppressive practice, they are skills that can be utilised in all our interactions with people, whether they are clients or colleagues. Underlying these skills sit notions of enhancing lives through humane, respectful and empowering social work practice. In the end, the family determines what humane, respectful, empowering social work practice it should be.

PART IV

Phases of the helping relationship: Intervention

13

TAKING ACTION: INTERVENTION

Ronnie Egan

The following three chapters focus on the client change process. There is an acknowledgment in these chapters that the notion of client change can be inherently flawed in that it shifts the responsibility for change from existing structural inequalities and barriers to those individuals most severely affected by these inequalities. In anti-oppressive practice, one needs to acknowledge the different levels of the change process: structural, cultural and personal (Mullaly, 1997). These levels, as suggested throughout this text, are not mutually exclusive. Rather, the relationship between broad macro changes and cultural and individual changes is a dialectical one, with each aspect exerting an influence on the others.

In this chapter, we define and contextualise the process of intervention using a solution-focused approach to demonstrate different strategies in the intervention phase. The tasks of intervention will be outlined to highlight the scope of the change process and the different roles undertaken by the worker. Chapter 14 focuses specifically on groupwork as an intervention, and provides a case example that highlights the similarities and differences between individual work and groupwork. Chapter 15 goes on to explore the use of constructive challenge as an intervention. Together, these three chapters focus on ways of facilitating change in our work with clients.

CONTEXTUALISING THE CHANGE PROCESS

Intervention is defined as the action phase of the work, where the client and worker collaborate to implement change (Cournoyer, 2008). For the purposes of learning, we discuss intervention as if it were a separate entity, describing its process, skills and tasks. In practice, however, there is considerable overlap between the phases of engagement, assessment, intervention and evaluation. As noted throughout this text, the relationship between all phases of the helping process is fluid and dynamic. In the intervention stage, both client and worker are narrowing the focus from the information-gathering typical in engagement and assessment to implementing an action strategy. Presenting the stage of intervention after engagement and assessment can be misleading, because it may be assumed that change can only occur in this sequence. For some clients, their decision to seek external support may create the required change and so become an intervention in and of itself (de Jong & Berg, 2007). However, for the majority of clients this will not be the case (Geldard & Geldard, 2005). The micro-skills discussed in earlier chapters on engagement and conducting assessments will also be used during the intervention phase.

Anti-oppressive practice draws the links between the individual, the external environment and the oppressive relationship between each of these elements. Mullaly's (2002) discussion of internalised oppression is useful in understanding client change. Internalised oppression refers to an individual's beliefs and behaviours that contribute to their own oppression. This occurs when a person internalises the dominant value and belief system of society, even when this discriminates against them as an individual. An example of this type of oppression is women feeling bad about themselves over issues of body image, and dieting to conform to how society believes females 'should' look.

This process of internalising oppression can affect both workers and clients. It can impact on an individual's capacity to exert power and their capacity to change. If an individual, or the group to which they belong, believes they are incapable of changing their circumstances, or that they are inferior to others, then their own actions and responses can contribute to ongoing personal oppression (Mullaly, 2002). In social work and welfare practice, the relationship between a worker and client can unintentionally reinforce this powerlessness.

ANTI-OPPRESSIVE PRACTICE IN THE CHANGE PROCESS

A worker's awareness of internalised oppression can be used consciously in the change process with clients by acknowledging the power and influence inherent in the worker–client relationship. For workers, this means having an awareness of their own systemic power through their organisational mandate and influence in the helping relationship. Table 3.1 in Chapter 3 outlines the different features of power *over* practice with clients as opposed to power *with* clients (McCashen, 2005). These features remind us of the potential power we have in relation to clients.

Translating the anti-oppressive foundation into practice can be a challenging task for two reasons. First, an understanding of oppression explains why it occurs, whose interests this serves, and who is disadvantaged and discriminated against. It is most powerful when explaining social or group phenomena. However, its use in the area of individual or small-group change is contextual rather than specific. For example, the worker may be able to assist clients wanting to change aspects of their external environment like accessing resources. Such external changes may not necessarily lead to internal changes for the client. The latter requires the use of other practice theories and skills that deal with the issue of change at this level. Second, workers who are anti-oppressive in their practice will experience acute tensions related to their role. More specifically, this tension is associated with providing individual services to clients who may be voluntary or involuntary, while simultaneously attempting to act as an agent of social change.

This tension can be felt most strongly during the intervention phase. Changes in the client system that are desired by both the client and worker may be impossible to achieve, such as gaining employment or income security. Clients will most likely desire a change in their personal circumstances to be demonstrated in some concrete way, such as having greater access to services or resources. Understandably, clients are often not interested in the worker's desire to facilitate change at a structural level. Nevertheless, it is important for the worker to have those skills that assist the change process with individuals while still recognising and noting the reality of a disadvantaged and discriminatory social structure. The challenge is to translate structural theory into skills which can empower clients within an oppressive organisational mandate. This empowerment can occur when the worker uses the notion of tapping into client strengths and exploring the client's previous success at change.

207

Exercise 13.1

You are working at a housing service with a family who has recently been evicted from a rental property. The family consists of two adults, Mary and Les, and two children, Gary (two years old) and Shantell (six months). Mary has two other children, Kim (aged seven) and Rory (aged nine), both currently in foster care. This is the fourth time the family have used the housing service in six months. You have been involved with the family twice before. Both adults receive income security payments and have substance abuse issues. The child protection system is currently involved. The family needs crisis housing assistance from you as its members all slept in the car last night. It is your role to deal with their crisis housing needs.

Divide into two small groups and adopt the role of the housing worker. In this exercise each group understands the family in different ways:

- One group is 'sick of this family' and does not want to assist them again.
- The other group recognises the 'no win' cycle of this family.

Both groups are to develop a rationale for assisting or not assisting this family.

1 What theory informs your decision and why?
2 How do you understand this family's needs?
3 How would you discuss your decision (to help or not) with Mary and Les?

In the large group, discuss and debate your differing positions.

USING A SOLUTION-FOCUSED APPROACH TO DISCUSS CHANGE

A solution-focused approach can be used to understand and provide strategies to assist during intervention. The approach shares with other systemic approaches the assumption that change is inevitable and constant. A worker needs to understand, test and think about this assumption, demonstrating to the client the belief that they can change. The client's motivation for change also needs to be explored. By asking the following questions, the worker can probe the client's investment in achieving a desired outcome:

- How confident are you that you can make this change?
- When was the last time you were able to change in this way?
- What would it take to make this change again?

Once the client's investment in achieving change is clear, a solution-focused approach aims to enable clients to build upon existing competencies. This approach is based on the assumption that clients will invite us into a conversation about what they want to change, and how they understand change will happen. The worker's use of questions is integral to facilitating this process. Questioning becomes part of the intervention strategy. De Jong and Berg (2007) believe that clients invite workers, in different ways, to shift from talking about their problem to seeking solutions. These 'invitations' may include direct or indirect verbal signals and non-verbal cues. The types of questions and comments by the client that might indicate to the worker that the client is ready to talk about change, solutions or action may include:

- What do you think about the options I'm looking at?
- What should I do about my problem?
- What would you do if you were in my shoes?
- Can you help me?
- Is there any hope for someone like me?
- Can you help people with problems like mine?
- Have you ever dealt with this sort of thing before?
- I'm not sure what to do.

These cues require the worker to listen attentively; Chapter 7 discusses the skills related to active listening (Geldard & Geldard, 2005). With a solution-focused approach, we are waiting for the client's conversation to move towards seeking change, so listening for this shift in focus from problem to solution is important.

Client comments like those listed above may have no other behaviour to signal the shift, or alternatively they might be matched by non-verbal behaviour. For example, a client may make the comment 'I'm not sure what to do', and accompany this with a sigh. You could clarify with the client their verbal and non-verbal messages to ensure your interpretation of the client's signals are accurate. You might ask the client whether they want some feedback about what the next step might be.

Non-verbal signals from clients that may indicate they are ready for change could include:

- pausing in talking about problems and looking expectantly at you;
- ceasing conversation, suddenly looking hopeless, overwhelmed or confused; or
- intermittently glancing at you while talking about their problems.

These signals are less clear, and do require clarification with the client to ensure you understand their meaning. Non-verbal behaviour, as suggested throughout the book, is often the behaviour most open to cultural misinterpretation. As such, seeking clarification is an important skill in the intervention phase.

Often clients are relieved if they do not have to talk about their problems and will readily respond to our invitation to take part in conversations about change. There are many possible ways for the worker to offer an invitation to talk about change. These include asking the following questions:

- How will you know when your problem is solved?
- How will you know when you won't need to see me again?
- Since things have been so painful in the past, what would you like to be different in the future?
- How will your [spouse/child/another worker/boss] know that you have begun to resolve this problem?
- How were you hoping I might help?
- What would be one of the first signs that your problem was resolved?

These same questions or variations of them can be used to invite people into conversations about action. From a solution-focused approach, there is no set rule for when to offer an invitation to a change in conversation. In general, the earlier the worker and client have this conversation, the better. It is in these conversations that we begin to identify what types of intervention the client is wanting.

In other chapters, we have explored some of the challenges of working with clients who are mandated to attend agencies. A solution-focused approach can still be used in these circumstances. For example, in the case material presented in Chapter 15, Steven is facing court attendance at a non-government program which will greatly enhance his prospects of not receiving a custodial sentence. His aim is to ensure that he does not go to prison. This aim opens up the possibility of a conversation between the worker and Steven about the changes the worker believes a court would want to see in him so that he does not receive a custodial sentence.

Your use of questions becomes part of the intervention strategy. The following questions suggest ways of discussing change from Steven's view of a different life:

- What is the first step you need to take to continue with the group?
- What will be different for you if prison is no longer a threat hanging over you?
- What difference would these changes make in your life?

Once the goals for change are clear, the tasks of intervention begin. These tasks generally involve the worker identifying the resources that are needed. Questions used to identify these resources could include:

- What will you need to do to take a small step towards your goal?
- What will you need to do to decrease problem areas?
- What are some possible strategies for intervention?

The focus in these chapters is on interventions with individuals, families and groups. Most interventions will involve accessing services or resources. The degree to which workers can act on any broader social change agenda will be determined largely by the organisation within which they are employed. In defining strategies for intervention, there is an inextricable link between the organisation in which the worker is employed and the worker's role in the change process with the client and elsewhere. For example, some competitive tendering processes for human service programs in both Australia and New Zealand require service conditions which mean that the successful service may be unable to comment publicly about service delivery for the funded program. The service workers may want to highlight the limited nature of the service able to be provided or publicise negative aspects of the service or structural barriers facing clients accessing their services. However, if the organisation signs a contract that means service providers cannot comment publicly, then the capacity for intervention about structural barriers may not be an option. The brief of the agency provides the parameters of intervention available. Three types of intervention strategies are now discussed:

- accessing resources and information for clients;
- maximising client strengths; and
- statutory intervention.

ACCESSING INFORMATION AND RESOURCES WITH CLIENTS

In using a solution-focused approach, the worker and client can collaboratively determine what resources and personnel are required in the change process (Compton et al., 2005). Clients may seek assistance because they want external resources. Internal resources will be discussed in the section on maximising client strengths. Clients may not know of available resources, or alternatively may be unable to access them. Assisting clients to identify and access available resources is a key task in intervention. There are four main ways to access resources. These include:

- directly providing services in cash or kind;
- referral to provider agencies;
- brokering for services;
- advocacy for services.

Direct provision of services in cash or kind

As suggested earlier, the type of agency in which the worker is employed will determine the types of resources available for clients from this setting. If, for example, a worker is employed in an agency that supplies emergency relief there should be little problem in accessing this kind of assistance. In contrast, an income support agency—like Centrelink in Australia or WINZ in New Zealand—does not provide emergency relief. Nevertheless, workers in these agencies should have access to current information about where to access material assistance. The provision of emergency relief is the type of service that changes depending on agencies' access to resources. At any one time, those agencies that do offer emergency relief will have only limited access to cash, food vouchers, transport tickets, pharmacy funds or other emergency items. There are rarely enough resources to service the level of demand for emergency relief. This, understandably, is frustrating for the client, particularly if resources are unavailable when they are needed. Students need to recognise the different and over-lapping roles they will play in trying to access resources for clients. Sometimes organisations provide resources directly or refer clients to other organisations.

Referral to provider agencies

Referral assists clients to access resources from other agencies. Clients often experience the referral process as frustrating, particularly if they are referred elsewhere and the second organisation is also unable to offer assistance. Workers can avoid this frustrating situation for clients by telephoning other agencies to determine the availability of resources before sending clients to them. Chapters 16 and 18 discuss the referral process further. Having up-to-date information about available resources and services can streamline the intervention process for the client. Unfortunately, practitioners are often unable to maintain current resource information because of multiple demands on their workload. Workers also feel frustrated in this situation of increased demand and limited supply of services and resources (Harms, 2007). Workers experiencing frustration could identify strategies for meso or macro change to address limited resourcing. For example, a local network could be established to regularly monitor the availability of emergency relief resources in the area. Such a network might use this monitoring process to publicise and lobby for increased resources. However, workers may be unable to prioritise such a strategy because of service contracts or workload pressures. This example of accessing emergency relief highlights the challenges for workers in accessing resources or referring clients elsewhere for service provision.

Exercise 13.2
You are a worker in a foster care agency. A single woman, Liz, has requested respite foster care for her two children under the age of five. Liz is expecting her third child. In the past, Liz has been investigated by Child Protection Services and your agency provided short-term foster care at that time. You know that Liz has made positive changes in her life since that notification. At this time, however, she feels that she needs a short break before giving birth to her new baby. Your agency currently has a waiting list for respite foster care. You need to access alternative arrangements with her by arranging a referral elsewhere. These arrangements may include other respite foster care agencies, local in-home support, alternative supported accommodation options or other child care resources.

In groups of three, allocate the roles of Liz, the worker and the observer. Role-play Liz's request for respite foster care with the worker.

The observer makes notes about how the worker and Liz interact during the interview.

1 How might the worker respond to Liz's request?
2 What resources might you be able to offer Liz?
3 What encouraged Liz to continue in the interview?
4 What did you observe as the most difficult part about the interview?
5 How did the intervention change during the interview?
6 In small groups, discuss your responses to this role-play and identify further strategies you might have used in the interview with Liz.

Brokerage

The worker in the role-play with Liz assumed the role of the broker. Brokerage is a task often required in the intervention phase of the helping relationship. Goldberg Wood and Middleman (1989) identify three expectations of the broker. They note that the broker should:

• have a current working knowledge of available resources;
• cultivate a range of differing resource options that can be used by clients;
• work towards creating resources in areas or fields where there are none.

They also suggest that the worker needs to stay in contact with the client to ensure the linkage with the new service is accomplished. Hopefully the worker would have existing positive relationships with different foster care agencies that may have foster care places available. However, foster care placements are increasingly in short supply across the country. The development of good networking for cooperative resource-sharing between agencies demonstrates how the worker can cultivate resources. Creating a local or statewide network of foster care providers to lobby government for increased resources or improved coordinated foster care provision demonstrates how to develop additional or even new resources. If no such alternative foster care options are available, the worker may also advocate for Liz to access services.

Advocacy

O'Connor et al. (2003) define advocacy as 'an effort to influence the behaviour of decision makers in relation to another or a group of others' (2003, p. 182). Seden (1999) also suggests that the worker may use their own power and influence in the interests of the expressed wishes of a client. Advocacy and brokerage are strategies central to translating the daily needs of clients into change at a broader systems level. In this way, workers have the potential to address and change larger structural impediments, which disadvantage or oppress the individual clients with whom they work. However, O'Connor et al. make an important distinction between case and class advocacy (2003). Case advocacy is the focus of this chapter. Class advocacy refers to those macro changes suggested in the emergency relief example earlier in the chapter. It is important to understand this distinction, as the strategies for case and class advocacy are different. O'Connor et al. (2003) identify four steps to facilitate case advocacy process (2003):

1 *Decide what is to be advocated.* For Liz, her priority is to access respite foster care services. You need to discuss possible options available. If other foster care agencies are unavailable, the organisation may have more power to pressure foster care providers for respite placements. Although wary of the Department, Liz agrees for you to contact them on her behalf. The worker is advocating for Liz's access to respite foster care resources.

2 *Identify the decision-makers.* You would need to discuss this option with your manager and collaboratively identify the appropriate departmental level and the person at that level who would have the most influence in processing an urgent foster care placement.

3 *Identify and understand the framework by which decision-makers (in the department) will make their decision.* You and your supervisor identify and understand that the department worker would be basing her decision to assist Liz on a risk-assessment framework. The argument you construct to advocate for Liz therefore needs to be based on this framework.

4 *Identify the manner in which the decision-makers perceive their relationship to the advocacy effort.* The departmental worker may recognise that an intervention of accessing respite foster care at this point could be a better option than having another child protection case return to the system. In this way, your efforts of advocacy on behalf of Liz might well be successful.

MAXIMISING CLIENT STRENGTHS

A strengths perspective focuses on the client identifying, harnessing and maximising their own strengths. De Jong & Berg (2007) highlight that clients with long histories of statutory involvement are often surprised when they are asked how they have survived this system. Many report that interventions in the past have focused on what they are not doing, or what they were doing badly. Such a focus can make change discussions difficult. Other solution-focused techniques, however, can help to draw out client expertise. Chapters 3 and 8 discussed the skill of searching for exceptions and use of the miracle question (De Jong & Berg, 2007).

As discussed previously, miracle questions are invitations to clients to think about what it would be like after their problem has been solved. You may preface a miracle question to Liz by noting that it might seem like an odd question. Then you would go on to ask: 'If a miracle happened, and the problem was solved, what would be different?'

An example of 'searching for exceptions' would be a discussion between the worker and client about past experiences in the client's life when the problem might reasonably have been expected to occur, but did not.

Exercise 13.3
1 In pairs, allocate the role of the worker and Liz.
2 The worker practises asking Liz the miracle question.
3 Role-play the conversation where a worker asks Liz the miracle question. Take it in turns to be the worker and Liz.
4 How might you preface your miracle question?
5 In the role of Liz, how does it feel to be asked this question?

STATUTORY INTERVENTIONS

Statutory interventions are those carried out by the worker which are mandated through legislation or a court order. These interventions may include actions such as removing a child from a family home, or facilitating the placement of a person into a residential facility when it would not be the client's choice to make such a move. These actions are generally used as a 'last resort'. Decisions such as these are never made by one worker. They are made in consultation with supervisors, managers or other senior staff. However, often this kind of intervention feels fraught when trying to practise in an anti-oppressive way. This tension is further exacerbated by an environment characterised by increased service demand and inadequate resources (Egan, 2008). However, for some clients statutory interventions may be viewed positively (Turnell & Edwards, 1999). This may occur, for instance, after a statutory intervention such as a family violence order, or a Children's Court order. In these cases, police or child protection workers may intervene by using a legal order to safeguard the children. It may be about protecting the most vulnerable people in each situation. Although initially this may be against the wishes of either or both parents, this intervention may ultimately generate positive changes in the lives of the children and parents.

BARRIERS TO CHANGE

When change does not occur as part of the intervention, there can be serious consequences. For example, in a statutory agency where a legal order requires the client to undertake a particular activity (such as drug rehabilitation), and they do not, there may be legal consequences. As such, it can be the responsibility of the worker to compel a client to attend the activity, knowing however that attendance has changed nothing for the client. This may be a common occurrence with mandated client–worker relationships. A solution-focused approach can offer workers a number of ways to think about why change may not have occurred. These could include the following:

- The goals of the intervention are not those of the client.
- The goals are not specific and concrete.
- The goals focus on something the client cannot control.
- The goals are too large.
- The goals focus on ending something the client wishes to hold on to.
- The goals do not motivate or interest the client sufficiently.

Exercise 13.4
Take some time to reflect upon situations where you have had decisions made for you by figures of authority (e.g. parents, teachers or employers). In small groups, discuss your experience of these situations.

1   How did you react to being told what to do? Try to recall both your thoughts and your feelings at the time.
2   What, if anything, motivated you to comply with the decision of the person in authority?
3   If you did not do as instructed, why was this the case?

CONCLUSION

This chapter has defined and contextualised the intervention phase of the helping process, highlighting some of the potential dilemmas and contradictions faced by workers. A solution-focused approach to practice is used to explore different ways of working collaboratively with clients. Strategies of change including accessing resources for clients, maximising client strengths and statutory interventions have been outlined. Chapter 14 will now examine groupwork as a change strategy, and Chapter 15 will discuss the challenges in the intervention when working with mandated clients.

14

FACILITATING CHANGE THROUGH GROUPWORK

Ken McMaster

GROUP EXPERIENCE IS FUNDAMENTAL

Being a member of a group, like our gender, class or ethnicity, is such an integral aspect of our lives that we often take for granted how much time we spend in groups or groups within groups. Over the past 25 years, a great deal of attention has been directed towards understanding the impact of gender and ethnicity on our lived experience, while at the same time surprisingly little attention has been given to understanding what it means to be a member or leader of a group. Attention has focused upon groups in the context of the wider community rather than on the method of groupwork.

In contemporary social work, while there is evidence of continuing interest in groupwork as a method, not enough attention has been given to 'either the knowledge base of group dynamics or to the practice base in groupwork method and skills' (Ward, 1998, p. 152). This chapter attempts to rectify this concern by focusing on method within the framework of strengths-based practice. For the purpose of this chapter, I will keep my focus on social-change groups, by which I mean groups that are generally run with the express purpose of assisting people to explore or change a behaviour that has become problematic for them. Examples of social-change groups include parenting groups, grief groups, stopping violence groups, victims' groups, psychiatric survivors' groups—the list is endless.

There are many forms of groupwork, but a strengths-based practice is anti-oppressive in its structure, purpose, and the relationships between leader and participants. Social-change groupwork is in essence about commonality of struggle, often against various forms of oppression; it therefore has the potential for reducing social exclusion, while at the same time creating the opportunity for greater social participation. Groupwork can offer:

- being known to others;
- consistency and predictability;
- experiences of diversity;
- energetic and stimulating contact with others;
- ownership and control—a sense of agency;
- the opportunity to meet a diversity of needs—physical, spiritual, cognitive and emotional.

A constructionist view of development is not about essentialism, but about the meaning we attach to events that impact upon us. As Saleebey (2002) notes:

> Human beings build themselves into the world, not with their meager supply of instinct, but with the capacity to construct and construe a world from symbols, images, icons, language, and ultimately stories and narratives. While culture provides these building blocks, we impart, receive, and revise meanings largely through telling stories, the fashioning of narratives, and the creation of myths. (2002, pp. 280–1)

Our entry into constructing our unique realities is our family, which is also our first experience of being in a small group. When we think about being in a family, there is not a chart of rules on the fridge—although more visible contracts are growing in popularity. The negotiation as to what rules, values or beliefs are acceptable within this group involves reinforcement for adherence and punishment for breaching them. This experience shapes us for future experiences of groups because we take these ideas with us into other group settings. However, we soon find that the rules, values and beliefs which are applied at home may or may not reflect the rules, values and beliefs in the wider society. We can therefore import into any subsequent group the basis for conflict and disagreement.

This chapter describes a strengths-based approach to groupwork. It is written from the perspective of a male group facilitator working within the New Zealand context, so reflects a bicultural emphasis rather than a multicultural perspective. However, the effective group facilitator is mindful of their position in the society *vis-à-vis* power, status and privilege that emanates from their ethnicity, gender, class and abilities, and as such takes this into account in their facilitation.

STRENGTHS-BASED VERSUS PROBLEM-FOCUSED GROUPWORK

For the purpose of this chapter, I focus upon what is commonly known as strengths-based approaches to social-change groupwork (Metcalf, 1998). Many traditionally run groups that have emerged in human service settings have utilised a psycho-educational approach in that group members are encouraged to reveal issues, express emotion as to what is occurring, search for insight and often be given the answers about how to resolve issues. While clients find these groups supportive, they can emerge from them with little in the way of concrete strategies that they can use in their own lives. In essence, they have spent too long focusing on what is wrong rather than looking at what is right and building from that position. They have become, in the language of White and Epston (1990), 'problem saturated'.

Strengths-based groups build upon the key idea that the role of the facilitator is to assist group members to construct new discourses and strategies while at the same time deliberately resisting the temptation to add to pathological discourses. The key facilitating style within a strengths-based approach to groupwork is as a guide or co-researcher rather than as a leader. That is not to say that the facilitator abdicates good leadership in working with the group to create a safe environment to explore what are often difficult and painful issues. The facilitator has the task of putting in place processes that allow group members to build upon and extend competencies that they already have. The role of the facilitator is also to allow group members to learn from each other through exercises and activities that allow for the sharing of strategies that others have found to be effective.

In a strengths-oriented approach, it is recognised that client problems do not occur constantly and that there are problem-absent times. These are labelled as *exceptions*, and the role of the facilitator is to identify the specific interactions, thoughts and behaviours that occur at these times and to utilise them in constructing a solution. The challenge is to look at what has been working in order to identify and amplify these solution sequences (de Shazer, 1982, 1985). For clients, this is profound in that they begin to view themselves as competent rather than incompetent, thereby building a greater sense of agency.

A number of key ideas form the basis of strengths-based approaches to social-change work. A starting point for the following ideas is the work of O'Hanlon and Weiner-Davis (1989, pp. 34–50), who identify a number of strategies for strengths-based practice. I have also added a number of additional key ideas that have emerged from my own group-work practice.

1   *Keep the group non-pathological by redescribing problems to open up possibilities.* Groups can often become problem saturated, which lowers energy and can make group members worse in their behaviour. Keeping the group non-pathological requires the skill of reframing from problem to solutions (O'Hanlon & Weiner-Davis, 1989). For example, if a group member describes the hassle of getting to the program, then a simple reframe can be to inquire how they managed to get to the session, despite the effort required. This is likely to generate a consideration of agency or an ability to have control in one's life.

2   *Build intrinsic versus extrinsic motivation.* Intrinsic motivation is more readily achieved by eliciting (drawing out) rather than telling. Very few of us respond to being told what to do and having others become experts on our lived reality. I hold the view, and state in training, that: 'We believe what we hear ourselves saying.' If we can work with people in groups to change their narrative—for example, about 'having to attend programs' to 'approach motivation'—where they argue for themselves the benefits of change, then we start to create movement in the direction of change.

3   *Focus upon the exceptions to the problems discussed during group interactions.* In other words, group members may describe behaviours or ways of thinking that are in direct opposition to the problem behaviour described. The key facilitator skill is to hear these exceptions, as this is the richness of strengths-based groupwork.

4   *When you notice a group member's competency in the group process, comment on it intermittently and gather other group members' thoughts on your discovery.* This is about noticing the

small changes. For example, if you hear a group member talking differently about a situation or problem, it is useful to ponder how this different thinking has come about and explore, by thinking differently, what people might notice about changes in behaviour. By creating 'news of difference', several skills are able to be practised —for example, listening, collaborative learning and feedback to others.

5   *Insight is one aspect of the change process. However, insight alone does not sufficiently provide group participants with the agency to act differently when they leave the session.* Strengths-based approaches are clearly targeted at changes in behaviour, so the person should always be able to leave the group session with something to try out or do differently. For example, reflective questions allow the participant to actively plan for the incorporation of insight into action. Useful questions that inquire as to what the participant is now aware of, and how this awareness will translate into behaviour outside the group room, is very rich material for strengths-based groupwork.

6   *Attempt to see group members as people with complaints about their lives, not as persons with symptoms.* Linked to this is the challenge to help group members view their problem as external to themselves. This will help them see the problem as a separate entity that influences but does not always control their lives. This is not to assume that they have no responsibility for behaviour, merely that problems are never the totality of a person's lived experience.

7   *Be aware that complex problems do not necessarily require complex solutions.* This is a time to assist your group clients to think in simpler ways. Solution-based practice often uses the following ideas: 'If it ain't broke, don't fix it'; 'Once you know what works, do more of it'; and 'If it doesn't work, don't do it again; do something different'. This recognises that significant aspects of our behaviour are habitual, and that if we interrupt the patterning, then we quickly shift behaviour.

8   *Adopt the client's world-view to lessen resistance and then work to discover less dangerous and interfering options with the person.* This is a fine line, and the skill of the facilitator is not to collude in disrespectful behaviour towards others. For example, if a client is in conflict with others in the group, then this can be viewed as useful because it will assist the group to discover ways to manage and work with conflict in a constructive way.

9 *Focus only on what is changeable.* Assist group members in thinking more specifically and less emotionally when setting goals for change.

10 *Go slowly and encourage members to ease into change.* Help clients see each strategy as an experiment, not as a technique that guarantees success.

11 *Strengths-based practice has the important goal of connectivity and social participation in the world.* An important aspect of the work is the legacy we leave for participants when they leave the group. Use of internalised other questions can be useful in building an audience for change: 'If [partner/children] were sitting with us listening to us talking, what would they say about your seriousness to sort out your issues?'; 'If [partner/children] were sitting with us listening to us talking, what would they say they would hope to be different as a result of our talking?'; and 'What advice might [partner/children/friends] give you about sorting out the issues affecting you if they were with us?'. The second step in this process is to inquire as to where the person is prepared to position themselves in relation to their partner, children and friends. I call these accountability referenced questions:

- 'On a scale of 1–100, how much do you share the hopes of your partner and children?'

If a person answers with a measure of 70 per cent, then you can ask a follow-up question such as:

- 'What would your partner make of that?' or
- 'What would we notice in the energy and commitment you would put into working with me to understand and get these problems out of your life?'

In summary, a strengths-based approach to social-change groups requires that we are vigilant for the dominant narratives that we, as facilitators and clients, bring into the room. Our role is one of walking alongside clients to discover alternative explanations to problem behaviour so that they can construct unique realities based upon meeting social needs in pro-social ways.

STAGES IN THE GROUP PROCESS

Group conditions change over time as a result of the interplay between the participants' need to attach and to separate. Observing and understanding the change in conditions is an important skill of groupwork practice. By examining the patterns of interaction and behaviour, it is possible to determine what needs prevail in the group at any given time and what, if any, intervention is required. Most writers describe a series of stages in the developmental life of the group. The model of group process favoured is that developed by Sarri and Galinsky (in Heap, 1977). They indicate that there are seven stages of the group process (see Figure 14.1). However, they do recognise that not all groups reach all stages, depending upon the nature of the group and the length of the group process. Outlined below and presented in Table 14.1 is an overview of these stages.

Table 14.1 Group members' behaviours and facilitator tasks through the life-cycle of the group

Stage	Group members' behaviours	Facilitator tasks
Pre-forming	Feelings of fear, resistance, negativity associated with preconceived ideas, apprehension	Prepare pre-course materials, conduct interview and assessment, communicate clearly defined course objectives and expectations
Formation	Feelings of anxiety, overwhelmed by work, family and peer group expectations, affected by past school histories, literacy and cultural issues—staunch attitudes. Some committed, enthusiastic and positive	Preparation, punctuality, establish group rules, ease the tension, welcoming, devise 'connecting' exercises, establish relationships, create a safe environment, introduce strategies to counter resistance

Table 14.1 Group members' behaviours and facilitator tasks through the life-cycle of the group (continued)

Stage	Group members' behaviours	Facilitator tasks
First working stage	Awareness of cultural, religious and class differences, bonding and formation of sub-groups, feelings of self-doubt, 'insider/outsider' divisions, establishment of goals	Reinforce ground rules, review process, be prepared for changing group dynamics, bring life and stimulus to program, be genuine, committed, encouraging, promote individual members' strengths, address transference of ownership issues
Re(vision)	Feelings of loss of interest, low energy, absenteeism. Revisit goals and set new goals/SMART	Evaluate progress of group, revise what's happened and discuss where group is going. Encourage members to revisit their goals, maintain energy levels, continue supervision and support
Second working stage	Increase of energy, group insight into cost/benefit of program, awareness of members' own strengths and weaknesses, a cohesive group dynamic and feeling of empowerment ('becoming')	Maintain leadership role, start talking about graduation, prepare for closure, maintain energy levels by role modelling, challenge opinions, affirm change and progress of group, offer insights, outline achievements
Closure	Boisterous feelings, personal issues revised, concerns of 'where to now'— loss—some withdrawal, anticipation and anxiety	Reaffirm ground rules, promote achievement, outline support networks, celebrate outcomes, encourage a feeling of ownership for the program's success

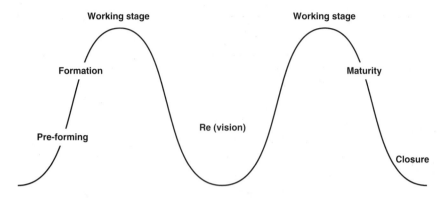

Figure 14.1 Group life-cycle

The utility of the framework shown in Figure 14.1 is that it matches what occurs on a sessional basis with what occurs over the lifespan of the group. For example, at each session the group has to reform and rebuild focus in order to get to the working stage. As you read through the following descriptions, consider a group you have been a part of.

Phase of origin

This refers to the pre-formation stage of the group and includes issues of resistance to working in a group, seeing the relevance of the purpose of the group, and the setting of the group. The functions of the facilitator include assisting members to develop group readiness, establishing the profile of the group in the minds of the potential members, and dealing with planning, building co-working relationships and the practical details of preparing for the group.

Formative phase

In this stage, group members are often energetic in a more diffuse manner. Members seek similarities in background, personal values and attitudes in their expectations of the group. Tentative relationships begin to emerge, giving rise to group structure, but this is in the context of a high level of anxiety in group members as they test out issues of safety, trust and boundaries.

The functions of the facilitator include assisting members to settle into the group by developing clear ground rules, establishing culture/ *kawa* (protocols)/norms for the group, energising the group into

227

activity to reduce levels of anxiety, and assisting members to begin building relationships with each other.

First working stage

The first working stage in the group is where interpersonal ties increase and greater cohesiveness is visible in the group. Sub-groups may start to emerge as a result of the move to commonality, and there is an increase in clarity around the purpose of the group at this stage.

The functions of the facilitator include assisting members to begin to work on the task of the group, engendering a sense of success in completing smaller tasks, and ensuring that cliques are managed appropriately and the ground rules are being adhered to.

Phase of revision

At this stage, the group will start to develop behaviours that are generally called 'storming'. Conflict begins to emerge in the group as differences in values become more evident. This is also often concurrent with challenges to the facilitator's leadership—in other words, the honeymoon is over.

The functions of the facilitator include the need for the culture of the group to be reworked and modified, further clarification of the purpose and commitment to the group's aims, and assisting group members to normalise conflict and find processes to resolve conflicts. Further tasks include assisting group members to reflect upon progress in meeting the group task and establishing goals for the next phase of the group, to re-establish a commitment to the group's purpose and aims.

Second working phase

This phase cannot work well unless the issues at the revision stage are resolved.

This is a more focused stage of working in the group in that group roles become clearer and more defined, resulting in a high level of cohesion, identification and stability of the group structure. Group members take on greater responsibility for monitoring and challenging anti-group behaviour.

The functions of the facilitator include increasing the pace and focus of the group and assisting group members to realise their renewed goals and work towards goal completion.

Phase of maturation

This refers to the mature stage in the life of the group, with clarity in the roles and responsibilities of the group. Group members own the group and see it as *their* group, and are protective of purpose as well as members. A team feeling has emerged. Group members begin a process of differentiation at this point (a move to more individual issues).

The functions of the facilitator include allowing group members to be more responsible for the life of the group, working with the individual issues that members bring to the group, dealing with group members who move into termination too early, and keeping the group moving so that it does not stall.

Phase of closure

The literature refers to this as the phase of termination, but I prefer the idea of closure or transition. This occurs when the goals of the group have been attained and there is no reason for the ongoing existence of the group, or when the group has been established for a defined number of sessions and these are now completed. The functions of the facilitator include assisting members to finish relationships with other group members in a meaningful manner. In closed groups, members can practise terminating relationships in healthy pro-social ways and the facilitator can assist members to plan for post-group change work and maintain changes made.

Since the development of this model, another phase is increasingly being identified as critical for the maintenance of changes in behaviour: the phase of maintenance. Prochaska (1999) argues that there is often a need in the post-action (working stages) of change for group members to access ongoing support from counsellors, sponsors, self-help groups and family/*whanau* if they are to succeed in maintaining a position of change. By locating themselves in an accountability framework, they are considering the impact of their behaviour on others, and are thus able to continue to resist the tendency to isolate themselves and return to previous patterns of behaviour.

By having knowledge of the stages in the life of groups, the group facilitator is then able to predict the group behaviours that are likely to emerge and plan accordingly. The following two exercises will assist you to consolidate the material covered so far in the chapter.

Exercise 14.1

First, reflect on the range of different groups you have been involved with over the last month:

- family/*whanau*;
- learning groups;
- sports groups;
- social action groups;
- social groups;
- project groups;
- lobby groups;
- study groups;
- support groups.

Once you have identified the groups you have been part of, identify the similarities and differences in the rules that govern their operation.

1   How do you manage participating in different groups with different rules?
2   What do you need to do to make the transition from one group to another?

Exercise 14.2

Consider one of the groups in Exercise 14.1 that you identified as having been part of for a reasonable length of time and relate the stage process to that group. What did you notice occurring at various stages in the life of that group? Which stages did the group move through? What stages were most difficult for the group?

Also draw up a chart and identify the types of behaviours that are likely to be most evident in participants at each stage. Then identify the tasks that the facilitator is required to undertake. Compare your chart to Table 14.1 above.

SKILLS OF AN EFFECTIVE GROUP WORKER

Facilitators have the important task of creating an environment where clients can explore solutions to existing issues through guided discovery or co-researching. The style of a strengths-based group facilitator is to draw forth exceptions and examples when dominant narratives or problem-saturated ideas are absent. In this section, a model of how to design a piece of program work from a strengths perspective is shared. Facilitators still have the responsibility to provide a process/structure around the session, while the group members generate the material. A number of key skills are required by the group facilitator, one of which is careful observation and noticing the small changes or exceptions in group members' behaviour or thinking. While effective facilitators use themselves in facilitating, the following skills will be defined in the remainder of this chapter:

- planning;
- group facilitation;
- collaborative problem-solving;
- using immediacy;
- self-advocacy;
- managing diversity.

Planning

Planning is the ability to consider what needs to occur in order for the group to function. In thinking from a solution-based perspective, we can identify three distinct phases of the change process. These apply just as much to individual work as they do to groupwork. If, as a worker, you take care to work with these phases, then you are more able to match your work with where people are at in their change process. The three phases are:

- talking about the talking;
- doing the talking; and
- reflecting upon the talking.

Talking about the talking is about creating the space for the conversation in the first place. If we have not cleared a pathway or engaged the person in the conversation, then we cannot progress to any depth when it comes to actually exploring the issue at hand. In terms of motivational approaches, this stage is the most significant in terms of change. Get this aspect right, and a very meaningful conversation will often develop.

Doing the talking refers to that stage when we know we are in meaningful conversation with another person. This is what I call the most active part of the process in that this stage allows us to unpack or deconstruct what is going on. This allows the group to develop solutions from their lived experience and communicate these to each other.

Reflecting upon the talking is the third stage; this is where we translate the talking into meaningful action. It is my view that unless we are able to translate the talking into action, we have somehow missed an important aspect of the process.

Group facilitation

This refers to the style or method of working in a group. Different groups demand different facilitator styles, and each group will require a variety of responses and behaviours from the facilitator as it moves through its phases of development towards greater capability and maturity. However, within a strengths/solution-based approach, the facilitator takes on the role of guide rather than expert. The facilitator's expertise is related to understanding group process and assisting group members to identify the exceptions to their presenting problems and building upon these. The first step in working with a group is to accept that you have been given the authority to influence and intervene in group experience. If you are reluctant to provide active facilitation, it can be very detrimental to the group at critical stages of transition when the group looks to you for guidance, reassurance and structure.

Facilitation is the design and management of structures and processes that help a group do its work and minimise the common problems people have working together.

Facilitation is a process that focuses on:

- what needs to be accomplished;
- who needs to be involved;
- design, flow and sequence of tasks;
- patterns of interaction;
- levels of participation and use of resources;
- group energy and capability;
- the physical and psychological environment.

One of the major challenges of groupwork is to maintain energy and focus while undertaking the task at hand. Many groups are easily sidetracked, particularly when group members have little experience of maintaining their own focus and view the group program as irrelevant to their situation. One of the most common traps that new facilitators can fall into is to focus on individuals within the group rather than relying upon the group itself to provide the energy and information required. This ultimately leads to group facilitators undertaking individual work with an audience. The downside of this particular approach to working in groups is that while the person who is the focus of attention may well be engaged in the work, other group members are not. They can become bored, distracted and disruptive in the group. We can minimise this by working with four levels of group interaction:

Level 1 Interaction with an individual;
Level 2 Interaction in a subgroup;
Level 3 Interaction with the whole group; and
Level 4 Interaction with a person outside the group.

The rationale behind using the four levels of interaction in groups can be reduced to a mathematical formula (see Table 14.2). For example, you may have a group of ten participants. If you work individually with these participants, the amount of time you have to spend with each is reduced to six minutes per hour. What this means is that for 54 minutes of that hour the other members of the group are not actively engaged in work for themselves. In a two-and-a-half-hour group session, this effectively means that each individual member has potentially fifteen minutes of time. Many of us would not think this was worth the investment of time and energy. Group members will agree.

Table 14.2 Different levels of interaction in groups

	Individual	Pairs	Sub-groups (4)
Time working	6 minutes	30 minutes	15 minutes
Time listening	54 minutes	30 minutes	45 minutes

If we are working in pairs for one hour, each individual has 30 minutes, interaction time—a vast improvement. I am not suggesting that this is an either/or situation; this example merely illustrates that by using robust and creative group interaction, the ability to maintain energy and focus within the group is greatly enhanced. This is important because one of the clear indications when groups are not working well is that its members do not feel involved or engaged.

Example of this model in action: A case study

This case study is from part of a session designed to deal with the issue of developing empathy in a group of men who had been referred for being abusive towards their female partners. The role of the facilitator is to put a process around the issues that the group members need to work with to avoid a continuation of the problem behaviour.

You will notice from Table 14.3 that the levels of change and the three phases of change are integrated to develop a dynamic and energetic experience. You will also notice that the facilitator is a guide and manager of the process. What is interesting from this approach is that the group members are effectively sharing strategies with each other, and are thereby empowered to search for solutions from within their own experience. An assumption is made that problem behaviour does not exist all of the time and that there will be times when participants have been able to make connections and experience empathic behaviour towards others. By taking this approach, participants are starting from a point of competence rather than incompetence.

Table 14.3 Phases of change in group process and levels of intervention

Phase in process	Task	Level of interaction
Talking about the talking	Introduce the topic: Our theme for today is to focus upon empathy— that is, putting yourself in the shoes of someone else.	Whole group
Talking about the talking	What would interest you most in learning about how to place yourself in someone else's shoes?	Pairs—five minutes
Talking about the talking	Process and list responses on a whiteboard or flipchart.	Whole group—five minutes
Talking about the talking	On a scale of 1 to 10, what is your interest level?	Whole group

Phase in process	Task	Level of interaction
Talking about the talking	Identify three things that might get in the way of learning more about what it is like to be in someone else's shoes.	Pairs—two minutes
Talking about the talking	Process and list responses on a whiteboard or flipchart.	Whole group—five minutes
Doing the talking	Think of a time when you have been open to hearing about what it is like for another person and answer the following questions: • What did you need to do in order to be so open? • What did you say to yourself to remain open? • What did you need to think about the other person in order to remain open? • How did it help you to understand that person's experience of the world more? • What impact did being open have on your relationship with that person? List your answers on flipchart paper.	Sub-groups (four)—twenty minutes
Doing the talking	Have the sub-groups report their findings to the whole group.	Whole group—fifteen minutes
Doing the talking	You all have the ability to put yourself in someone else's shoes. Now put yourself in the shoes of your partner or children. What would they say about the impact of living with violence? How might they describe it?	Pairs—five minutes
Doing the talking	Have the pairs report their findings to the whole group.	Whole group—fifteen minutes

Table 14.3 Phases of change and levels of intervention *(continued)*

Phase in process	Task	Level of interaction
Reflecting upon the talking	What have you become aware of through doing this exercise? What will you be doing differently as a result of what you have learnt? What will others in your life notice in your behaviour?	Pairs—three minutes
Reflecting upon the talking	Who needs to know about what you now know? What do you need to tell them? How will you tell them?	Pairs—three minutes
Reflecting upon the talking	Have each member of the group state what they have learnt and what they will do as a result. This helps to achieve two goals: • building accountability for change with other group members; • translating learning into action that can be evidenced.	Whole group—ten minutes

In the above case study, the outcome is both evidenced and visible to others. Insight is not the goal of the process but an ability to build upon existing skills and then change behaviour in an accountable way. In other words, it means building connections with others through responsibility for behaviour and publishing these changes with others.

Exercise 14.3
1 What do you notice about the process used and how might you adapt this to working with your cultural group?
2 What concepts in your culture relate to the cultural concepts used in the above example?
3 What would you add to or take out of the above process to make it culturally responsive to your culture or the cultural background of the clients you work with?

Collaborative problem-solving

Collaborative problem-solving refers to using the strengths and experiences within the group to assist in problem-solving. It is assumed that in any group of people there will exist many examples of effective problem-solving. The challenge for the facilitator is to trust that this is the case and to view participants as having competence rather than incompetence. For example, if a group member attends a session expressing concerns about a problem, then it is the role of the facilitator to assist the group to identify a number of strategies that might work. By having the group members consider and generate possible solutions, in addition to assisting the person with the stated problem they assist each other, while at the same time reminding themselves of their own competency.

Using immediacy

Using immediacy refers to the group being in a place where members can get immediate feedback on how they are in the world. Once the group gets beyond the formation stage, group members often face similar issues to those they experience outside the group. Sometimes people—often unknowingly—play games when interacting in a group. They develop strategies to help them avoid emotions that they would rather not face, such as fear or anger. They sometimes act in ways that distort reality and create barriers that prevent or inhibit creative responses to resolving issues. One of the key challenges of groupwork is to make the invisible visible. When an individual is using an avoidance strategy, they can—through feedback and other techniques—gain awareness that they are doing so and thus have the opportunity to develop an alternative way of interacting. The challenge is to develop more honest processes of interaction.

Self-advocacy

Self-advocacy refers to the ability to have agency in the world. A key aspect of strengths-based practice is to be able to translate the talking that people do in a session into action or behaviour. In this way, we can evidence that any talking we have done has made a difference in the person's life. It is therefore important to ensure that new understandings are consolidated for the person, and that this is translated into action. I firmly believe that people have agency, and the test of good

237

intervention is in my view that they are able to exert influence on the world around them. For example, it is possible for the facilitator to inquire with the group member about what will be different as a result of the new understanding or what others would notice in terms of changed behaviour. This allows the group member to visualise changes outside of the group.

Managing diversity

Managing diversity refers to the ability to get along with others and deal with differences. Social-change groups, by their very nature, allow us to be with other people with whom we may not otherwise choose to associate. In this way, we are challenged to sit in a room with others and work with our assumptions and prejudices. We therefore have to develop the ability to manage diversity, which can be a strength in the world outside of the group. Inevitably, conflict will emerge as group members become more comfortable with each other and intimacy increases within the group. The key skill for the facilitator is not to be afraid of conflict, but to manage it in a way that ensures the group remains safe, group members can deal with the conflict and all can learn from the experience.

CONCLUDING THOUGHTS

In this chapter, I have explored a strengths-based approach to social work intervention with social-change groups. I have argued that being a member of a group is one of the fundamental experiences that we have as humans. I have also covered the developmental stages that groups go through and the key skills that a facilitator using a strengths-based approach is required to have.

Groupwork continues to be an under-utilised resource within the human services profession, but in my mind it has the potential for significant change. If we consider that everyone who attends a group impacts on at least 25 other people, then this can start to make a serious difference in our communities. The challenge for students and practitioners in the human services is not only to give greater consideration to groupwork as a method, but also to utilise strengths-based approaches that are empowering rather than problem saturated.

15

USING CONSTRUCTIVE CHALLENGE DURING INTERVENTION

Delia O'Donohue

This chapter addresses the issue of challenging clients in the context of direct practice with individuals, families and groups. Challenging or confronting clients often creates anxiety for both workers and clients, and is one of the skills that many beginning practitioners are most concerned about using. The risk of eliciting an angry response or alienating clients seems to be of greatest concern to workers.

In this chapter, the skills required for effective confrontation will be identified and discussed with reference to an ecological-systems approach and strengths-based perspective. Incorporation of this approach will help to identify the possible consequences of confrontation, not only for clients but also for others within the client's system. It will also help the worker to explore possible sources of resistance to, or support for, change.

The integration of a strengths-based perspective is also useful and important as it encourages workers to identify and focus on positive aspects of the client's situation and to refrain from negative and aggressive approaches to challenging that involve 'blaming' and 'shaming' the client.

WHEN IS CONSTRUCTIVE CHALLENGE APPROPRIATE?

Constructive challenge is generally appropriate when:

- particular behaviours or beliefs are negatively affecting the client;
- clients' behaviour is inconsistent with their goals;

- clients minimise the positive aspects of their behaviour, and of their resources and strengths;
- clients' verbal responses in interviews are superficial or inconsistent;
- clients' verbal responses contradict or are inconsistent with their non-verbal communication;
- clients minimise the negative impact of their behaviour;
- there are inconsistencies between the accounts of two or more people;
- there are discrepancies between how the worker and the client understands the situation;
- clients are engaged in behaviour or actions that are illegal, violent, abusive or detrimental to their health and the health and well-being of those associated with them;
- clients are ignoring your service or program guidelines and causing difficulties for staff and other participants.

Challenging or confronting clients should occur in the context of a supportive counselling relationship. Ideally, it should only occur after a rapport has been established with the client, although there may be some circumstances—particularly in work with involuntary clients— where it is necessary to challenge behaviour even during the assessment phase of the relationship. However, even in these circumstances, confrontation or challenging should always be done in a respectful manner.

The process of challenging involves three important phases: identifying discrepancies and incongruities; discussing these issues with the client in a respectful and factual manner with a view to resolving the conflicts; and evaluating the effectiveness of your challenge or intervention (Ivey & Ivey, 1999, p. 196).

The following types of discrepancies have been identified and discussed in detail by Hepworth et al. (1997, pp. 549–51). They commonly occur and are frequently interrelated:

- Cognitive/perceptual discrepancies may occur due to a lack of understanding or 'accurate information', or due to clients' 'misconceptions' about themselves (Hepworth et al., 1997, p. 549).
- Affective discrepancies 'include denying or minimising actual feelings, being out of touch with painful emotions, expressing feelings that are contrary to purported feelings' (Hepworth et al., 1997, p. 549).

- Behavioural discrepancies involve actions or behaviours that are dysfunctional and/or incongruent with the client's stated goals or the goals of your program/service.
- 'Resistance to change' often manifests itself when clients are ambivalent about change because they derive particular benefits from maintaining their current situation. (Hepworth et al., 1997, pp. 549–50).

Exercise 15.1

Consider your responses to being challenged by family, friends and/or supervisors at work or on placement. Do you tend to become defensive when challenged? What range of emotions do you experience?

Skills required to effectively challenge clients include:

- empathy;
- timing;
- flexible approach—from minimal challenge to assertive confrontation;
- consideration of the influence of the broader system;
- a focus on the client's strengths.

These skills will be discussed with reference to the following case study:

Exercise 15.2: Case study

Steve decided to attend a group-counselling life-skills program, conducted at a non-government welfare agency. He came along with two of his friends, citing boredom and a pending court case for assault as providing motivation to attend.

Steve was 23 years old and had a long history of alcohol and marijuana use, as well as several convictions for theft and burglary. He was at risk of going to prison if convicted at his pending court case. Steve had no family support, having left home and school when he was fourteen years of age after being abused by his alcoholic step-father for many years. He was living in transitional housing with friends who were also drug users. He had been employed in a few short-term jobs, but had never had any long-term employment.

Steve presented as angry, depressed, bored and determined to make trouble in the group program. He was disruptive, constantly seeking attention and undermining group discussions and activities. The staff conducting the group were frustrated and initially wanted to bar him from further attendance, citing concern about the impact of Steve's behaviour on other group participants. One of the group facilitators met with Steve individually and explained the group rules to him again, including the need for respectful communication. Steve said he would comply with the guidelines in future, but then failed to turn up to the next two sessions. He then attended again and was as disruptive as ever.

Steve was interviewed individually again and a contract was made with him that clearly stipulated the rules of the program, staff expectations and also what he could expect from the staff, other program participants and the program. Steve agreed to sign the contract and to attend individual counselling—a condition of his continued attendance in the group program. It was clear that Steve's motivation for agreeing to these conditions was fear of imprisonment, and that he was under considerable pressure from his lawyer to attend the program.

In individual counselling, the practitioner focused on exploring Steve's background and the experiences that had led to him to the point where he was facing a possible prison sentence. The counsellor also spoke with Steve at length about his self-perception and the negative self-images that he had internalised from years of abuse at home and years of failing to achieve at school.

There was clearly a need for the worker to challenge the beliefs that were negatively affecting Steve and inhibiting him from making progress in achieving his goals: to reduce his substance use and offending behaviour, obtain more permanent accommodation and undertake some job-skills training. Adopting an ecological-systems approach and strengths-based perspective, the counsellor worked with Steve over a period of six months—his court case being adjourned to allow him more time in the individual and group counselling programs. Progress was slow, as Steve's motivation to attend counselling fluctuated. However, his attendance and behaviour in the group program improved markedly during this period. Both the counsellor and the group facilitators used positive reinforcement, boundary-setting, modelling, negotiation, consultation and conflict-resolution skills to engage Steve and to strengthen his motivation to achieve his goals. They had to resist the temptation to terminate the counselling relationship when Steve appeared 'stuck' and seemed to be reverting to old patterns of behaviour that negated the progress he had made.

EMPATHY

As discussed in Chapters 5 and 6, understanding your client's situation fully and conveying empathy are important elements of effective communication and confrontation. An authoritarian approach that involves overt criticism of the client or the client's circumstances is unlikely to achieve positive results. Many clients have experienced significant emotional abuse in their lives, and some have been subject to formal intervention by statutory authorities over a number of years. As in Steve's case, they are often bitter and resentful of authority figures and will respond negatively to challenges that are experienced as rebukes. It is therefore important to use confrontation sensitively and as a 'selective skill', rather than as a 'style of practice' (Hepworth et al., 1997, p. 551)

Consideration of client feelings, and understanding the concerns and fears that underlie their inability to change, are important components of effective challenging. As workers, we often have high expectations of our clients. Some examples of this are when we expect them to conform to our program guidelines without allowing them any input into the formulation of those guidelines; when we expect them to communicate respectfully knowing they have poor communication and social skills; or when we expect them to instantly abstain from substance use when they have been dependent for many years. It is important that workers understand the fears, concerns and risks clients perceive when they come to counselling to contemplate major life changes, and acknowledge these when challenging resistance.

Working with clients who are very resistant to change can be frustrating. Many are either formally or informally 'involuntary' clients who are attending for counselling due to pressure from statutory organisations, pending court appearances, family members, unhappy partners, schoolteachers, and so on. As in Steve's case, they may communicate in an abrasive or indifferent manner and stubbornly refuse to take responsibility for their situation. It may be tempting to prematurely terminate contact with such clients; however, perseverance is often the key to successful engagement of clients who initially appear resistant to change

(Hepworth et al., 1997, p. 561). Aggressive confrontation about the need for change only serves to entrench their position. Instead, these clients should be encouraged to explore both the advantages and disadvantages of change, and workers should focus on mediating between the various systems operating in the client's life to strengthen their connections and the support for change.

In order to be able to complete the first phase of the challenge process—identifying incongruities and discrepancies—and to successfully convey empathy, it is important that workers utilise effective communication skills. Observing, reflective listening, paraphrasing, summarising and use of silence are all important skills that help workers to convey empathy.

Beginning practitioners are often wary of silence, and some avoid it altogether by jumping in and providing clients with optional answers. It is important when challenging clients to make appropriate use of silence as it can both highlight your level of concern about the issues raised and, importantly, gives clients time to reflect seriously on the issues that you have identified.

The worker's tone of voice and non-verbal communication are also very important in conveying empathy and concern for the client's situation. Maintaining awareness of your own reactions and non-verbal communication is as important as noting your client's reactions when being confronted or challenged.

It is also important to give consideration to cultural factors that may be influencing a client's communication style and presentation. Some workers may label clients as 'resistant' or 'reluctant' when in fact cultural factors are influencing their communication style.

In the case study presented, the worker was careful to adopt a client-centred approach in his work with Steve, and used attending and listening skills to gradually develop a rapport with him. At the same time, the worker was clear about the boundaries of his role and reinforced the importance of compliance with group and agency rules.

TIMING

The timing of challenges is also of critical importance. Before using confrontation or being challenging, it is important to consider the developmental stage that your client is at and whether their behaviour is in fact consistent with their developmental stage. It is also important to assess their psychological state and whether there are any specific mental health issues that may be contributing to their difficulties.

Aggressive confrontation in initial interviews will usually elicit a defensive response. As noted above, it is important to develop a rapport and an appreciation and understanding of your client's circumstances before challenging discrepancies and negative behaviour patterns: 'Ill-timed and poorly executed confrontations may be perceived by clients as verbal assaults and may seriously damage helping relationships' (Hepworth et al., 1997, p. 546). Clients should not be challenged when they are distressed or in a state of crisis, as this may exacerbate their feelings of distress.

Prochaska and DiClemente (1986) have developed a 'stages of change' model that provides a useful tool or framework to assist workers to decide when it is most appropriate to challenge clients in relation to discrepancies between their behaviour and goals. It is a model that is used widely in the drug and alcohol field, but it is also relevant to other fields of practice. They suggest that people tend to go through five stages of change, although progress is not always linear. The five stages they have identified are:

- pre-contemplation;
- contemplation;
- action;
- maintenance;
- relapse.

The authors maintain that clients need to be confronted or challenged when they are in the 'contemplation stage' of change. In this stage, clients have become increasingly more conscious of the existence and extent of their problem and begin to re-evaluate themselves and to consider taking action. During this stage, they 'are most open to consciousness raising interventions, such as observations, confrontations, and interpretations' (Prochaska & Di Clemente, 1986, p. 19). The authors maintain that the premature use of confrontations or challenges will often result in a loss of rapport and communication breakdown between the worker and client. In the pre-contemplation stage of change, the focus of attention should be on providing information, and increasing the client's perceptions of potential harms and the consequences of the behaviour that has been defined as problematic.

Whilst Steve's outbursts and difficult behaviour suggest he was in the pre-contemplation stage of change, his attendance in the group program suggests he was open to considering the need for some changes in his life. Although the threat of imprisonment may have been the primary motivating factor for this, when dealing with such difficult and complex cases, it is important to 'capture' whatever motivation is present, no matter how fragile or disingenuous it may seem.

FLEXIBLE APPROACH

Once a decision has been made to challenge incongruities or discrepancies that have been observed, workers and students need to give consideration to the appropriate level of confrontation required from minimal challenges through to more assertive confrontation.

Minimal intervention

When challenging clients, workers should first consider using reflective questions that encourage clients to consider discrepancies and incongruities in their behaviour and/or responses themselves. Encouraging 'self-confrontation' is the most 'respectful' and least intrusive method of intervention (Hepworth et al., 1997, p. 545). Some clients have sufficient insight into the contradictions in their behaviour and are able to begin to analyse discrepancies and incongruities with minimal intervention from the worker. They can then move on to initiating positive changes in their lives with encouragement and support.

Reflective questions should be formulated carefully with a clear focus on exploring feelings or facts. Non-judgmental language should be used—labelling and criticism are inappropriate.

Assertive challenges

Sometimes more assertive confrontation may be necessary, particularly when clients are involved in harmful behaviour or where attempts to encourage self-confrontation have failed. However, as stated earlier, this level of confrontation should be used sparingly and should not be used as a customary method of practice. Unfortunately, some workers—particularly in statutory settings—adopt a confrontational approach consistently in their work with clients, often reinforcing and perpetuating labels that constrain and limit the client's potential. It is important, even when using assertive confrontation techniques, to work on developing the client's sense of self-worth by confronting risk-taking behaviour in a respectful and concerned manner.

Ivey and Ivey (1999) suggest summarising the dimensions of incongruities by using the following types of model confrontation statements:

'On the one hand . . . but on the other hand . . .'
'You see it that way, I see it this way . . .'
'You say . . . but you do . . .'
'Your words say . . . but your actions say' (1999, p. 199)

By using these types of statements, you can present concerns about inconsistent responses made by the client, differences in attitudes and perspectives between the worker and client, and discrepancies between goals and actions. In the case scenario presented, the worker challenged the client about the discrepancy between his goals and his actions in the group program using this type of approach:

On the one hand your attendance here suggests that you are motivated to make some changes in your life, but on the other hand your behaviour suggests that you're afraid to explore the issues that are affecting your ability to make changes. What's going on here?

In formulating this challenge, the worker acknowledged that the client's attendance was positive but at the same time he was direct about the lack of constructive input into the group. He was careful not to label or overtly criticise the client, expressing a genuine desire to understand Steve's behaviour and the actions that were undermining his progress.

This challenge led to a discussion of the difficulties of exposing oneself in a group situation. The worker explored with Steve his negative experiences at school and how he adopted the role of 'class clown' and the 'bad sheep' to compensate for his lack of academic progress. Underlying these earlier life experiences were feelings of failure, loneliness and helplessness—feelings that he was fearful of experiencing again in the group program. The conversation helped to increase the worker's understanding of the emotions underpinning Steve's disruptive behaviour and presented an important new dimension for them to focus on in their work together.

CONSIDERATION OF THE INFLUENCE OF THE BROADER SYSTEM

The ecological-systems approach

This approach encourages workers to view clients' circumstances holistically, and to take into consideration their immediate and broader network when deciding upon goals and strategies for intervention. It moves away from the traditional focus in psychology on the individual and individual pathology, emphasising the importance of considering and identifying the impact of social and environmental influences on a client's situation. Refer to Chapter 12 for earlier discussion about systems theory.

The emphasis of ecological-systems theory is on the 'goodness of fit' between clients and their environment:

> The purpose in formulating the ecosystems perspective was to encourage workers to view situations holistically, attending simultaneously to people, their families and whatever other systems might be important to their needs. Furthermore, the desire was to create a theory that would encourage us to recognise on an ongoing basis that these different 'levels' are always reciprocally influencing each other—ecological systems are inherently transactional in nature. (Lehmann & Coady, 2001, p. 69)

What does this mean in terms of practice? In addition to assessing a client's developmental stage and psychological state, workers need to focus on how family, community, social, economic and political factors are impacting on the client's situation, before challenging or confronting a client in relation to behaviour or responses that may initially or superficially be regarded as dysfunctional. Numerous factors contribute to a client's situation—there is rarely just one factor that directly causes a social problem (Ambrosino et al., 2001, pp. 68-9).

Clients are sometimes labelled as being resistant to change and confronted about this in a negative or aggressive manner when in fact their progress is being hindered by external factors. In the above case example, both Steve's lack of positive family support and structural factors inhibited his progress at various times. Systems theory emphasises the importance of families having open boundaries and being receptive to input from outside. Families with closed boundaries tend to become isolated and often lose their ability to continue functioning effectively. Steve's family was closed to outside input. His step-father's own history of alcoholism and offending contributed to the family's social isolation and family members' entrenched negative attitudes towards authorities. This meant that Steve was unable to receive support or assistance with his school problems as 'helping professionals' were viewed with suspicion and education was not highly valued.

The structural factors impacting on Steve's situation included: a lack of affordable housing for unemployed young people; a lack of access to informal flexible pre-employment training programs; and a lack of mentor support in the workplace for young people with complex needs. These all contributed to Steve's situation and his inability to achieve his goals.

It would be simplistic to view his problems as simply stemming from his substance misuse or psychopathology. Economic policy and social policy have a direct impact on the provision, availability and diversity of housing, health and welfare services, and access to economic participation for young people like Steve. The impact of these policies needs to also be considered before workers begin to challenge clients about discrepancies between their behaviour and stated goals, and advocacy should be a key skill utilised in work with and on behalf of such clients.

Another important aspect of work using an ecological-systems approach involves encouraging and facilitating the development of positive emotional and affiliation supports (Lehmann & Coady, 2000, p. 74). Many clients with long histories of substance abuse have limited social networks. Often their sources of support have diminished over years of abuse, and they may appear isolated and solely dependent on drug-using peers. It is important to identify whether it is possible to work with the client on building some positive family relationships, even with an extended family member. This is not always possible or appropriate, particularly if there has been abuse in the family, so encouraging the development of alternative support networks through building community connections and through mentor programs can be a very important aspect of work with this client group (Jesuit Social Services, 2006).

Relevance of the ecological-systems approach to challenging

The ecological-systems approach is sometimes criticised for placing too much emphasis on the broad social environment and too little on the individual's contribution to their situation. Some critics state that as a theory it is too abstract, others that it gives minimal attention to intra-psychic issues and to the issue of personal responsibility:

> Proponents of the systems/ecological framework argue, however, that the individual is perceived as a highly valued system itself and that intrapsychic aspects and psychological aspects, which incorporate the individual's capacity and motivation for change, are parts of any system involving individuals that cannot and should not be ignored. (Ambrosino et al., 2001, p. 63)

In my view, the approach does emphasise some important issues that need to be considered before challenging or confronting clients:

* Is the client's system open or closed, providing positive or negative support in regard to the changes the client has identified that he/she wants to implement?
* What role does this individual play within his/her network and what impact will changes made on an individual basis have for the broader system?
* How will significant others in the client's system deal with the client's reaction to being challenged? Consideration of this issue is particularly important when dealing with clients who have a history of aggression and/or violence. If the client responds poorly to confrontation, what will be the consequences for both you as a worker and those in the client's immediate network?

FOCUS ON STRENGTHS

The ecological-systems approach and strengths-based perspective have much in common. Many of the key components of these approaches have a similar focus, so it is easy for workers to integrate both perspectives together in their work with clients.

The basic principles on which the strengths perspective is based have been outlined by Saleebey (1992) and DeJong and Miller (1995) as follows:

* *Empowerment*—This involves encouraging clients to identify their strengths and potentialities and fostering those strengths to assist the client to resolve their issues and concerns.

- *Membership*— Many clients are isolated and do not have stable reliable support networks. Workers need to work collaboratively with clients and foster links and roles with and in communities that provide some sense of belonging and meaning.
- *Regeneration and healing from within*—The role of the worker is to assist clients to discover and use 'their own (inner and outer) resources for healing' (Saleebey, in De Jong & Miller, 1995, p. 734).
- *Synergy*—This is the belief that people working collaboratively can achieve more beneficial results than if they had tried to resolve their issues and concerns alone. The emphasis is directed as much to 'enhancing the relationships between clients and their contexts as it is to expanding the inner resources of clients' (De Jong & Miller, 1995, p. 735).
- *Dialogue and collaboration*—The emphasis is on negotiation and consultation between the worker and the client, in contrast to providing expert advice.
- *Suspension of disbelief*—The strengths perspective encourages workers to respect the client's perceptions and story, and to avoid the tendency to question and doubt their statements and perspective.

The inclusion of this approach in the area of challenging and confronting clients marks a shift away from traditional approaches where the expert informs the client where the client is going wrong and then prescribes solutions. Instead, the emphasis is on sharing concerns, identifying strengths and abilities to address these concerns, and working collaboratively to expand the client's inner resources and enhance their support networks and community context.

When formulating challenges, it is important to acknowledge client strengths and also utilise them as a source of motivation: 'The questions social workers ask are critical. They may reinforce the worst of external conditions and internal experience or they may guide the client to recognition and acknowledgement of their own sense of self-worth and possibility' (Graybeal, 2001, p. 240).

'Exploring for exceptions' is an interviewing technique employed in solution-focused approaches that can be used effectively to challenge clients to identify their strengths and successes. This technique has been discussed in Chapters 10 and 12. It involves encouraging clients to reflect on times when the problem they are currently experiencing didn't occur, and how 'the client may have contributed to making the exceptions happen' (De Jong & Miller, 1995, p. 732). Exploration of exceptions focuses attention on how a person has survived and coped, in contrast to focusing on mistakes and failures.

Note the differences in focus and language in the two examples of challenging clients that follow:

> It is clear from our discussion that you are a serious alcoholic. You manage to stop drinking for periods of time but then always relapse, so we need to get you into long-term treatment.

> Although you feel at the moment that there are no solutions to your drinking problem, I remember in our first interview that you said that you didn't use alcohol at all for a period of three months last year. What was different then? How did you manage this achievement?

The second example is a clear demonstration of a strengths-based approach to challenging: it encourages the client to reflect on his past success and the factors that helped sustain it for a period of time. It contrasts greatly with the first example of an authoritarian and aggressive approach to challenging.

RELEVANCE OF THE STRENGTHS PERSPECTIVE TO THE USE OF CONSTRUCTIVE CHALLENGE

Some critics of the strengths perspective regard it as 'naïve' and 'simplistic', and state that it also ignores individual pathology and advances in psychoanalytic models of practice (Graybeal, 2001, p. 234). However, others maintain that a focus on strengths does not ignore problems or pathology but instead places concerns 'in the context of the belief that the client also holds the clues and creativity that will lead to solutions' (Graybeal, 2001, p. 241).

Exercise 15.3

Role-play the case scenario outlined in this chapter where confrontation is required. Analyse your approach in this role-play and discuss it with the members of your group. Did you adopt an authoritarian approach/minimise your concerns/focus on strengths/use minimal or assertive confrontation techniques?

STRATEGIES FOR STAYING SAFE IN THE WORKPLACE

As noted in the introduction to this chapter, one of the main concerns about using confrontation is that it may in some circumstances elicit an angry or violent response from the client. Research undertaken in Australia and overseas suggests that violence towards human services workers is increasing, particularly in areas such as child protection and psychiatric services (Stanley & Goddard, 2002). Some studies suggest that up to one-third of social workers will experience some verbal or physical violence in the course of their work (Rey, 1996; Puckett & Cleak, 1994). It is therefore imperative that both agency managers and individual workers recognise this risk, and work together to develop and implement appropriate strategies for staying safe in the workplace.

Many clients feel powerless in the face of organisational and bureaucratic policies and procedures that they experience as either confusing, meaningless or oppressive. Some are unable to control their anger and frustration when they are refused services they require, or find that outcomes and decisions they disagree with are non-negotiable. In recent years, welfare agency budgets have been cut 'while case loads have risen, inhibiting the effectiveness of social workers. The worker who can deliver less help but must still uphold bureaucratic regulations may be seen less as a helper than as an agent of social control' (Rey, 1996, p. 1).

In such a climate, it is important that workers use confrontation appropriately, with the minimum level of intervention required to encourage progress. If clients sense that you are trying your best to work collaboratively with them, that you allow them to have a voice and contribute to the development of agency guidelines and program development, and that you are genuinely listening to their concerns and are prepared to advocate on their behalf if their requests are reasonable, then they are more likely to respond in a reasonable manner than if they experience your approach as bureaucratic and uncaring.

However, unfortunately even the most skilled workers will at times encounter angry, abusive clients in their practice. So it is important to ensure that your agency has guidelines for staying safe in the workplace and that you are familiar with these guidelines.

GUIDELINES FOR STAYING SAFE IN THE WORKPLACE

1 *Assess the likelihood of violence.* Before commencing an interview where you plan to challenge or confront a client, gather as much

background information in relation to your client's behaviour as you can: read file notes and reports that are available, and talk to other staff who have dealt with your client. In some situations, it may be appropriate to communicate with professionals from other agencies who are also working with your client to ascertain their assessment of the client's situation and likely response to being challenged. If the client has a criminal record and this is available to you, check to see whether the client has a history of violent offences. Research suggests that 'major predictors of violence include past history of interpersonal violence, fire setting, cruelty to animals, use of weapons, involvement with gangs, alcohol and drug use and addiction, head trauma, and diagnosis of psychosis or antisocial personality disorder. Presenting problems known to trigger violence include domestic violence, divorce and child custody, denial of benefits, and involuntary hospitalisation' (Rey, 1996, p. 4).

2   *Make appropriate preparations for interviews.* If you are concerned that a client may react angrily or violently in an interview, make sure that you alert other staff in the organisation before commencing the interview. In some situations, it may be appropriate to have your supervisor or another staff member interview the client with you— although an assessment needs to be made about whether this will escalate the client's and your level of anxiety and tension. Ensure that other staff stay in close proximity to the interview room. Do not leave clients waiting in reception for long periods of time—it only adds to their frustration and anxiety.

3   *Familiarise yourself with agency policies and procedures in relation to worker safety.* Students and workers should make sure that they become familiar with the agency's safety policies and procedures as part of their initial orientation to work or placement. If agencies do not have such policies in place, you should advocate strongly for them.

4   *Create a safe environment.* Agency managers should always provide safe working conditions for staff. This includes the provision of interview rooms that have alarms, telephones and seating for staff close to exit doors. These facilities are now commonly provided in statutory settings, but are less common in small non-government welfare agencies—often because of funding constraints but occasionally due to denial on the part of managers and workers as to their necessity. Workers should strongly advocate for the provision of these facilities, and should not be made to feel that if a client

becomes aggressive they must deal with the situation on their own or that it is due to their incompetence.

When interviewing clients, always sit closest to the exit door and close to any alarm or panic buttons that have been provided. Ensure that the room does not contain any items or furnishings that can be thrown or used as weapons (Newhill, 1995, p. 635). Do not interview clients in the office alone outside normal working hours.

5   *Clarify your role.* Be very clear about your role, and about your ethical and legal responsibilities and obligations. Role clarification is a very important aspect of work with clients, and role confusion is a potential source of anger, hurt and frustration. If you are employed in statutory organisations, your clients should have a very clear understanding of any obligations that you may have to the courts or other legal bodies to report on their progress (Trotter, 1999). This is further discussed in Chapters 6 and 8: 'Avoid making promises or guarantees that cannot be kept or that are beyond your control' (Bowie, 1989, p. 46).

6   *Awareness of client's and worker's reactions.* It is important to maintain an awareness of your client's verbal and non-verbal reactions, particularly when confronting or challenging them. Follow your instincts and, if you feel that a client is becoming agitated or potentially violent, take action to address the situation and to ensure your safety: 'Many violent incidents have occurred because social workers felt that they should be able to handle situations alone, believing that asking for help meant that they were inadequate practitioners' (Newhill, 1995, p. 635).

7   *Defuse or exit when necessary.* If a client is becoming angry and defensive, it is worth trying to defuse the situation. One of the best ways to do this is to 'try and engage the person in a dialogue. This cannot be forced but most people want to be understood. Many have serious grievances about the unfair way they have been treated and their current behaviour may be some form of retaliation. It is important to listen to their story' (Trevithick, 2000, p. 21).

However, this approach does not always work. Some clients may become irrational, and attempts to try and understand their perspective and negotiate with them have no impact. If this is the case, and the client's level of aggression is escalating, then it is imperative that you remove yourself from the situation immediately and seek assistance.

8 *Plan home visits carefully.* Home visits to clients for the first time should always be conducted in the company of another worker. Whilst you may be familiar with the client through office interviews, their actual living circumstances and the people they live or socialise with are unfamiliar. Care must be taken to find out as much about the client's background, their home environment and particularly about any other people who may be at their residence during the home visit before the visit is undertaken. Students should not be expected to undertake home visits on their own in the course of their placements.

If clients have a history of violence or the purpose of your visit is to discuss placement of the client's children in the care of Child Protection Services, then you should be accompanied by a senior staff member or, in some circumstances, by the police. Office staff should always be informed of your destination, time of departure and time of expected return (Rey, 1996, p. 5).

9. *Utilise debriefing services as required.* Most welfare services now have access to professional critical incident stress debriefing services, and workers should not hesitate to use these services when required. Students and workers should also expect debriefing from their supervisors and support from their colleagues when they have experienced some form of verbal or physical abuse from a client.

Exercise 15.4: Case scenario

An Aboriginal man has begun attending a drug counselling program. He is not communicative in interviews and does not maintain eye contact with the worker. He says he has come for counselling because his lawyer told him to. The worker challenges him by stating that he is not serious about wanting to rehabilitate. The client responds by becoming aggressive, abusive and departing from the program.

1 What cultural factors should the worker have considered in this case?

2 Formulate a more appropriate method of challenging this client.

CONCLUSION

Constructive challenge is an important skill in direct practice that helps clients who are experiencing difficulties to recognise and resolve discrepancies and incongruities in their behaviour and responses. The aim of constructive challenge is to help facilitate change (Ivey & Ivey, 1999, p. 213). It is most effective when used in the context of a positive working relationship and should only be used when genuinely required. The inclusion of a focus on client strengths is more likely to result in a positive response to challenges. However, workers should always be prepared for a range of reactions from clients, and advocate for the provision of safe working environments in their agencies.

Exercise 15.5

1 How do you decide when to challenge a client?
2 Should all challenges include a focus on strengths? Are there some circumstances where an authoritarian approach to challenging may be required?
3 Should you avoid challenging clients who are potentially violent?
4 What cross-cultural factors do you need to consider when contemplating challenging clients?

PART V

Phases of the helping relationship: Evaluation and termination

16

UNDERSTANDING ENDINGS: EVALUATION AND TERMINATION

Jane Maidment

In this chapter, issues related to practice evaluation and termination of client contact are covered. The chapter begins by discussing the rationale for evaluating practice, followed by an outline of differing types of evaluation procedures. The second part of the chapter focuses on the expected and unexpected ways in which clients and workers may draw their professional contact to a close. Students will be asked to complete an exercise that will demonstrate an understanding of the Integrated Framework outlined in Chapter 1 and referred to throughout the text.

EVALUATION OF PRACTICE

The delivery of welfare services in New Zealand and Australia occurs within a political context characterised by economic rationalism, rising litigation against service providers, intense public scrutiny and fervent competition for government funding (Ife, 1997; Fook, 2002). It is therefore not surprising that, in this climate, client evaluation of service provision has won a legitimate and critical place in the social work process. Quality evaluation ensures that:

- consumers are able to give frank feedback about service delivery;
- consumers have a voice in the planning and delivery of future service;

- workers have the opportunity to modify their performance in response to feedback, enabling practice development;
- agencies can monitor the effectiveness of their programs;
- accountability for service provision to clients, funding expenditure and service value is made transparent;
- funding providers are supplied with data to assist with decision-making about how to allocate scarce resources.

There are three main types of evaluation. These are *progress* evaluation, *client outcome* evaluation and *program* evaluation (Miley et al., 2007). Progress evaluation refers to the ongoing process that occurs with the client to see how, or whether, goals are being met, and how the client perceives the worker's involvement. A review of progress of this nature would occur most times when the client and worker meet. These evaluations therefore include dialogue about both client progress and worker style in facilitating client progress. Workers can use this type of ongoing feedback to modify their own practice if necessary, in order to be of more assistance to the client. It is important for workers to encourage and be open to client views on the helping process. As discussed in Chapter 2, client feedback is a critical tool for developing better practice.

Progress evaluation is likely to take the form of an informal discussion of this nature:

Worker: So last time we met you mentioned you wanted to organise a night out for yourself, but you would need to get a babysitter. How did that go?

Maria: Well . . . like I said, organising the babysitter would be hard, as I don't know anyone who could do it, and I don't have the money to pay for one . . . but I did actually get my hair cut and I took the kids with me.

Worker: Well that's fantastic and must have taken a fair amount of organisation on your part.

Maria: Yeah it did . . . but I used that checklist we put together a few weeks back, to get myself organised . . . and the kids had an afternoon sleep so they didn't go wild in the shop. They just played with the toys we took, and ate their snacks.

Worker: So the checklist system worked for you?

Maria: Well I used it . . . but didn't do everything on it.

Worker: Before we go on to work out how we are going to use the time today, I just wanted to ask how you have found these sessions so far . . . in terms of how we have worked together.

Maria: Well . . . as you know, I didn't really want to come here, but my doctor kept saying it would be good for me to have someone to talk to about things, and it is. I do sometimes feel pressured by you to do things I don't feel ready to do, and like, you might think less of me if I haven't done the things we decided would happen in the week ahead. Maybe that's my own pressure . . . I am not sure . . .

In this conversation, the worker refers back to a short-term goal discussed with the client in the previous session (going out for the night), and seeks feedback about how the client is experiencing the working relationship. In the conversation quoted above, the client notes that she feels pressured, and then wonders whether it's her own internal pressure. This is a fruitful line of inquiry for the worker to pursue in the session. It may provide clues as to how the worker can modify her style, or it may be an opportunity for the client to consider her own self-expectations. Either way, client feedback of this kind is critical for developing better practice, as discussed in Chapter 2.

Exercise 16.1

Refer back to the definition and discussions on critical reflection outlined in Chapter 1.

Imagine you are the worker having the conversation with Maria. After the interview, you decide to check in with your supervisor. You are surprised that Maria felt pressured by you.

1 Using the critical reflection process, identify the concrete experience (e.g. the fact that Maria found you pressuring), and reflect upon what this feedback means to you.
2 In class, or with your supervisor, discuss the attitudes and values that have contributed to your response to Maria's feedback.
3 How might this discussion inform your practice in the future?

Outcome evaluation is likely to be more of a formal process that occurs at the end of client contact. It involves examining the overall degree of client goal attainment (Miley et al., 2007). Common forms of outcome evaluation include consumer satisfaction surveys, and agency follow-up telephone or mail questionnaires post termination. In some clinically-oriented services, the outcome evaluation may include completion of a questionnaire for use in single-subject design research. This research technique involves the comparison of data pertaining to the same set of variables as set out at the beginning of the intervention, and measured in the first session, with data measured at the end of intervention. To conduct single-subject design research, the client goals must be measurable, and include reliable, valid outcome measures where the data can be displayed graphically (Grinnell, 1997). This type of evaluation is an example of a quantitative design more commonly used in services where the worker is part of a health-oriented multi-disciplinary team.

Program evaluation is used to gauge the extent to which a designated group or service is meeting its overall objectives and providing effective assistance to clients. Evaluation processes also establish baseline data that can be developed to produce new models of practice, are useful for agencies to address gaps in service delivery, and help in providing evidence of accountability to outside funding sources. Program evaluation involves a research process where data are collected that gauge the degree to which the program provided meets agency-set objectives and expected outcomes. There is a range of models that can be used to conduct program evaluation (Owen, 1993; Timmreck, 1995). Practical and ideological factors are considered when selecting a model to conduct evaluation. There needs to be a degree of fit between the model used and the work of the agency. Given that program evaluation entails a research process, practitioners will need to be mindful of the debate regarding the efficacy of using quantitative or qualitative data to gauge effectiveness.

EVALUATION APPROACH

Decisions regarding which research method to use are influenced by several factors, including personal values, time and expertise (Creswell, 1994). Nevertheless, debate about the relative merits of using either qualitative and/or quantitative approaches for evaluation has been long-standing and at times heated. This debate has been founded on differing philosophical positions regarding the interpretation of 'truth' and 'reality' (Hartman, 1994, p. 11). Until recently, use of the differing methodologies has almost always been associated with distinct epistemological positions (Bryman, 1992).

Proponents of quantitative approaches have argued that qualitative material lacks rigour, whereas those using qualitative methods have suggested that quantitative analysis over-simplifies the complexities of real-life situations (Trute, 1997). Recent discourse on research methodology has explored ways in which qualitative and quantitative methods may be blended to provide a productive integration of the two models (Brannen, 1992; Creswell, 1994; Trute, 1997). Supporters of an integrated approach have put forward a number of compelling arguments that support using mixed methodologies. These arguments are summarised below.

Using several levels of inquiry to examine a research problem facilitates the investigation of diverse aspects of the problem (Fielding & Fielding, 1986). The validity of findings can be enhanced when similar results are found using different methods (Denzin, 1970), and results from each method can be compared to highlight contradictions that require further investigation and explanation (Brannen, 1992). Using combined methods can provide a more complete picture of under-represented populations. The qualitative approach ensures that the population in question 'gives voice' to its issues, whereas the quantitative approach serves to measure the extent and patterns of inequality (Brannen, 1992, p. 22).

Whatever method is chosen to evaluate progress, outcome or programs, it is essential to ensure the process of conducting the research has client empowerment as a key principle underpinning the research process. Lee (2001) argues that research can be used to inform empowering practice in the following ways:

> It may help localities discover the nature and scope of yet unknown or unmet human needs, it may give a voice to the most vulnerable as they tell their own stories and define their own needs, it may give support and documentation to social workers and others in their advocacy of the needs of the most vulnerable in society and their attempts to make systems more responsive, and, finally, it may empower the most vulnerable with the common concerns (beyond individual concerns) and the data they need to advocate for themselves. (Lee, 2001, p. 419)

With the above objectives in mind, it is vital for practitioners at all levels to integrate progress, outcome and program evaluation into their work.

Exercise 16.2: Case study

The purpose of this exercise is to develop beginning knowledge and skills in two areas: outcome evaluation and presentation.

You work in a community outreach service that runs an emergency accommodation program for homeless men, many of whom have psychiatric conditions. Local residents have complained to the council about the program on the basis that it attracts men into the community who seem to behave unpredictably.

Securing funding for the emergency housing program has been difficult, and it is currently operating out of a property owned by a local church group. The church group has agreed to rent out the premises at a negligible rent, and the council approved this arrangement when the program began. There is to be a public meeting for interested parties to attend, and you wish to provide evidence at that meeting of how the program is meeting a range of differing needs in the community.

1 What are the differing sources from which you could access evaluation data and what form might such data take—for example, the use of quantitive data or case studies?

2 Role-play a conversation you have with one of the homeless men about the emergency accommodation service. In this conversation, you want to hear first hand about the benefits or hazards the client has encountered using the emergency accommodation.

3 What types of quantitative data might you present at the public meeting?

4 How would you ensure that you presented the data in a way that was empowering and not denigrating to clients of your service?

5 With another person, develop a ten-minute presentation of made-up 'data' that you will give at the public meeting. This data may include personal accounts from residents, figures on occupancy rates, collateral benefits from occupancy (such as monitoring of residents' health), or feedback from local professionals about the program. Your data-collection is not limited to these sources. Organise the presentation of your data so that they will be clearly seen, heard and understood by the audience. You may need to develop a summary of documentation for the

audience. Conduct your presentation in the classroom setting or online using a PowerPoint presentation, audio recordings (for classroom settings) or transcripts (if working online).

TERMINATION

The second part of this chapter focuses on termination of client contact. This final phase of the social work process is also referred to in the literature as closure, ending or finishing (Harms, 2007; Cournoyer, 2000). This phase is related to concluding the work with clients. The ending of work together can throw up many opportunities to further consolidate progress made, affirm and celebrate positive changes, and reiterate plans for how future challenges for the client will be responded to. Ideally, the end stage of work will provide a rich context for the worker to use a strengths perspective, where the client and worker together identify internal and external resources, successful outcomes or new learning and change that has occurred as a result of the work done. Termination of a positive nature is more likely to occur when it is planned. It is possible, however, for closure to happen in both expected and unexpected ways.

Factors that influence termination

Two factors have a marked influence on the way in which termination occurs between the client and worker. These are the agency mandate and the nature of the work that has been completed between worker and client.

Agency mandate
The purpose of the agency service, the scope of that service, and the length of contact between worker and client may be quite explicit in the agency mandate or contract with funding providers. Some interactions between clients and workers are mandated through court orders, such as would happen when a person is on a supervision order administered through the Corrections Department. In this instance, persons on probation may be required by law to attend fortnightly sessions of one hour with the probation officer for six months. This expectation is clear from the court order, and both client and worker will know almost to an exact date when the termination of contact will occur.

Conversely, a person attending the Accident and Emergency Department at a hospital may have a series of conversations with a worker over the course of just one day, as was demonstrated in the case study with Nan in Chapter 6. Clearly the relationship between worker and client will be different in these circumstances, given the context in which the work is carried out and the voluntary or involuntary nature of the client's status. Residential workers can have contact with clients that spans a number of years. Understandably, worker–client termination of contact in the residential setting will be different to that encountered in the Accident and Emergency Department where the client and worker will have had much less to do with each other.

Nature of the work to be done

Some situations require workers to simply provide information, characterised by very short-term intervention. This is the case when a worker assists a client to complete an income benefit form, or provides information on different types of home help services available in the community. While workers in these situations need to remain sensitive to the feelings of their clients and mindful of the broader issues of oppression and marginalisation, much of the work is time-limited and task-focused.

Other situations require a greater degree of delicate, responsive and insightful handling, such as counselling with women who have been subject to domestic violence or sexual abuse. Clearly, the nature of the work done between the client and the worker will influence the way termination occurs.

Exercise 16.3

1 Identify a time when you have engaged a professional service and been left 'high and dry'. This does not necessarily need to be a 'helping' type of service. Write down a few adjectives to describe what you thought and felt about the service.

2 Next, identify a time when you experienced a good 'farewell'. This does not necessarily need to be associated with finishing up work with a professional helping agency, although it might. Note down what the termination process consisted of, and what you thought and felt at the time.

3 Finally, with a partner in class or online, discuss your examples and draw up a list with two columns. In the first column, note

down what you both believe to be essential practice elements or tasks for successful closure. In the second column, note down the guiding principles or values you would associate with effective closure. Share your list of practice and principles with other class members.

There is a range of conditions under which termination between client and worker may occur. The context in which the termination occurs will clearly influence how the worker and client experience the process. Ideally, termination is planned; however, sometimes it may occur suddenly, or on terms that leave the worker with a challenging situation to address. This can happen when the client:

- terminates contact without warning, by not showing up to appointments;
- expresses extreme dissatisfaction with the service delivery and leaves the service;
- resists the termination process and wants to remain 'friends' with the worker.

Whatever the circumstances that lead to closure, the worker has an ethical obligation to ensure the client has an opportunity both to give feedback about the service received and to be made aware of how to access services in the future. In cases of unexpected termination, the worker needs to follow up with the client either by letter or telephone to ensure the client knows of future options for service delivery and to facilitate some form of closure.

Not surprisingly, there are instances when just one worker or single agency is unable to provide the range of resources needed by the client or client group. In these circumstances, the client is often referred to an alternative service.

Referral

A worker may refer a client to another agency for a number of reasons, including accessing more services or targeted expertise. For this reason, as discussed in Chapters 12 and 17, it is important for workers to become familiar with the formal and informal local community resources, as well as the eligibility criteria for services available. Taking a structured approach to liaise and personally network with staff from other agencies ensures that workers are knowledgeable about how to access available resources, and can in time develop inter-agency collegial relationships. These personal contacts, along with liaison and advocacy, are key components in accessing additional services for clients. In order to successfully carry out these tasks, workers must take a proactive approach to continually developing ongoing community networks in practice.

When referring a client to another service, it is important that the worker is mindful to 'smooth the transition, maintain client motivation, and incorporate any progress achieved so far into the work of the subsequent helping relationship' (Miley et al., 2007, p. 448). By putting time and care into the processes of termination and referral, the worker is conveying genuine respect to the client, while ensuring that good work already done is duly acknowledged and not jeopardised or compromised. It may be possible to convene a transfer interview, where the client meets the new worker, with the original worker present. Unfortunately, workers are not often in the position where they can conduct transfer interviews. The referral process may therefore occur in writing or over the telephone. The content of any referral letter needs to be discussed with the client before it is sent. If the referral is made over the telephone, it is best that the telephone conversation between workers occurs when the client is present and can hear what is being said. After a referral has been made, it is incumbent upon the original worker to ensure that the client has successfully linked in with the next service, rather than 'falling between the cracks' in the process. This will require the worker to follow up with the client and agency to ensure the parties have connected and that the next stage of work has commenced.

Exercise 16.4

Role-play the following termination conversations with these different clients. Observers of the role-play need to note down the specific skills used and possible alternative ways to handle the situations.

Debrief with the 'worker' and the 'client' after each role-play, provide feedback and repeat role-plays using different strategies suggested.

Case study 1: Gillian

You have been seeing Gillian for some time. She had experienced depression, resulting in a stay in hospital; this is where you first met

---

her eighteen months ago. You engaged well with Gillian, despite her low mood at the time, and have had ongoing contact with her since her departure from the ward. Gillian's mood has lifted and she is coping well at home.

You have just found out that you have been appointed to a new job in another agency, and ring Gillian to let her know that you will no longer be her contact person in the agency, but reassure her that another worker can be contacted. Gillian feels let down by you and says so.

• Role-play your telephone conversation with Gillian.

Case study 2: The Jones family
You are a child protection worker and have been working with the Jones family for several weeks. Staff from the local school became concerned about the Jones girls (Heather, aged six, and Jo, aged eight) when both talked explicitly about sexual matters in the classroom. You have just had a long meeting with Mr and Mrs Jones, where foster care options were discussed. You struggled to gain any rapport with the couple, who presented as being rather hostile about your involvement. The next morning, they arrive at the office and demand to see you. They say you are incompetent at your job and they want to have contact with another worker.

• Role-play your second meeting with Mr and Mrs Jones.

Case study 3: Sharnelle
You work in a small community agency that supports homeless youth. Over the course of several months, you have struck up a good rapport with Sharnelle, who is sixteen. In fact, you have got to like her and quite enjoy the times when she calls in for a cup of tea. She is bright and open to suggestions about how she can improve her health and employment prospects. She has been very motivated to make positive changes, and has done so in several areas. One day, Sharnelle calls in with a young man you have not met before (Paul). Paul appears to resent the time Sharnelle spends with you, speaks to her in an aggressive way and shows no respect for her. The next week, Sharnelle calls in to say she is moving to Sydney with Paul.

• Role-play your conversation with Sharnelle.

In each of the role-plays in Exercise 16.4, the endings reflect the 'messiness' and unpredictability of practice. While it is the ideal to have a planned and celebratory closure, many different circumstances can lead to a different kind of client and worker closure. As a worker, it is critical that you are able to put aside your own feelings of defensiveness, hurt or loss when endings occur unexpectedly. Just as you make great efforts to build rapport and strong working alliances during engagement, you need to ensure you incorporate a strengths perspective during closure. This process involves:

- affirming any positive changes that have occurred during the intervention, no matter how small;
- drawing attention to the client's internal and external resources;
- reiterating the connection between the personal and political dimensions of presenting issues;
- providing information about how to access resources in the future;
- acknowledging the specific learning and experience that your work with the client has contributed to your own understanding and practice development.

In this way, the principles of empowerment, reciprocity and collaborative partnership that underpin anti-oppressive practice are demonstrated in termination. During the final interview between worker and client, there needs to be some discussion about what will happen to the client file, noting who will have future access to file notes. The fate of client files is very much dependent upon the mandate and structure of the social service agency in question. These matters relating to confidentiality and client records will also have been discussed during the engagement phase of client contact.

In rural, remote and even regional areas, it is quite possible that the worker and client could have continuing social or professional contact in the future, outside of this particular 'helping' context. If this is the case, earlier discussions about the client–worker roles need to be revisited at termination. In some cultural contexts, the notion of professional boundary-setting is not clear-cut. Lynn et al. (1997) remind us that in work with Torres Strait Islanders and Aboriginal people, worker self-disclosure is used much more than would be the case in 'Western' helping styles. Endings are likely to be characterised by extended storytelling, humour, sharing of food and leaving the door wide open (1997, pp. 18–23).

Using rituals

Rituals serve a number of purposes when incorporated into the termination phase of social work practice. They are particularly useful in terms of embedding additional therapeutic value into the ending process. Rituals:

- provide the client with a 'bridge' between the past and future events;
- provide a vehicle for expression of thoughts and feelings about closure;
- acknowledge and celebrate successful completion of goals;
- acknowledge client strengths as well as the development of additional external resources;
- provide a space for both the worker and client (or client group) to focus on practical and emotional matters related to finishing the work together.

Different rituals can be used to mark the end of the helping relationship. As Lynn et al. (1997) have noted, it is not unusual in Indigenous cultures to punctuate endings with the sharing of food. This process was illustrated in the Samoan family case-study discussed in Chapter 10, where a difficult family meeting was concluded with prayer and a shared meal. In some instances, the ritual may be specifically related to an aspect of the work the client and worker have done together. For instance, when a young client is leaving a residential setting, a ritual can be performed where other residents and workers help the client to pack their bag. In this ritual, the workers and residents who will remain at the setting metaphorically give a gift of something for the young person to take away with them. These 'gifts' may include strong friendship, self-esteem or a new skill, such as reading or creative arts. The gift is usually related to the individual relationship each person has had with the resident who is leaving. Other rituals to mark endings and new beginnings can incorporate aspects of art, music, dance and speech-making.

Much of the social work and welfare literature on termination of contact focuses on the notion of loss, connecting this stage of the helping process to theories on grieving (Lee, 2001). Needless to say, it is therefore critical at this stage for the worker to facilitate a closure that will reaffirm the generation of client hope and empowerment. Combining the cognitive functions of client outcome and program evaluation with the affective and more emotive functions of closure and ritual enables endings to be structured yet powerfully meaningful events. In this way, the final stage of the helping process can potentially be very significant in terms of cementing enduring, positive change.

Exercise 16.5

This exercise is designed to consolidate your understanding of the Integrated Framework (see Chapter 1). In small groups, refer back to the case scenarios of Gillian, the Jones family and Sharnelle in Exercise 16.4 and select one of these to complete the following exercise.

1 Discuss how each of the theoretical approaches listed in the table below would influence the way your work with these clients would finish. You will also need to articulate an anti-oppressive understanding of the situation of the client/s.
2 Next, identify the skills and tasks you will use in termination, and complete Table 16.1 accordingly.

Table 16.1 Application of theory and skills to the termination phase of client contact

Theoretical perspective	Anti-oppressive understanding of issues	Skills used	Tasks
Crisis intervention			
Solution-focused			
Ecological-systems			

17

'FINISHING WELL'

Mark Furlong

INTRODUCTION

It is easier to locate material on engagement—indeed, almost any technical or theoretical aspect—than on the final phase of casework (Nursten, 1997). In the references available, the traditional term used to describe this ending period has been 'the termination phase'—a frame so loaded with negative associations that it causes all but the most hardened to wince. Less frequently, this stage of the casework process is referred to as the 'ending phase', 'disengagement', 'closure' or, occasionally, 'celebration' (Timms & Timms, 1977; Jackson & Charble, 1980; White, 1995; Merrett, 2004; Chenoweth & McAuliffe, 2005; Harms, 2007; Welsh, 2006). In this chapter, the concluding stage of the casework process will be considered as the phase of 'finishing well' (Relph, 1985)

That the ending phase of case work has received less attention than other phases is not surprising if this absence is viewed from a critical perspective. Unlike the certainty preferred in modernist accounts, there is often an inherent instability in the interactions that are in play as the final contact is approached. This characteristic defies straightforward description, and reflects a subtle yet contradictory dance being conducted—for example between intentions and emotions and between the 'adult' and 'child' behaviours participants express.

It is difficult to name, and then to work with, this opaque quality. In part, it is this confusing nature to endings that helps explain why there is an incomplete body of scholarship available to practitioners. Yet, in addition to the above, the relative lack of attention given to the final phase of case work also reflects the mindset of our broader culture: in the West, we continue to live in a 'death-denying' environment, a milieu where we have been acculturated to feel far more comfortable talking about beginnings—'let's turn a new page', 'hit the restart button', and so forth—than to feel comfortable sitting with, and holding together, what is missing and what is now present (Faludi, 2008).

In this chapter, an attempt is made to represent, and to offer suggestions for working with, the opposing moments that are characteristic of the context that is invoked as the participants approach 'the end'. That is, an effort is made to name the practical, as well as the emotional, elements that are relevant to those workers and consumers whose aim is to *finish well*. Similarly, an effort is made to link the ideological with the technical—particularly with respect to employing strengths and narrative 'technical' innovations to further the principles of a practice approach that is critical and values centred.

The contention leading the current attempt is a simple one, at least one that is simple to state: finishing well requires the worker to support a process that is inclusive of both the practical and the emotional— what are sometimes referred to as the instrumental and the expressive—aspects of the casework project towards the purpose of 're-pairing' what has been incomplete. First amongst the elements that need to be re-paired is the 'during' and 'after' status of the client: in order to be regarded as initially eligible for a service, the client has been judged to be 'in need' and/or 'at risk'—yet, at the conclusion of this service, this status has to be regraded towards the client having their sense of capacity and connectedness restored.

In what follows, initial attention is given to theory. Three theory streams are outlined that build towards a base that is capable of informing a considered approach to the ending phase of casework practice. Second, several matters of technique are outlined as an entry point to a general description of practical guidelines. Third, a concluding section summarises the material that has been developed. Across each of the sections, a degree of attention is given to the important question of evaluation; that is, how this 'instrumental' aspect of practice can be linked to the more 'expressive' dimension—the touchy-feely aspect—that is always present, even if not always talked about openly. In order to set the stage for this material, a case study will be introduced. This case study has been prepared to introduce the key themes involved in attempting to finish well.

> ## Case study of Jan
> After more than eighteen months' contact, today is the last meeting with Jan (aged 50), her de facto partner Jim (aged 60) and her adult son Nic (aged 23). Jan had initially been referred to the family centre where I worked after leaving a slow-stream rehabilitation setting— a service to which she had been admitted following a severe industrial accident. This meeting, like nearly all contacts I had with Jan and her family, took place at their flat.
>
> Jan's accident had left her with chronic back pain, poor (and probably deteriorating) mobility and a moderately severe head injury involving significant frontal lobe damage and impairment to her sensory function. As a result of the accident, Jan had lost her 'well-ness', her livelihood, her identity as a self-reliant worker and, to a great extent, as a partner. When I first met her, Jan presented as an agitated, anxious and depressed woman.
>
> Jan and Nic lived in a two-bedroom flat; Jim had his own unit but 'stayed over' two or three nights a week. These three had a close bond, even if over the first year or so of our contact there were large adjustments that had to be made to the structure of their relationships. Throughout my contact with Jan and her family, Jim remained employed while Nic was (mostly) unemployed and Jan continued to receive a WorkCover entitlement. Casework consisted of a mixture of face-to-face counselling and support with more or less active periods of advocacy with respect to Jan's complex legal and medical situation.

Given the nature of Jan's initial difficulties, there was no doubt Jan, her partner and her son had made clear progress. Mindful of the importance of not playing down their losses and pain, each had been able to develop a (far more) positive appraisal of what they were now. For example, Jan was now—and directly saw herself as—more assertive and self-affirming. Moreover, this family had surprised themselves with their toughness and togetherness in managing to deal with the traumas and anxieties of the last years.

At this last meeting, it was clear to all of us that there had been significant progress; it was also clear that much had been lost that would never be recovered. I had worked well with, and directly admired, each of these people as it was clear that the family had closely engaged with

277

me. We had planned to finish at this time some months earlier, and had worked progressively toward evaluating what had occurred: to document the important successes that had been accomplished, such as Jan's much-improved mood and the fact that she had come to mostly regard herself as a 'personal success' (rather than as a pale shadow of what she had once been). As well, this time of ending clearly witnessed that there remained important deficits that would forever remain as an enduring burden.

Despite this thoroughness, and despite the 'textbook' way I had tried to prepare for this moment, right there with these people it was hard—really hard—to clearly and unambiguously say goodbye. I felt an abiding affection for this hardy and admirable 'tribe'. I felt strongly tempted to let my role as a caseworker slip, to let my admiration and affection for these people shape the way I positioned myself, the way I responded to the openings this last session occasioned. Should I say 'I'll give you an informal ring in a month or so' or 'Do drop in when you are in the area'?

COMMENTARY

In this situation, the technical term 'termination' presents as the most obvious reference. Yet, as a frame for understanding the ending phase, 'termination' is incomplete as it focuses attention on only one dimension: the aspect of loss. The alternative term 'celebration' has also been put forward, yet once more this frame draws attention to only a single dimension—the joyful, even triumphant, aspect of the situation. Far better is a frame that highlights the 'bittersweet' quality of the final session and sets the task as that of 'finishing well', as attending to both the sad and the celebratory (Relph, 1985). Theorising these contradictory emotional moments led me to want to steer the final sessions towards a practical sense of closure, however uncomfortable and ragged particular moments might have been.

In the received literature, we have been told that it is important to plan in advance for, and thoroughly discuss with the participants, the ending phase of casework. This is the traditional wisdom of the profession: plan for the ending and do so from the first session/contact; be prepared to raise the (often awkward) matter of finishing up; as far as possible, maintain a calmness—a steady 'holding environment' to use the psycho-dynamic term (Winnicott, 1965; Maluccio, 1979)—by avoiding unexpected interruptions and events. And, of course, there is good sense in observing these principles. These ideas are particularly useful if the ending phase is predicted, yet do they apply when the ending is unexpected—for example, when it is the worker who is the leave-taker?

Such events can confound the worker, who is relying on received theory and, more generally, expects the client to respond 'sensibly' (when in fact the client might have experienced the worker's departure as a rejection or even betrayal). I remember being shocked the first time I 'copped a serve' in this way: with rage and hurt, a client said 'So, who are you going to slough me off to?' when I told him I would be leaving to take up another job. In either case—whether it is a long-planned exit or a sudden rupture—it is the worker who must take the lead in trying to end the process well.

THE THEORY

Mindful of the importance of aligning narrative and strengths approaches, a distinguishing point of emphasis in the approach developed in this chapter is the use of Andrew Relph's article 'The last time: A metaphor for leaving' (1985). In the ending phase, Relph suggests one door is closing as another opens—an ambiguity that evokes the two faces of Janus. Janus, the ancient Greek god of doorways and passages, can be said to offer to us a word-picture for the nature of healthy endings.

That this final phase can be bittersweet is to denote only the flavour, if not the intensity, of the experience of leave-taking. Yes, leave-taking can be touching and palatably bittersweet, yet in their rawer forms, endings can be played out in ways that are jagged and mis-taken. Leave-takings can stir up memories and associations, connections that might be more or less conscious. Finishing up can therefore be endowed with echoes of the losses and ruptures that have previously occurred to our clients, as this stage can also cue what has happened to us as individuals with our own less than ideal past histories (Maluccio, 1979; Relph, 1985; Nursten, 1997; Baum, 2004).

Clients and workers alike have experienced sudden deaths, traumas or separation—in short, a set of more or less unprocessed partings. These memories can be reactivated predictably, for example around anniversaries, or when you go to a movie that you expect will resonate with what you have experienced. Such examples of resonance—what can be seen as examples of the 'soft spots' everyone has—can also be prompted by what occurs unexpectedly when we chance upon a reminder of that what is regretted or has gone missing.

Repeating, or repeatedly avoiding, what is awkward and mis-taken around endings can be a pattern that cartwheels across some people's lives. For example, we are all familiar with the person who will 'get in first' by being overly eager to say 'this relationship is not working for me—I'm out of here'. Yet, while most of us don't do this, it is also true that each of us can relate to the attractiveness of this position—of the logic of withdrawing in ways that are defensively self-protective. Further, few amongst us have never 'slipped away', unobtrusively leaving a workplace, party or last meeting, without saying our goodbyes. Such examples are all too human, even if it is more likely that such avoidances and clashes will present as patterns in the lives of those who are our clients.

Against this background, if the final stage of the casework process can be accomplished to a reasonable degree, this success has the potential to deliver a restorative impact in itself, even if the 'presenting problem' has not fundamentally been resolved (Relph, 1985; Nursten 1997; Anthony & Pagano, 1998). The opposite is also true: if the presenting problem has been positively addressed, yet the ending phase is accomplished poorly, this can undermine the client's sense that the outcome has been positive and their efforts have been productive. That is, if a 'technical success' is not well processed symbolically and emotionally, this can erode—even disqualify—the good work that had been done.

Just as dealing positively with the thorny issue of confidentiality at the beginning of the casework project can be so crucial in setting up the chance to have accountable and inclusive relationships with our clients, if we can thoughtfully manage the complex elements that arise in the final phase, this integration can itself be therapeutic. This final stage is about completing the process at these multiple levels, dimensions that include the practical, the symbolic/narrative and the emotional. Yes, there has been a beginning, a middle and now this is the end—although of course it is not really the end for the client or for you. *Finishing well* provides a solid base for hopefulness and a positive trajectory, for a further reaching towards a pairing of the qualities of agency and connectedness, towards a restoration of the client's pre-contact sense of wholeness and, in a symbolic sense, of the here and now as a two-faced passageway between what has come before and what will follow.

You have to be negatively branded to receive a service

The initial presenting problem may be resolved, may be ameliorated or may seem more profound at the conclusion of the case-work process. And, given that these options are all possible, this chapter takes a particular position: irrespective of whether formal success has occurred, if we can 'finish well' with our clients, we can often assist these people to contest the sense of 'personal failure' that frequently accompanies so many lives (White, 2002). A short detour may clarify the grounds upon which this claim is based.

White, along with more theoretically oriented researchers who have studied the process of 'individualisation' (Bauman, 2001; Beck & Beck-Gersheim, 2002; Giddens, 2002), argue that Western citizens are immersed in a culture that presses everyone to measure themselves against criteria which are impossible to satisfy: Are you living up to your potential and making the most of your life? Are you managing your health and your relationships effectively? Am I taking responsibility for managing the risks and choices that are important to my life? Such questions can never be positively and finally addressed, an outcome that leads to an endless and often punitive self-scrutiny.

Yet what if a person is not an 'ordinary citizen', but is someone the competent authorities have subjected to a naming procedure, the effect of which has been to downgrade that individual's personal status? These rituals are commonplace, albeit symbolically significant: Children's Courts that have marked a parent as 'neglectful' or 'unfit'; mental health experts who have conferred upon a person a psychiatric diagnosis; rehabilitation specialists who place upon a person the label 'head injured' or, more generally, all those who are eligible for a service as they have been deemed 'excluded' or 'currently at risk'. Following such a definitional ceremony (White, 1995, 1999), it makes sense to expect that the person is likely to suffer an even sterner process of self-interrogation than is usual for the general citizen.

Moreover, this self-scrutiny occurs within a context where a relentless media stirs the pot further. Often boosted by 'concerned' expert professionals, the popular media underline the problem of 'broken homes', 'failed marriages' and 'dysfunctional families', and singles out those who are 'dole bludgers' or 'bad mothers', those who are said to be likely to reproduce 'the poor parenting' they themselves received. Spurred by this attention, the net of self-suspicion wraps itself ever more punishingly around, and into, those who have been castigated. Over time, these helpfully conferred labels tend to become the surnames, the tags and badges, of a person's lived identity.

According to critical theorists, these labels become the inscriptions of a demoralising culture, the internalised negative self-report that comes to haunt the subjectivity of so many. And being haunted, even stalked, by a disqualifying inner narrative—a chorus that originates in dividing practices that set up an absolute moral nomenclature based on simplistic yes/no criteria—makes for a 'difficult' experience of selfhood and, in all likelihood, a compromised behavioural life. Inadvertently, an interaction with the 'helping system' tends to potentiate a process of negative self-scrutiny.

In this circumstance, if the client comes to take up a cooperative attitude—what is often referred to as 'having insight'—this person will internalise a disabling self-description; if, on the other hand, the person 'resists' the categorisation conferred by the agency, the agency reserves the right not only to maintain the initial ascription of pathology but to add to this disqualification an additional signifier: the person is now deemed to be 'uncooperative', 'in denial' and/or 'insightless'. Mindful of this inadvertency, it makes good sense that the final stage of the case-work process *contests* the process of disconfirmation and negative self-narration that clienthood bestows.

We social workers have long been on the front line in the endless war that is fought over what-should-it-be-called: should client X be seen as one of the 'deserving poor', or as an 'indigent?'; should client A see himself as 'ill', or should he regard himself as more or less willfully deviant? The terms used may change, but the effects of these polarising practices go on. Mindful of this dynamic, social workers have at least some capacity to be co-creators of new maps and to be companions in the process of clients creating new forms of identity.

As happened in the work with Jan and her family, we can also act as ambassadors and translators, even as culture-jammers. Especially as the casework process moves towards its conclusion, we can have an advocacy role in developing 'preferred narratives' (White, 1999, p. 56) that contest the taken-for-granted and routine habits of thought repro-duced by traditional service systems. By seeking innovative ways to confer and sustain alternative accounts of identity, we can work towards finishing well. Narrative approaches can play a particular role in this respect. White argues:

> If the stories that we have about our lives are negotiated and distributed within communities of persons, then it makes a great deal of sense to engage communities of persons in the renegotiation of identity. So,

regardless as to whether I am meeting with an individual, a couple or a family, I am thinking . . . about how this audience might be invited to play a part in the authentication of the preferred claims that are emerging in the process of therapy. (White, 1994, p. 78)

Working towards realising these goals organises our actions, irrespective of whether contact is short- or longer term, or occurs in a straight-up sequence or one that meanders on more jaggedly.

We can take the trouble to write letters to clients that draw attention to, and act as enduring documents of, positive descriptions (Epston & White, 1990); we can seek to 'recruit an audience' that can witness these descriptions (White, 1995) by way of organising 'refecting teams' and other 'witnessing circles'. Such public performances of new identity are about the progressive use of the power/knowledge linkages as they are clear about who should write the rules and who should own the game. Such approaches also have the benefit of strengthening the 'relational self' (Paterson, 1996; Furlong, 2003, 2007) as the importance of connectedness is acknowledged. Seeking to 'finish well' is to proceed mindful of this mission.

Much of the above aligns well with the precepts of the strengths-based approach. For example, if an ending is unexpected, the practitioner may be prompted to ask questions which 'presuppose people's ability'—for example: 'So, when the respite centre closed down, how were you able to cope?' (McCashen, 2005).

On transitions: The emotional awkwardness of endings

Ideas about 'witnessing circles', 'inviting an audience' and 'preferred identities' are important concepts, even if they can be misconstrued as instances of technique. This noted, how do they become integrated into practice when our work tends to be experienced in a rush, as a hurly-burly of embodied immediacies rather than as a sequence of steps towards the confident execution of a plan. To a marked degree, many expert accounts do not articulate how much of a struggle good practice actually is. There is nothing out of the ordinary—nothing out of order—about this messiness. Rather, this lack of clarity is simply the way it is.

If the focus is on the ending phase, it is especially true that the worker has to contain high levels of uncertainty technically as well as personally. In this location, there are likely to be 'invitations' to lose one's calm and the structure of the exchange. For example:

283

- The client might not arrive for, may become unsettled during, or may not want to finish abruptly a last session.
- You might feel tempted to arrange 'just one more meeting', even though this would be likely to subvert the steadiness that is offered by a firm boundary.
- Perhaps most problematically of all, a client might introduce important information—and do so at exactly the time you were trying to bring about a sense of closure (Barton & Marchell, 1986).

I remember all too clearly the last meeting with Jan when both of us, figuratively and literally, were hopping from one foot to the other not knowing whether to shake hands, to embrace or risk saying too much about how we felt.

These uncertainties are always stressful—perhaps all the more so to those who like to feel in control. For example, in these unstable moments there is likely to be a particularly strong challenge to those who have naturalised the indirect forms of communication characteristic of digital technology (Elliot & Lemert, 2006). In these modes—like what happens on Facebook or when you text the message that you are ill and will not be coming to work—the consumer is taught to be intolerant of interpersonal awkwardness: anonymity and user control are characteristics of digital modes of communication. Yet, in the ending phase, it is anything but anonymous and one should not send in a text message that wards off discomfort or arrange to have your connection 'drop out' when the going gets tough.

Why is the ending phase a point of so much high anxiety? This tension is present because endings are a transition—a transfer frame between different states: between what has been dreamed of and what is; between being in role—you as a client and me as a practitioner—and our (more) naked selves as ordinary individuals, humans who may shake hands, perhaps touch, yet who are trying to say goodbye as fully as we can. Transitions are border crossings, zones of heightened tension, which means the energy level is high. This state of arousal can be expressed in a spectrum of emotional vectors, often in a form that is guarded or even non-verbal. So, if the practitioner thinks he or she might have a line on what is happening emotionally or symbolically, is it always the best option to share your thinking?

Three communication options

Three different communication options are possible in the ending phase, as they are throughout the ongoing casework process. You can *internally register* what you think is going on—in other words, not say this idea out loud to the client, but rather act mindful of this hypothesis. For example, even though you think a client might be tempted not to attend an approaching last session, you might decide to say nothing directly to the client about this. Following the same scenario, a second alternative is to *name it*, to note your idea with the client, but to do so only in passing. This alternative can often be useful, as those things that are named are to an extent normalised, an action that may make the difficulty less likely to be acted out. Third, one might *make it a theme*— that is, put some focus to the idea that the client might be likely to find the finishing-up stage a difficult challenge. In this case, over a part of a contact, or contacts, this idea might be explored.

As with any choice point, there are risks and benefits to consider. And, having made the judgment, if you have gambled and got it wrong, a new course can be plotted. For example, if the client does not arrive for their last session, perhaps a letter might be written that documents the achievements made, the resilience shown or the fact that you might have done better if you had forewarned the client that the ending point might be hard to manage.

It is not sensible to psychologise the question of endings. There are many real-world difficulties that can occur: a family crisis; a broken-down car; scarce money might have to be prioritised. This structural matter acknowledged, it is important to try to conduct a process that aims to finish well in a manner that is 'socially intelligent' (Goleman, 2006) and 'emotionally literate' (Orbach, 1999). Role erosion is a real possibility, especially when the sense of intimate connection risks eclipsing the more technical understanding of the encounter.

In finishing, we have to be in an awkward place, one where there will hopefully be at least a degree of celebration. Yet, to the degree that celebration is present, there is also likely to be an aligning moment of sadness. For some, this latter moment can re-evoke loss, or even the rage of dependence and abandonment. Like being in that dream when you are on stage and do not know your lines, in the finishing stage there tends to be a flash of semi-public nakedness that is the opposite of being anonymous.

285

TOWARDS A POSITIVE CONCLUSION

As the end of contact approaches, unplanned events may occur: a child becomes ill, the car breaks down, an attack of hopelessness overcomes the plan to attend a last session. As is less frequently discussed, the unexpected can also overtake the worker: the agency reorganises case loads, the worker gets a new position, funding is withdrawn—the list is endless. In these instances, it may still be possible for the worker to find innovative ways to reach towards closure: a ritual may be arranged, a perseverance to end well be demonstrated, a thoughtful letter composed. Such actions document and witness an alternative account.

This kind of effort can be productive even if the initial contact was not welcomed by the client. When many people no longer receive any mail except for official rebukes, such as summonses and eviction notices, the fact that a worker has taken the trouble to document an acknowledgment can speak with a voice that long echoes. ('Texting' such a note probably does not have the same significance.) And it works both ways: I remember receiving a photo of a smiling young daughter from a family I had finished seeing a year earlier that still means an awful lot to me.

Whether planned or not, it remains possible to work to the same goal: as far as is possible, the worker needs to conduct the ending phase in such a way as to restore to the client their sense of connectedness and personal worth. As historically articulated, this goal has been referenced to individual capacity (empowerment, self-determination, choice, and so forth). More recently, the 'goalpost' has been reformulated so that the quality of a client's connectedness and social inclusion is also emphasised (Folgheraiter, 2004; Furlong, 2007). An example of practice where the client is someone from one of the many 'diverse' populations who tend to personalise their relationships with professionals might illustrate this point (see Case study of Marika).

Case study of Marika

You have just received the good news that you have a new position, a promotion that means you will be leaving the agency and will have to finish up with many clients well before you had planned. These 'cases' are at different points, but you are keenly aware that there are some situations that are more sensitive than others. Marika, an ex-street dweller, is one person with whom you have a sense of engagement. You know Marika has a well-earned reputation

---

for being direct, even confronting, yet you also know she is fragile and prone to intense feelings of hopelessness and isolation.

You bring up your 'good news' as soon, and as evenly, as you can. You know, as she does, that it is you who is abandoning her by moving on while your relationship is in mid-course. In that moment, Marika gives you the 'cold shoulder', stays very quiet for several moments and then changes the subject. Summoning your reserves, a little later you re-raise this touchy matter and assure her that you will work with her to find a new worker. Again, she says nothing to this and just gives you another cold look.

You would have much preferred if she had got angry with you, if she had told you she was 'dirty' on you for planning to 'slough me off', that you were 'a typical skip prick' for 'pissing off so you can off to do your bigger and better things'—all the ideas you thought she had in her head at that time. Then, after some reflection, you ask her directly: 'How can we make sure you have a support team there for you if you come adrift? Who are the people you and I might speak to if you decide an insurance policy is a good investment?' Several meetings later, Marika and you have managed to talk over what she has achieved, as well as what has not (anywhere near) been achieved. She has toughed it out, and so have you.

Being able to collect one's thoughts, and then to 'talk when the talking is tough' (Miller, Donner & Fraser, 2005), is a technical—as well as a personal—accomplishment. If at all possible, it is better if we can review how satisfactory, or unsatisfactory, progress has been with respect to the specific goal(s) that have been decided. It is also possible that unplanned accomplishments can also be identified. For example:

- 'Looking back over our work, what do you think you have been able to have the most success with?'
- 'What has been most surprising to you about your success?'

So this does not get into a phoney celebration, it is important to ask for 'the other side' to be articulated:

- 'So, what have you been most disappointed about in me/in you?'
- 'What's still on your agenda/what seems not finished?'
- 'What do you think might be your next step?'

As usual, the questions one asks are 'interventive' (Tomm, 1988) and actively shape the understanding, and to some extent the intersubjective experience, of not only the casework ('how useful was it?; how well have I served you and your interests?', etc.) but the sense of personhood of the client ('how capable/much of a learner/survivor have you been, as illustrated in the work we have done together?'). It is often useful to anticipate slippage/relapses. Many authors stress the importance of making sure the client does not expect that progress and/or success will be even (Relph, 1985; Morgan, 2000). For example, Westcott, Dafforn and Sterne (1993, p. 269) suggest that 'relapses are inevitable', and that it can be useful to plant the seed that a temporary 'spin-out' or 'minor relapse' is not the sign of a permanent reversal.

It is important not to come over as a Pollyanna who silences the disappointment or hurt that is hard to put into words. On the other hand, it is important to keep a focus on what can be constructed as positive in what has happened. Putting these distinct threads together is part of working towards a process of re-pairing. The consideration of this question raises the matter of evaluation.

EVALUATION: WHO DEFINES SUCCESS AND FAILURE?

It has long been held that the clearer the goal, the clearer an evaluation is able to be. For example, Marsh and Doel (2005) recommend that SMART goals are negotiated—goals that are Specific, Measurable, Achievable, Realistic and Timely. The capacity to sensibly evaluate the work that is done therefore depends on how clear, and how enduringly relevant, goal-setting has been, as non-measurable or global goals—the 'I want to feel better' kind of goal—are said to be far less helpful than a more behavioural aim, such as 'I want to keep my son out of care for the next three months.' Also relevant here is the distinction between 'progress' and 'outcome' evaluations, the former being undertaken immediately at cessation of contact and the latter six or more months after contact has concluded, as discussed in Chapter 16.

Mindful that many agencies have their own in-house programs of evaluation tied to their funding and service agreements, if the objective is to encourage individual practitioners to undertake thoughtful, as opposed to exhaustive, evaluations of practice, two points might be helpful to emphasise. First, Duncan and Miller (2004) have put forward a series of relatively low-tech, collaborative processes for goal-setting and the evaluation of goal attainment. Aligned with the solution-focused approach that has been so well developed with mandate and semi-voluntary presentations (Turnell & Edwards, 1999), Duncan and Miller stress the importance of investing considerable care, time and creativity in co-constructing the goals of practice (an emphasis that is examined in Chapter 10).

A second point to emphasise is that the process of evaluation between worker and client requires both parties to be accountable, a condition that can only be approximated insofar as the participants are each able to communicate directly. That we can talk 'when the talking is tough' (Miller et al., 2005), yet do this with compassion and without sentimentality, is to seek an impossible-to-realise ideal. To take up, and to make one's own, the aim of finishing well is to seek a direct dialogue with one's own demons. Specifically, it is necessary to value—but not over-value—what one has to offer if 'we', the client and I, are to examine what went well, and what did not, without either sentiment or hubris. At the risk of over-using a metaphor, this is to engage with one's journey as a practitioner, a process that can run along a whole professional life course (Rønnestad & Skovholt, 2003). In finishing up, one has to be comfortable being evaluated and to be able to sit in the place where the practitioner is, in one strong sense, a peer—where one sits alongside, or even behind, the client (White, 1994).

That this goal is impossible to fully realise is not a problem; rather, it is in the demonstration that one desires to do this as fully as possible that the scope for finishing well can be furthered. This is all the more important given that the nature of many social problems is acknowledged to be increasingly complex (Green, 2008). It is now recognised that an increasing prevalence of presentations exists where there are multiple causes for concern—for example, where at least two of the following are present: substance abuse, poverty, mental health, accommodation or protective issue, (ACOSS, 2007). This situation has been said to challenge the usefulness of traditional arrangements where specific 'service silos' (Keene, 2001), such as Mental Health and Child Protection, were expected to offer services organised on a circumscribed symptom/treatment model (Keene, 2001; DHS, 2002).

Not only do these complex presentations challenge the design and effectiveness of current services, but the presence of multiple problems makes the task of evaluation more demanding. This is especially the case if:

- there is a recursive, and apparently intractable, quality to the relationship between these problems;

- the employing agency favours short-term measures of success, which are used to demonstrate the effectiveness, or otherwise, of the work that is done; and
- the definition of one or more of these problems is not shared between the 'consumer', the 'worker' and the 'manager'. For example, preventing mental health admissions, which keeps costs down, may be an indicator of success from a manager's point of view, while a particular practitioner might see a consumer recognising their need for treatment and securing an admission as a sign of success.

Similar variations can be identified right across the contested terrain of the human services, even if these disputes are particularly vital in the child protection field (Furlong, 1996). This disputed context is brought into particular focus as the casework process draws to its conclusion. It is usually not possible to 'hold all the variables' that might impact on the effectiveness of the work that has been done, nor is it always clear 'who owns the game' when it comes to evaluation: is it the client/consumer, the service provider or the manager/policy-maker who is to judge success? Given these many ambiguities and disso-nances, it follows that the ending phase has a particular scope for reconciling, for re-pairing, what is dissonant—at least to a significant, if not ever to an absolute, extent.

THE PROMISE OF A GOOD ENDING

Western citizens are increasingly being swept along by the tide of prag-matism. A side-effect of this thinking is that we are all supposed to have the 'you must be ready to move on' mindset. This is an apolitical attitude, one summed up in an adage that is particular to this time: just build a bridge and get over it, don't get bogged down if you are upset or feel slighted (Furlong, 2008). Yet, if we pause and reflect, the better angels of our nature know it is rarely this simple.

We are reminded of the importance of remembering if we think about South Africa's Truth and Reconciliation Commission. In this instance, it is clear that the 'move on' metaphor is counter-articulate: it is not possible for a people to get over it and move on without a polit-ical, symbolic and practical process that acknowledges, and to an intense degree relives, the injustices and the traumas that have been experi-enced. The importance of remembering, of not succumbing to the 'let's move on' mantra, was reiterated in 2008 by Mary Simon, an Inuit spokesperson, on the occasion of the Canadian Prime Minister officially apologising to the country's Indigenous people for the long-standing official policy of 'killing the Indian child within' by separating children from their kinship groups: 'Let us not be lulled into believing that when the sun rises tomorrow, the pain and scars will be gone. They won't. But a new day has dawned' (Simon, 2008). The same logic applies whether a nation, a team or a single individual is involved: one does not really move on by forgetting; rather, real progress occurs by re-pairing, by doing the remembering that reconnects. With respect to grief, White (1988) said many years ago that the task was not to 'let go' but to 'say hello' in the here and now to who and what is no longer physically present. The task is to balance two competing imperative—'lest we forget' and its opposite, 'too much remembering'.

Human service managers, like the culture they represent, do not tend to understand the importance of the process of re-pairing. This should not surprise us, as managers understand professional practice in concrete, rather than process-sensitive, terms: professionals deliver services, undertake episodes of care, and so forth. This language constructs practice as a disembodied, 'interactionless' procedure where the expert does it to a passive other (Furlong, 1997). This kind of language denatures the realities of person-to-person practice. Terms such as 'case management' can also be used in this impersonal and disguising kind of way. Thus, images of practice that direct attention away from, even formally deny, the complex emotional, practical and symbolic realities of working with people are unhelpful to practitioners.

On the other hand, the worker and the service user are not, and should not view themselves simply as, peers or friends. To elide from one's understanding those aspects of the contact that speak to the formal nature of the work is to be as counter-articulate as manager-speak. And it is especially at the end of the process of practice that we are most confronted by this tension.

Exercise 17.1

1 How comfortable are you with 'saying goodbyes?' Do you ever tend to avoid these situations?
2 If you do find yourself 'in the middle of an ending' kind of exchange, are you more likely to underplay or dramatise?
3 Can you identify a 'low-key' ending in your everyday life where there is an opportunity to practice *finishing well*?

18

MORE THAN 'JUST THE END': CLOSURE WORK WITH CLIENTS

Wendy Bunston

Common sense tells us that life is full of endings. To get where you are today you have most likely finished primary school or its equivalent to begin secondary school, and ended your secondary education to commence your tertiary studies. You may have ended (or had ended by others) intimate relationships, friendships, jobs, volunteer work, membership within a social group, or studies. These endings may have occurred suddenly or been protracted, they may have been mutually decided or unwanted, painful or pleasant, overdue or premature. With so much experience in endings this far in your life, then, why the fuss in how to end a working relationship with a client?

This chapter will explore why the attention you pay to how you end your work with clients is just as important as how you begin, and relies on much more than common sense. In using a strengths-based perspective to inform your work, you do not simply reframe everything to create a positive spin, particularly for clients who have encountered more than their fair share of trauma, tragedy and loss. To utilise a strengths-based approach in this manner may feel superficial and even disrespectful to your client. Rather, such a perspective is about enabling clients to access a true, solid and constructive narrative about themselves that recognises their capacities, resilience and growth. 'Ending work' calls on the same belief in people's capacity to move forward and grow (Phillips & Cohen, 2000).

What we can do, and how we can do things, are also impacted by other variables. Anti-oppressive practice (AOP) further complements a strengths-based approach through broadening a client's appreciation of the larger context within which they exist, enhancing their 'ability to understand the operation of power dynamics and of different forms of oppression as they arise in "real life" situations . . . it also depends on a willingness to engage positively and constructively with difference' (Turney, 1997, p. 116).

This chapter begins by exploring how we define 'endings', also known as terminating or creating closure, and examining the difference between planned and unplanned endings. It will then look at how your approach to this phase of your work should honour your client's strengths and integrity as well as respect their context and culture in order to create endings that can be considered beneficial. Just how you 'end' your work with clients may call for as much exploration of your own experience of endings as that of your clients. The chapter ends with a discussion of the corresponding tasks, processes and skills required to create thoughtful closure and in particular the micro-skills of *referral*, *normalising* and *affirmation*.

DEFINING HOW WORK 'ENDS'

The work of social workers and welfare workers is relationship-based. Much is written about how you commence your relationship with a client, the intricacies of the engagement process and how to go about building a strengths-based relationship. How you end with clients (or they with you) is less written and talked about. Maybe this has something to do with the fact that endings are in reality sometimes messy, and can often leave you feeling conflicted—even when things do go to plan (Gibney, 2005). To think of 'the end' as 'the end' in relationship-based work is a mistake.

What occurs at the conclusion of work is that you stop seeing the client and the client stops seeing you. This may be forever or they may come back to see you, or maybe another worker, at different intervals. The experience, the memory, the occasion of that relationship, whether short or long, can last a long time. Should you have had a traumatic encounter with a worker within the helping professions, you may feel anxious or even distressed at the prospect of meeting another. How might you as a worker be attentive not just to the phases of the working relationship that occur over time, but to fostering a 'beneficial' ending with your client?

Planned endings

As students, you already know when your placement will end. This can both liberate and restrict what you offer. This time limit can create a momentum for change, harnessing your energy and that of your client in achieving set goals and outcomes. Equally, it may prove restrictive, as arbitrary time limits disregard the unique journey each client takes in order to achieve change, potentially setting them up as failures if goals are not met in time (Hepworth et al., 2002). How might this outcome be avoided? By doing what we do best: 'talking about it'.

Turney (1997, p. 115) believes 'Social Work could be described as an essentially language based activity' where empowering clients involves helping them find their own voice. AOP also requires that you talk honestly about the structural constraints you work under, explaining your role as 'student' and being upfront about the 'when', 'why' and 'how long' of what you can realistically offer, as well as what options and alternatives are available. This approach presumes an already different working relationship, one that offers choice, affording your client the power to continue knowing the limits of what is on offer, or to choose not to proceed.

Exercise 18.1

In a small group, brainstorm how a strengths-based and anti-oppressive practice approach would inform how you talk to a client openly and honestly about the constraints under which you work, what you can realistically offer and how you might mutually determine when and how your sessions should end.

How could you ensure that this discussion is open to review throughout the course of your work together?

Some services may leave the decision of terminating up to the individual worker. This decision is best made in collaboration with your client, although on occasion you or your client may feel all that can be achieved has been achieved (Lewis, 2002; Hepworth et al., 2002). It is important to reflect on our own experiences of endings and consider how they may influence our decisions to end. Even when endings are mutually determined it is still important to keep 'checking in' with clients and reviewing progress.

It is not unheard of for clients to continue contact with a worker out of politeness or because they feel disempowered and unable to question the worker. Workers are also vulnerable to making decisions based on past experiences or contextual pressures (Hunter & Kottler, 2007).

Exercise 18.2: Case study

My first social work placement occurred within the Oncology Department of a hospital. I had been assigned to work with a child who was admitted to hospital for a series of check-ups while in remission. She was admitted for tests over a few days as the family lived some distance from the hospital, and this proved more convenient. I assisted the family with finding affordable accommodation and other practical supports and I felt that I formed a very successful relationship with this girl and her family. Not long after this child was discharged, my supervisor asked me to provide a written transcript of an interview with a child or family during my placement to assess my interviewing skills. As I felt I had engaged well with this family, I decided to ring and ask whether I could make the trip to their home for a follow-up appointment. I set up the appointment for a week later and made the long drive out to their home. When I arrived, I was full of anticipation and eagerness, ready to record every word of our meeting to prove how well I had worked with this family. What I found was a very polite but extremely anxious mother, dreading to hear but anxious to know what must be the 'bad news' about her daughter's tests, as understandably she assumed 'surely the hospital would not send someone out so far unless the news was awful'. When the 'check-up' admission ended for this family, so too did their worry. My decision to continue in order to prove my skill in interviewing created unnecessary anxiety and distress for the family.

Consider the case study described above and, with a partner, discuss how you may have handled this case differently. Describe what were the possible pressures on the worker that contributed to this outcome. Bring your discussion back to the large group and compare your comments.

Unplanned endings

Clients often terminate contact with little or no forewarning. Perhaps the urgency or direction of their attention has changed. They may feel their concerns are so overwhelming that nobody can help them or they simply feel they don't 'connect' with you as their worker. The reasons for clients not attending may be many and varied, and as a new worker it is most demoralising when clients don't return and you can immediately assume the worst—'It must be because of me!' Irrespective of the cause, it is helpful to reflect on your practice and learn from each client contact.

Ritvo and Ritvo (2002) suggest we pay attention to more than simply trying to understand our client's internal and perhaps unexamined motivations for prematurely terminating work. What of the internal world of ourselves as workers? How might we make space to acknowledge what meaning we give to saying goodbye, as well as the psychological challenges we experience?

Is there a way we can recognise our own experiences of endings or make conscious our own preferences for how we want work to end while respecting that clients may have a different preference which is equally valid and valued? When clients finish work early or simply do not turn up, are we able to respect their choice—or further still, are we able to build into our work an overt agreement that clients can choose to finish when they need to? Your work together might be on how to end in a way that respects both the client and the worker.

Clients who are actively suicidal, or where there might be protective concerns regarding children, or where attendance is court ordered may need specific contracts around what occurs if there is failure to attend. In these instances, an AOP approach would encourage a full discussion about the power differentials that play out in work undertaken where the worker is required by law and/or ethically to respond if a client places themselves or others a risk. When there are no clear or obvious risk factors and prearranged contract involved, there is no specific obligation on the part of clients to continue.

Follow-up can, however, be considered where clients fail to show up for a session. This may be via a letter or by phone. Some clients may in fact be pleased that you have made the effort to follow up with them. Some services or the worker may routinely follow up with these clients in order to gain insight into how the client experienced the contact with themselves or their service as a mechanism for continuous improvement (Cournoyer, 2000).

General follow-up tasks are legitimate undertakings as long as they are conducted in a manner that respects the integrity of the client and are not coercive. Done well, follow up may in fact leave the client feeling empowered and their opinion valued. Working with respect and transparency involves informing clients about the policy or practice of the organisation regarding 'follow up' with clients, and if possible forming some prearranged agreement about how this might occur that is mutually acceptable.

Ending a session

Clearly stating what time has been allowed for this appointment, what commitments or understanding the client has about the length of time needed or allocated, and allowing the client some say in finishing early if they feel this is needed works on the premise of shared decision-making. When a session is drawing to a close, it is useful to flag that there is only a certain amount of time left, summarise what achievements they have made, what issues have been covered and, in the time remaining, what else needs to be addressed (Geldard & Geldard, 2005). Revisiting the decision to continue with more sessions is also very helpful, making it overt that clients have a choice to stop or continue, and should they choose to stop, this does not preclude the possibility of further work being continued in the future (Gibney, 2005).

How to facilitate a 'beneficial' ending

A 'beneficial' ending is one that 'should be of service to the client, and as such, it should be therapeutic, in and of itself' (Gibney, 2005, p. 52). This does not only apply to therapeutic settings. In any role you undertake as a welfare or social worker, your ability to create 'beneficial' closure is based on a commitment to respecting the abilities of your client, leaving them in a position of strength and having facilitated a relational experience that is reparative and hopeful (Bunston & Millard, 2006).

The tasks, processes and skills involved in ending are complementary and overlap. For example, a particular ritual marking the end (e.g. concluding a children's art activity group with an exhibition of their work for family and friends) is both task- and process-orientated. The task is the event of the ritual (i.e. the exhibition); the process is the preparation inherent, both physically and psychologically, in drawing the work to a close. The skill set of the worker ensures these tasks and processes are undertaken with sensitivity, awareness and respect for the emotions, challenges and strengths of the client. Influencing how this all comes together is the culture and context within which the worker and the client exist.

CONTEXT AND CULTURE

As outlined in Chapters 1, 2 and 3, understanding our own socio-economic, cultural, historical and political positioning requires a questioning of what informs our own judgments, value base, the assumptions we make, how we understand our own limitations and how much we are prepared to learn from and accept others. Acknowledging the power imbalances that may exist between you and your clients, the policies and values of the organisation you work for and where your accountability lies facilitates the potential for 'real conversations' to occur about how to approach the task of ending your work together (Turney, 1997).

Openness to understanding others means genuinely asking for your client's input, and respecting their race, religion, gender or social class. Being sensitive to the context and culture of your clients, and demonstrating competency in your professional approach (Chenall, 2006), are prerequisites for working collaboratively and ending appropriately.

TASKS

One of the most important tasks of ending is celebrating and reinforcing your client's accomplishments through evaluating your work together, reviewing goals achieved, and anticipating that positive outcomes will continue past your session's ending. It is also useful to elicit strategies, or devise a maintenance plan the clients themselves can use on an ongoing basis (Hepworth et al., 2002).

Another important task may include developing culturally and contextually appropriate rituals or ceremonies that mark the occasion of ending. This may take on the form of together creating some token that is symbolic of the working relationship or perhaps giving, or receiving, a small gift that acts as a memento or reminder of the relationship (Hepworth et al., 2002).

Solution-focused and narrative practice approaches see clients as the 'expert' within their own lives, and as more than able to successfully negotiate the difficulties life throws their way (Morgan, 2000). See Chapter 3 for an earlier discussion about skills in both solution-focused and narrative approaches. Narrative therapists may use letters, documents, journals or certificates to evidence change throughout the course of working together, as well as to offer a tribute to its ending.

Exercise 18.3

As a group, brainstorm and discuss:

1 the different methods you might use to review, evaluate and celebrate the goals achieved by clients in their final session/s;
2 how age and gender may influence your choice of finishing-up activities, such as rituals or ceremonies with clients;
3 the appropriateness or inappropriateness of receiving or giving gifts.

Referral

As discussed in Chapter 16, ending sessions should involve a review that considers all the options open to clients, including their transfer to another worker or perhaps referral to another service. Should transferring be decided upon, it is a matter of who to, and how. Arranging a handover session, with the existing worker introducing the new worker, can enhance the likelihood of successful transfer, especially when clients are apprehensive about their ability to engage with someone else. It is not always possible to organise a handover session when referring on to another service, and if working in a time limited service you may need to discuss what their options are for ongoing work and if you or they make contact with other services in order to facilitate this.

Transferrals work well when you know of and can confidently recommend another professional or agency. Sometimes, transfers to other workers occur not because the worker is leaving but because the issues or dilemmas presenting in your work together may be met better by a different worker in the service or because the client has the confidence to ask for another worker. These scenarios can be delicate and need to be managed with the best interests of the client in mind and ensuring this closure work also occurs respectfully. Keeping up to date with and well connected to other agencies and organisations that offer services that complement your own is invaluable to the referral process.

Exercise 18.4: Case study

Dionne and her eleven-year-old daughter Alhia participated in our groupwork program for children and mothers affected by family violence. Both mother and daughter found the ten-week program

---

299

very helpful and expressed their anxiety at the group coming to an end. They had previously felt extremely isolated and, although the perpetrator of the violence had left the family home six months ago, over the ten years he had lived with the family he had ensured they were 'cut off' from family and friends. Dionne in particular felt she had made a strong connection with one of the facilitators of the program. While the other group participants lived within our catchment area, Dionne and Alhia lived just outside our region and we had made an exception in accepting their referral as there was no such similar program operating in their local area. Facilitators met with Dionne individually for our standard 'end of program' feedback session two weeks after the program finished. She expressed how angry she was that the program was not run for a longer time period and how she felt discriminated against as some of the other mothers' children were being referred on into our service directly for ongoing individual and family work. We reassured Dionne that we would follow up with her local Child and Adolescent Mental Health Service (CAMHS) and find out what women's support programs might be available in her local community.

We found the task of referring on this mother and daughter more difficult than we had anticipated. Her local CAMHS informed us that this mother would have to call their intake service directly and they were unable to give us the name of any particular worker as they could not guarantee who might be the intake worker on any given day.

Similarly, we found that there were no current women's support programs running and that the next available group, while still technically within her region, would be further to travel to via public transport than it would be in getting across to our region. We contacted Dionne by phone to give her the details we had collected. Although our exchange with her was positive, we lacked confidence in both the information we were passing on to her as well as her motivation to follow through. Two months later, when holding our reunion for the group on a date already arranged, Dionne and Alhia failed to attend, despite us sending a formal invitation by post and leaving a number of phone messages. We never heard from Dionne or Alhia again. What seemed like a very positive therapeutic experience in the group ended on a sour note, both for ourselves as facilitators and, we suspect, for the family.

1 Consider what cultural, contextual and closure issues and dilemmas come to mind when considering this case study.

2 What might the feelings have been for both mother and daughter about ending with the groupwork program?

3 What feelings in particular might Dionne have felt with regards to the facilitator with whom she felt a strong connection?

4 What do you imagine were the feelings of the facilitation team?

5 In hindsight, what might we have done better?

6 What aspects of this case study demonstrate a strengths-based and anti-oppressive approach?

7 What are the implications for service planning and resource allocation?

PROCESSES

As already noted, tasks are the 'what to do' while processes are more concerned with the 'how to do'. Whether your work is time limited or open ended, a reasonable amount of time should be given to the process of terminating with your client, preferably at a time mutually determined and with an acknowledgment of the emotions involved (Lewis, 2002).

Normalising

Both the client and the worker are subject to a range of reactions to termination. For the client these may involve:

- a sense of satisfaction and anticipation about the future;
- feelings of ambivalence, combining a sense of achievement and excitement with a sense of loss and anxiety at losing the relationship;
- anger or disappointment at the ending of work, particularly if the work ends due to the worker leaving;
- denial about the relationship ending, and under-estimating the importance of the relationship in order to avoid feeling the full impact of this loss;
- a sense of slipping backwards or urgent new problems emerging (Hepworth et al., 2002).

These varied reactions are a normal part of endings, and in fact pay homage to the importance of the relationship and the work undertaken. The more comfortable the worker is with acknowledging their own responses, the easier it is to be attuned to those of your clients. In some instances, voicing how you feel about your work together ending may enable your clients to do so as well (Cournoyer, 2000). The feelings you as the worker face may also involve a sense of ambivalence or even guilt at not being able to do more or stay on longer than the time allocated through your placement. If your relationship with a client has proven difficult, you may well feel relief that it has come to an end (Hepworth et al., 2002).

Recognition of these mutual reactions does not have to equate to resolution. We may always feel a sense of sadness or ambivalence about certain relationships ending. The strength we imbue in ourselves and others is our capacity to respect the place of endings in our lives, to honour them for what they are and what meanings we attribute to them, and recognising that endings are invariably linked to beginnings.

AFFIRMATION

Chapter 10 introduced the notion of affirmation in work with clients. Strengths-based work calls on harnessing the resources and competencies of the client themselves and of the support and resources their environment offers in facilitating ongoing growth. Your work needs to identify what these are and amplify the transferability of these skills into other arenas as well as establish other options for support. These are tasks that involve the skill of the worker in collaborating with the client to see new possibilities and decrease the need for worker involvement while building the client's own internal and external sources of support.

'Once specified outcomes have been reached, rather than continuing a cosy but perhaps dependency-inducing relationship, it is important to review progress and plan to finish up in the belief that people can cope without the worker' (O'Connor et al., 2003, p. 124). Hope and affirmation are amongst some of the most important ingredients we can bring to the client–worker mix and they should be fostered throughout and particularly reinforced at the conclusion of your work. An ability to highlight, affirm and consolidate the strengths of your client, to explore what are the barriers to their growth, as well as what enhances it, is pivotal to the development of a 'health-inducing' relationship.

Some people have received very little affirmation in life and may be naturally suspicious, sceptical or perhaps feel unworthy of it. Others may have experience life as extremely oppressive and have effectively been denied the chance to make their own choices.

Exercise 18.5: Case study

I was seeing a young girl, Lily, who had been abused by her sister. She enjoyed coming to sessions as long as the subject of the abuse was not discussed. She clearly revered her older sister and felt distressed by, as well as blaming herself for, the fact that her sister no longer lived in the family home. Lily was quieter at home and school but overall was doing well and had a strong and healthy relationship with her parents. Her parents were struggling to resolve their feelings of guilt about the abuse and were keen for me to continue seeing her until she could speak about what had happened. As the sessions progressed, it became clear to me that she was not ready to discuss this and we were both feeling the increasing pressure to 'talk about it'. I suggested to the parents that Lily discontinue counselling and that I continue to see them to assist in sorting through their feelings and supporting them to support their daughter. I discussed my thoughts with the girl and after she indicated her preference to stop I invited her to come back in the future if she felt ready and wanted to. I continued to see the parents over the next six months. Five years later, I received a phone call from the mother of this young girl who was now an adolescent. Lily had asked her mother to ring me as she wanted to talk about what had happened.

1 Discuss what might be the complexities involved in ending work with clients, particularly when more than one client is involved.
2 What are the power differentials you need to consider in working with children and who decides when work ends?
3 Discuss how you, as a worker, might manage your own anxieties when clients want to end work even though you may believe they are not yet ready.

SUMMARY

Endings, like people, are unique. They can evoke a myriad of reactions and, if not managed well, the impact it leaves can be traumatic and long lasting. Whether endings occur in a planned or unplanned way, they require forethought and attention in order to be beneficial to your client. This involves:

- fulfilling the tasks of regular reviews, evaluating progress, seeking feedback as part of a plan that includes when and how to end, and where appropriate facilitating *referral/s* on to other supports and services;
- attending to the processes that accompany these tasks and *normalising* the range of reactions and responses of both the client and the worker to ending your work together; and
- using your skill in building the capacity of your clients through an attention to a genuine *affirmation* of strengths and progress in order to assist their growth well past the cessation of your work together.

Respecting the culture, context and wishes of clients, being upfront about what you can and can't offer, acknowledging the structural and organisational constraints you work under, and building a relationship of collaboration bodes well for a good beginning, middle and end to your work.

PART VI

Conclusion

19

CONCLUSION

Ronnie Egan and Jane Maidment

. . . each possible misunderstanding
Is your responsibility. Or it can be unambiguous
And take the contradictions out of things; is it too unambiguous?
—Bertolt Brecht, 'The Doubter'

This text locates the teaching of practice skills within an anti-oppressive ideology. Throughout, most authors have drawn upon a strengths perspective to demonstrate how skills can be used in a way which is consistent with this theory. We have attempted to do this by presenting practice examples from both the Australian and New Zealand context. They cover a range of cultures, ages, identities and practice contexts. These examples are used to demonstrate how to integrate practically the ideology, theory, phases, skills and organisational context in the work with individuals, families or groups. It does this using the Integrated Framework as a template (see Figure 1.1). Central to understanding these examples is the importance of respect for cultural and other differences.

The case studies highlight dilemmas which workers face daily in their practice. These tensions focus on care and control issues where clients are often mandated to attend services, and where workers grapple with the issue of where the focus of change should be, at an individual or social level.

Throughout the text, we articulate these contradictions. Each chapter contains exercises which provide practice for readers to reflect upon these dilemmas. Struggling to manage these contradictions is an ongoing task for human service practitioners, not only for beginners, but for all practitioners. By failing to engage with this struggle, we risk failing our clients and ultimately ourselves as workers.

MORE THAN JUST COMMON SENSE

The subtitle of this text, 'More than Just Common Sense', as suggested in Chapter 1, acknowledges the importance and limitations of everyday common sense in our practice. However, in using this title we place culture squarely in the teaching of practice skills. Whose commonality are we speaking about? Whose interests does this common sense serve? Who's applying the common sense? The notion of commonality is steeped in one view of the world, the dominant one which fails to allow for the diversity of commonalities we face in practice. This is found in Brecht's poem, 'The Doubter', which cautions us all against ignoring the contradictions. While 'common sense' is indispensable to our work, we must also recognise that it is something that the challenges of our practice require us to go beyond. We need to understand and appreciate the impact of ideology on practice, to reflect upon the relationship between theoretical and practical knowledge, its impact on the different phases of the helping process, upon how we develop interpersonal skills and the organisational context in which we practise. This text explores these components which, as the title suggests, go beyond common sense.

The Integrated Framework introduced at the beginning of this text provides a template for students and teachers. It is used to promote an understanding of these components and to form the foundation for work with individuals, families, groups and community. In this chapter, we will use the different components of the model to highlight the importance of integrating them into practice.

ANTI-OPPRESSIVE PRACTICE

The foundation of the model is the ideological basis from which we practise. In this text, an anti-oppressive ideology forms this foundation. It assumes that the worker can appreciate and acknowledge the diverse

308

oppressive influences operating on both themselves and clients. These refer to the structural, cultural and personal oppressions impacting on the lives of both clients and workers. These dimensions impact on the nature of the work undertaken by the worker and client. In Chapter 12, Samoan parents Louana and Joseph are trying to deal with their adolescent son, David. This case highlights how workers can consciously respect the cultural differences of the family by recognising the pressures which impact upon them at individual, cultural and structural levels. This recognition is translated into practice with the worker's focus on family strengths and culturally responsive interventions.

We have also examined the differences in cultural understanding between Australia and New Zealand. The emphasis in Australia is on culturally diverse approaches, whereas in New Zealand the approach to human service work is focused on a bicultural understanding. Both approaches provide important insights into our respective histories and provide lessons for students as workers, regardless of which side of the Tasman we practise on.

The discussion focused on mental health assessment in Chapter 11 demonstrates how cultural competence is critical to ensure workers have a sound understanding in a case like that of Samia, a young Afghani woman. Without such a cultural perspective, the worker will fail to appreciate Samia's world or the family concerns relating to mental health issues. Practice examples are used to highlight the dilemmas facing workers who are struggling to translate an anti-oppressive foundation into practice in the current human services context.

THEORY AND PRACTICE IN THE CURRENT HUMAN SERVICE CONTEXT

The linking of theory with practice can only be understood in relation to the broader social context in which services are delivered. This is represented as social norms, expectations, political ideology and ideas of legitimacy. The relationship between theory and practice, as presented in this text, is symbiotic and dynamic. The theoretical analysis that underpins our practice informs our assumptions and values, our interventions and, ultimately, the skills we use. A strengths perspective has been used in each chapter to translate the anti-oppressive ideology into practice.

Parallel to this theoretical analysis, there is recognition of the current context in which human services are delivered. This context is characterised by uncertainty and widening economic and social inequalities. Client eligibility criteria are used to prioritise limited resources, while risk assessment is seen as a way of further prioritising services and targeting resources. As discussed by Christine Morley in Chapter 10, models of risk assessment become a way of organising and classifying information related to risk, in order to enhance decisions regarding prioritisation. Throughout, there are examples of how different solutions for dealing with agency economic constraints have been utilised in practice. Chapter 4 draws attention to the increased use of phone and online service delivery options that has significantly reduced the need for face-to-face staffing requirements. Interestingly, these developments have also promoted significant forms of client agency and empowerment through accessible peer self help, advocacy and social activism online.

Even so, the focus on cost-cutting is further evidenced with the emphasis on time-limited, contracted and user-pay service delivery. The case of Nan, the hospital inpatient in Chapter 7, again demonstrates these economic imperatives. The worker's role is to facilitate Nan's move out of the hospital Emergency Department. The worker, who operates in a position secondary to that of the medical staff in the hospital, has to deal with the competing demands of the hospital medical hierarchy and Nan. As discussed in the exercise, these demands are unlikely to be the same. Crisis intervention theory provides a method to guide such work in practice.

TRANSFERABILITY OF SKILLS

Another component of the Integrated Framework is the skills used by workers. In this text, we argue that there is a range of techniques which, when joined together, form the basis of our communication with others. These techniques are transferable across different contexts and different levels of practice. We acknowledge that there is no one set of skills for work with individuals and a different set for work in social action contexts. The streamlining and rationalising of services demand generalist skills, which are transferable across different job expectations and contexts. This transferability of skills thus becomes central to a human service delivery that increasingly values worker flexibility, measureable outputs and demonstrated competencies.

PHASES OF THE WORK

A generic model has been used in Part II–V of the text to demonstrate the different phases of the work. This has been done for teaching purposes because students who are preparing for practice highlight the value of this model for understanding the different tasks of interpersonal communication in the helping relationship.

Exercise 19.1

Take a moment to reflect upon the following questions:

1 What are the key things you have learned in this subject?
2 What is the nature of this learning, in terms of skills, theories, practice examples, ethical dilemmas?
3 What excites you about the next stage, going on placement?
4 What are the skills you want to develop further on placement?
5 What dilemmas in the case studies caused you most anxiety?
6 What are the hurdles that could get in the way of your professional practice?
7 How are you going to deal with these hurdles?

THE FUTURE FOR PRACTICE SKILLS TEACHING

All professional practice needs to be responsive to context. Fook et al. (2000) suggest 'professional expertise lies in the ability to translate skills rather than holding domain specific substantive knowledge in the first place' (2000, p. 242). Further, they argue that it is the judgment, the socialisation and the cultural learning that go into making knowledge contextually relevant. We have encouraged you to make professional judgments by first reflecting on your own values and ideology and the impact these might have on your work. The challenge is to become socialised professionally to critique and appreciate the structural barriers facing the clients with whom we work.

Understanding cultural diversity is central in appreciating the worlds of the individuals, families, groups and communities with whom we work. The Integrated Framework is intended to act as a guide in order that skills learning does not occur in isolation from the theory, the ideology or the phase of the process. We believe that these components need to be woven together to provide an informed and responsive service to clients.

It is hoped, therefore, that students will develop an understanding of the complexity of the contradictions they will face in their work, while also being able to articulate and work with the individual components. The challenge for skills teachers is to motivate and inspire students to constantly and creatively experiment with their learning styles, and to understand the impact they will have on the lives of their clients.

We hope that students and educators alike have been able to use the material in these chapters to be travellers in learning practice skills rather than tourists who may have missed out on the real adventures along the way.

BIBLIOGRAPHY

AASW (1999), *Code of Ethics*, Australian Association of Social Workers, Canberra.

Abikoff, H. & Gittelman, R. (1985), 'Hyperactive children treated with stimulants: Is cognitive training a useful adjunct?', *Archives of General Psychiatry*, 42(8): 953–61.

Aguilera, D. (1998), *Crisis Intervention: Theory and Methodology*, 8th ed., Mosby, St Louis, MO.

Alston M. & McKinnon J. (2001), *Social Work: Fields Of Practice*, Oxford University Press, Melbourne.

Ambrosino, R., Heffernan, J., Shuttlesworth, G. & Ambrosino, R. (2001), *Social Work and Social Welfare*, 4th ed., Brooks/Cole, Pacific Grove, CA.

Andrews, L. (1980), Listen to the Silence, unpublished paper, University of Melbourne.

Anthony, N., Cronin, M., Mitchell, S., Raquel, T. & Tatchell, L. (2000), *Inside Out, Outside In: Wounding While Healing*, Northern Centre Against Sexual Assault, Melbourne.

Anthony, S. & Pagano, G. (1998), 'The therapeutic potential for growth during the termination process', *Clinical Social Work Journal*, 26(3): 281–95.

APA (1994), *Diagnostic and Statistical Manual of Mental Disorders, 4th Edition*, American Psychiatric Association, Washington, DC.

—— (2000), *Diagnostic and Statistical Manual of Mental Disorders (DSM-IV-TR) 4th Edition, Text Revision*, American Psychiatric Association, Washington, DC.

Archard, D.W. (2003), *Children, Family and the State*, Ashgate, Aldershot.

Askew, S. & Lodge, C. (2000), 'Gifts, ping-pong and loops—linking feedback and learning', in Susan Askew (ed.), *Feedback for Learning*, RoutledgeFalmer, London.

ATSIC (1993), *Annual Report of the Aboriginal and Torres Strait Islander Social Justice Commissioner*, ATSIC, Canberra.

Audette, N. & Bunston, W. (2006), *The Therapeutic Use of Games in Groupwork*, Royal Children's Hospital Mental Health Service, Melbourne.

Australian Council of Social Service (2007), *Australian Community Sector Survey: Paper 145*, ACOSS, Sydney.

Baines, D. (2006), 'If you could change one thing': Social service workers and restructuring', *Australian Social Work*, 59(1): 20–34.

Barbour, R. (1984), 'Social work education: Tackling the theory-practice dilemma', *British Journal of Social Work*, 14: 557–77.

Barrie, S. (1996), 'Video-based assessment of clinical competence in speech and hearing science students', in A. Yarrow, J. Millwater, S. De Vries & D. Creedy (eds), *Practical Experiences in Professional Education*, QUT Publications, Brisbane.

Barton, B. & Marshall, A. (1986), 'The central trauma emerging during termination', *Clinical Social Work Journal*, 14(2): 139–49.

Baum, N. (2004), 'Social work students' treatment termination as a temporary role exit', *The Clinical Supervisor*, http: www.haworth press.com/web/CS

Bauman, K. (1981), 'Using technology to humanize instruction: An approach to teaching nursing skills', *Journal of Nursing Education*, 20(3): 27–31.

Bauman, Z. (2001), *The Individualized Society*, Polity Press, Cambridge.

Baxter, K. (1992), 'Starting from scratch: Sexual assault services in rural areas', in J. Breckenridge & M. Carmody (eds), *Crimes of Violence: Australian Responses to Rape and Child Sexual Assault*, Allen & Unwin, Sydney.

Beck, U. & Beck-Gernsheim, E. (2002), *Individualization: Institutionalized Individualism and Its Social and Political Consequences*, Sage, London.

Becvar, D.S & Becvar, R.J. (2000), *Family Therapy: A Systemic Integration*, 4th ed., Allyn and Bacon, Boston, MA.

Beddoe, L. & Randal, H. (1994), 'New Zealand Association of Social Workers: The professional response to a decade of change', in R. Munford & M. Nash (eds), *Social Work in Action*, Dunmore, Palmerston North, NZ.

Bembry, J. & Ericson, C. (1999), 'Therapeutic termination with the early adolescent who has experienced multiple losses', *Child and Adolescent Social Work Journal*, 16(3): 177–89.

Benard, B. (1994), 'Applications of resilience', conference paper presented at the Role of Resilience in Drug Abuse, Alcohol Abuse, and Mental Illness conference, National Institute on Drug Abuse, Washington, DC.

Berg, I.K. (1994), *Family Based Services: A Solution-Focused Approach*, W.W. Norton, New York.

—— (1999). Foreword, in A. Turnell & S. Edwards (eds), *Signs of Safety: A Solution and Safety Oriented Approach to Child Protection Casework*, W.W. Norton, New York.

Bessant, J. (2003), 'The science of risk and the epistemology of human service practice', *Just Policy*, 31: 31–8.

Bishop, A. (2001), *Becoming an Ally*, Allen & Unwin, Sydney.

Blundo, R. (2001), 'Learning strengths-based practice: Challenging our personal and professional frames', *Families in Society*, 82(3): 296–304.

Bonner, M., Campillo, L. & Cosier, G. (2002), 'I have learnt how to ask questions: Implementing screening for domestic violence', paper presented to Expanding Our Horizons conference, University of Sydney, Sydney, pp. 1–9.

Bowie, V. (1989), *Coping with Violence*, Karibuni Press, Sydney.

—— (1996), *Coping With Violence: A Guide for the Human Services*, 2nd ed., Karibuni Press, Sydney.

Brannen, J. (ed.) (1992), *Mixing Methods: Qualitative and Quantitative Research*, Avebury, Aldershot.

Briggs, L. (2001a), 'Refugees and migrants: Issues of multiculturalism in Aotearoa New Zealand social work', in M. Connolly (ed.), *New Zealand Social Work Contexts and Practice*, Oxford University Press, Auckland.

—— (2001b), 'Multi-cultural issues in New Zealand social work', in M. Connelly (ed.), *Social Work in New Zealand*, Oxford University Press, Auckland.

Brill, Naomi (1995), *Working with People: The Helping Process*, Longman, Chaplin, New York.

Brown, R. (2001), 'Australian Indigenous mental health', *Australian and New Zealand Journal of Mental Health Nursing*, 10: 33–41.

Browne, E. (2001), 'Social work in health care settings', in M. Alston & J. McKinnon (eds), *Social Work: Fields of Practice*, Oxford University Press, Melbourne.

Bryman,A. (1992),'Quantitative and qualitative research: Further reflections on their integration', in Julia Brannen (ed.), *Mixing Methods: Qualitative and Quantitative Research*,Avebury,Aldershot.

Bubenzer, D., West, J. & Boughner, S. (1994), 'Michael White and the narrative perspective in therapy' (interview), *The Family Journal: Counselling and Therapy for Couples and Families*, 2(1): 71-83.

Bunston, W. & Millard, P. (2006),'Understanding the life of a group: An "extended" developmental perspective', in W. Bunston & A. Heynatz (eds), *Addressing Family Violence Programs for Infants, Children and their Families*, Royal Children's Hospital Mental Health Service, Melbourne.

Burke, B. & Harrison, P. (1998),'Anti-oppressive practice', in R. Adams, L. Dominelli & M. Payne (eds), *Social Work: Themes, Issues and Critical Debates*, Macmillan, London.

Burke, C. (1999),'Redressing the balance: Child protection intervention in the context of domestic violence', in J. Breckenridge & L. Laing (eds), *Challenging Silence: Innovative Responses to Sexual and Domestic Violence*,Allen & Unwin, Sydney.

Cabrera, A., Nora, A., Crissman, J. & Terenzini, P. (2002), 'Collaborative learning: Its impact on college students' development and diversity', *Journal of College Student Development*, 43(1): 20-34.

Calder, M.C. (1995),'Child protection: Balancing paternalism and partnership', *British Journal of Social Work*, 25(6): 749-66.

Camusso, M.J. & Jagannathan, R. (1995), 'Prediction accuracy of the Washington and Illinois Risk Assessment Instruments: An application of receiver operating characteristic curve analysis', *Social Work Research*, 19(3): 174-83.

Carling,A. (2002),'Family policy, social theory and the state', in A. Carling, S. Duncan & R. Edwards (eds), *Analysing Families: Morality and Rationality in Policy and Practice*, Routledge, London.

Cassata, D., Ray, M. & Clements, P. (1977),'A programme for enhancing medical interviewing using video-tape feedback in the family practice residency', *Journal of Family Practice*, 4(4): 673-77.

Centre Against Sexual Assault (CASA) House (1992), *Desperately Seeking Justice: A Resource and Training Manual on Violence Against Women in a Culturally Diverse Community*, CASA House, Melbourne.

Chenall, R. (2006), 'Psychotherapy with Indigenous Australians: Group work in a residential alcohol and drug treatment setting', *Psychotherapy in Australia*, 13(1): 62-8.

Chenoweth, L. & McAuliffe, D. (2005), *The Road to Social Work*, Thomson, Melbourne.

Cherlin, A.J. (1992), *Marriage, Divorce, Remarriage*, Harvard University Press, Cambridge, MA.

Child Welfare Information Gateway (2001), 'Understanding the effects of maltreatment on early brain development', *A Bulletin for Professionals*, October.

Clark, R. (2000), *It Has to Be More Than a Job: A Search for Exceptional Practice with Troubled Adolescents*, Deakin University, Policy and Practice Research Unit, Melbourne.

Cleak, H. (1995), Health care in the 1990s: 'Practice implications for social work', *Australian Social Work*, 48(1): 13–22.

Cleak, H. & Wilson, J. (2007), *Making the Most of Field Placement*, Thomson Learning, South Melbourne.

Commonwealth of Australia *Privacy Act* (1988, reprinted 21 December 2001) (with amendments up to Act No. 159, 2001), AGPS, Canberra.

Compton, B., Galaway, B. & Cournoyer, B.R. (1998), *Social Work Processes*, 5th ed., Brooks/Cole, Pacific Grove, CA.

—— (1999), *Social Work Processes*, 6th ed., Brooks/Cole, Pacific Grove, CA.

—— (2005), *Social Work Processes*, Brooks/Cole Thomson Learning, CA.

Connolly, M. (1999), *Effective Participatory Practice: Family Group Conferencing in Child Protection*, Aldine de Gruyter, New York.

—— (2001a), 'Every child has a silver lining: Domains of resilience in child welfare', *Social Work Review*, XII(4): 41–3.

—— (2001b), 'The art and science of social work', in M. Connolly (ed.), *New Zealand Social Work: Contexts and Practice*, Oxford University Press, Auckland.

—— (2003), 'Cultural components of practice: Reflexive responses to diversity and difference', in T. Ward & D.R. Laws (eds), *Sexual Deviance Issues and Controversies*, Sage, Thousand Oaks, CA.

Connolly, M. & Crichton-Hill, Y. (2005), *Culture and Child Protection: Reflexive Responses*, Jessica Kingsley Publishers, London.

Cooper, L. & Bowden, M. (2006), *Footprints on the Airstrip. Interim Report: Development of a Framework for Indigenous and Remote Projects*, Flinders University, Adelaide.

Cooper, S.M. (2002), 'Classroom choices for enabling peer learning', *Theory into Practice*, 41(1): 53–7.

Coulshed, V. & Orme, J. (1998), *Social Work Practice: An Introduction*, Macmillan, London.

317

Council for Aboriginal Reconciliation (1995), *Going Forward: Social Justice for the First Australians*, AGPS, Canberra.

Cournoyer, B.R. (2008), *The Social Work Skills Workbook*, Thomson Brooks/Cole, Belmont, CA.

—— 2008, *The Social Work Skills Book*, Wadsworth, Belmont, CA.

Cowger, C. (1992), 'Assessment of client strengths', in S. Saleebey (ed.), *The Strengths Perspective in Social Work Practice*, Longman, New York.

—— (1994), 'Assessing client strengths: Clinical assessment for client empowerment', *Social Work*, 39(3): 262-8.

Cox, A.L. (2001), 'BSW students favor strengths/empowerment-based generalist practice', *Families in Society*, 82(3): 305-12.

Cox, D. (1989), *Welfare Practice in a Multicultural Society*, Prentice Hall, Sydney.

Craft-Rosenberg, M., Kelley, P. & Schnoll, L. (2006), 'Family-centered care: Practice and preparation', *Families in Society*, 87(1): 17-25.

Creswell, J. (1994), *Research Design: Qualitative and Quantitative Approaches*, Sage, Thousand Oaks, CA.

Crothers, C., McCormack, F. & New Zealand Families Commission (2006), *Towards a Statistical Typology of New Zealand Households and Families: The Efficacy of the Family Life Cycle Model and Alternatives*, Families Commission, Wellington, NZ.

Dalrymple, J. & Burke, B. (2006), *Anti-oppressive Practice: Social Care and the Law*, 2nd ed., Open University Press, New York.

Davies, L & Leonard, P. (2004) (eds), *Social Work in a Corporate Era: Practices of Power and Resistance*, Ashgate, Aldershot.

Dean, R. (2001), 'The myth of cross-cultural competence', *Families in Society: Journal of Contemporary Human Services*, 82(6): 623-28.

De Jong, P. and Berg, I. K. (1998), *Interviewing for Solutions*, 2nd ed., Wadsworth, Belmont, CA.

—— 2007, *Interviewing for Solutions*, Brooks/Cole, Pacific Grove, CA.

De Jong P., and Miller S. (1995), 'How to interview for client strengths', *Social Work*, 40(6): 729-36.

DePanifilis, D. (1996), 'Implementing child mistreatment risk assessment systems: Lessons from theory', *Administration in Social Work*, 20(2): 41-59.

Department of Human Services (2002), *Literature review: To inform a Department of Human Services project to people with high and complex needs*, Thompson Goodall Associates, East Brighton.

de Shazer S. (1994), *Words Were Originally Magic*, New York, Norton.

—— (1985), *Keys to Salutations in Brief Therapy*, W.W. Norton, New York.

Dodson, M. (1993), *Annual Report of the Aboriginal and Torres Strait Islander Social Justice Commissioner*, Commonwealth of Australia, AGPS, Canberra.

Dominelli, L (1997), *Anti-Racist Social Work: A Challenge for White Practitioners and Educators*, Macmillan, Basingstoke.

—— (2002), 'Anti-oppressive practice in context', in R. Adams, L. Dominelli & M. Payne (eds), *Social Work: Themes, Issues and Critical Debates*, 2nd ed., Palgrave, New York.

Doueck, H.J., Bronson, D. & Levine, M. (1992), 'Evaluating risk assessment implementation in child protection: Issues for consideration', *Child Abuse and Neglect*, 16: 637–46.

Duncan, B.L., Miller, S.D., & Sparks, J. (2004), *The Heroic Client: A Revolutionary Way to Improve Effectiveness through Client-Directed, Outcome-Informed Therapy*, 3rd ed., Jossey-Bass, San Francisco.

Durie, M. (1994), *Whaiora Maori Health Development*, Oxford University Press, Auckland.

—— (1998), 'Te mana te kawanatanga', in *The Politics of Maori Self Determination*, Oxford University Press, Auckland.

Dutton, D. & Kropp, R. (2000), 'A review of domestic violence risk assessments', *Trauma, Violence and Abuse*, 1(2): 171–81.

Eagleton, T. (2000), *The Idea of Culture*, Blackwell, Oxford.

Edleson, J.L. (1998), 'Responsible mothers and invisible men: Child protection in the case of adult domestic violence', *Journal of Interpersonal Violence*, 13(2): 294–8.

Education for Social Justice Research Group (1994), *Teaching for Resistance*, University of South Australia, Texts in Humanities and the Centre for Studies in Educational Leadership, Adelaide.

Egan, G. (2007), *Skilled Helper*, 8th ed., Thomson Higher Education, Belmont, CA.

Egan, Ronnie (2004), 'What's happened to supervision: A critical comment', in *Weaving together the strands of supervision: Conference proceedings of the supervision conference*, Auckland College of Education, Auckland.

—— (2005), 'When outside is in and inside is out: The provision of external supervision in social work in Victoria', Australian Counselling and Supervision conference 2005, QUT, Brisbane.

Eliot, T.S. (1974), 'East Coker' from 'Four Quartets' in *Collected Poems 1909–1962*, Faber & Faber, London.

Elliot, A. & Lemert, C. (2006), *The New Individualism: The Emotional Costs of Globalization*, Routledge, London.

Elliott, B. (2000), *Promoting Family Change: The Optimism Factor*, Allen & Unwin, Sydney.

Epston, D. & White, M. (1990), *Narrative Means to Therapeutic Ends*, New York, Norton.

Errington, E. (1997), *Role-play*, HERDSA Green Guide 21, Higher Education Research and Development Society of Australasia, Jamieson Centre, Canberra.

Faludi, S. (2008), As quoted from an interview with Decca Aitkenhead, *The Age*, 12 April, pp. 28–29.

Federal Race Discrimination Commissioner (1997), *Face the Facts: Questions and Answers About Aboriginal People and Torres Strait Islanders*, http: home.vicnet.au/~aar/factfile.htm, the Commission, Sydney.

Fenichel, M. (2004), 'Online behaviour, communication, and experience', in R. Kraus, J. Zack & G. Stricker (eds), *Online Counselling: A Handbook for Mental Health Professionals*, Elsevier, London.

Ferguson, R. (2005), 'Telephone helplines for parents', in R. Wootton & J. Batch (eds), *Telepediatrics: Telemedicine and Child Health*, Royal Society of Medicine Press, London.

Fielding, N. & Fielding, J. (1986), *Linking Data: Qualitative Research Network Series 4*, Sage, London.

Findlay, R. (2007), 'A mandate for honesty, Jeff Young's No Bullshit Therapy™: An interview', *Australian and New Zealand Journal of Family Therapy*, 28(3): 165–70.

Folgheraiter, F. (2004), *Relational Social Work: Towards Networking and Societal Practices*, Jessica Kingsley Publishers, London.

Fook, J. (1993), *Radical Casework: A Theory of Practice*, Allen & Unwin, Sydney.

—— (1999), 'Critical reflectivity in education and practice', in B. Pease & J. Fook (eds), *Transforming Social Work Practice*, Allen & Unwin, Sydney.

—— (2002), *Social Work: Critical Theory and Practice*, Sage, London.

Fook, J. & Pease, B. (eds) (2002), *Transforming Social Work Practice: Postmodern Critical Perspectives*, Allen & Unwin, Sydney.

Fook, J., Ryan, M. & Hawkins, L. (2000), *Professional Expertise: Practice, Theory and Education for Working with Uncertainty*, Whiting and Birch, London.

Fortune, A. (1987), 'Grief only? Client and social worker reactions to termination', *Clinical Social Work Journal*, 15(2): 159–71.

Fortune, A. & Pearlingi, B. (1992), 'Reactions to termination of individual treatment', *Social Work*, 37(2): 171-8.

Fox, E.F., Nelson, M.A. & Bolman, W.M. (1969), 'The termination process: A neglected dimension in social work', *Social Work*, 14(4): 53-63.

Freeman, E.M. & Couchonnal, G. (2006), 'Narrative and culturally based approaches in practice with families', *Families in Society*, 87(2): 198-208.

Frey, R., Roberts-Smith, L. & Bessell-Browne, S. (1990), *Working with Interpreters in Law, Health and Social Work*, State Advisory Panel for Translating and Interpreting in Western Australia for the National Accreditation Authority for Translators and Interpreters, Perth.

Friess, S. (1999), 'Cyber activism', *The Advocate*, 2 March, p. 35.

Furlong, M. (1997), 'How much care and how much control? Looking critically at case management', *Australian Journal of Primary Health—Interchange*, 3(4): 72-89.

Furlong, M., Young, J., Perlesz, A., McLachlan, D. & Riess, C. (1991), 'For family therapists involved in the treatment of chronic and longer term conditions', *Dulwich Centre Newsletter*, 4: 58-68.

Gannon, M. (2001), *Working Across Cultures*, Sage, Thousand Oaks, CA.

Geldard, D. (1998), *Basic Personal Counselling: A Training Manual for Counsellors*, 3rd ed., Prentice Hall, Sydney.

Geldard, D. & Geldard, K. (2005), *Basic Personal Counselling: A Training Manual for Counsellors*, 5th ed. Pearson Education, Sydney.

Germaine, C.B. (1991), *Human Behaviour in the Social Environment: An Ecological View*, Columbia University Press, New York.

Germaine, C. & Gitterman, A. (1996), *The Life Model of Social Work Practice*, Columbia University Press, New York.

Gibney, P. (2005), 'Termination and discontinuities in psychotherapy', *Psychotherapy in Australia*, 11(2): 50-5.

Giddens, A. (2002), *Runaway World: How Globalization is Re-shaping our Lives*, Profile Books, London

Gitterman, A. (2001), *Handbook of Social Work Practice with Vulnerable and Resilient Populations*, 2nd ed., Columbia University Press, New York.

Glicken, M. (2004), *Using the Strengths Perspective in Social Work Practice: A Positive Approach for the Helping Professions*, Allyn & Bacon, New York.

Goddard, C., Saunders, J., Stanley, J. & Tucci, J. (1999), 'Structured risk assessment procedures: Instruments of abuse?' *Child Abuse Review*, 8: 251-63.

Goldenberg, I. & Goldenberg, H. (1985), *Family Therapy: An Overview*, 2nd ed., Brooks/Cole, Pacific Grove, CA.

Goleman, D. (2006), *Social Intelligence*, Hutchison, London.

Gong-Guy, E., Cravens, R.B. & Patterson, T.E. (1991), 'Clinical issues in mental health service delivery to refugees', *American Psychologist*, June, 642–8.

Graybeal, C. (2001), 'Strengths-based social work assessment: Transforming the dominant paradigm', *Families in Society: Journal of Contemporary Human Services*, 82(3): 233–43.

Green, D. (2008), 'Complexity and twenty-first century social work' (unpublished manuscript), La Trobe University, Melbourne.

Green, L. (1998), 'Single session therapy: An interview with Moshe Talmon', *Psychotherapy in Australia*, 4(2): 26–31.

Greer, P. & Breckenridge, J. (1992), 'They throw the rule book away: Sexual assault in Aboriginal communities', in J. Breckenridge & M. Carmody (eds), *Crimes of Violence: Australian Responses to Rape and Child Sexual Assault*, Allen & Unwin, Sydney.

Grinnell, R. (1997), *Social Work Research and Evaluation*, 5th ed., F.E. Peacock, Itasca, IL.

Guillen, M. & Suarez, S. (2005), 'Explaining the global digital divide: Economic, political and sociological drivers of cross-national internet use', *Social Forces*, 84(2): 681–708.

Haas, L., Benedict, J. & Kobos, J. (1996), 'Counselling by telephone: Risks and benefits for psychologists and consumers', *Professional Psychology: Research and Practice*, 27: 154–60.

Hambly, G. (1984), *Telephone Counselling*, Joint Board of Christian Education for Australia and New Zealand (JBCE), Melbourne.

Hamm, M. & Adams, D. (2002), 'Collaborative enquiry: Working toward shared goals', *Kappa Delta Pi Record*, 38(3): 115–19.

Hantz, P. (1999), *Suicide Risk-Assessment Tool: Guidelines for Use*, Barwon Health, Geelong, Vic.

Hardiker, P. & Barker, M. (1991), 'Towards social theory for social work', in J. Lischman (ed.), *Handbook of Theory for Practice Teachers in Social Work*, Jessica Kingsley Publishers, London.

Harms, L. (2007), 'Finishing the work' in *Working with People*, Oxford University Press, South Melbourne, pp. 227–41.

Harrigan, M.P., Fauri, D.P. & Netting, F.E. (1998), 'Termination: Extending the concept for macro social work practice', *Journal of Sociology and Social Welfare*, 25(4): 61–80.

Hartman, A. (1994), *Reflection and Controversy: Essays on Social Work*, National Association of Social Work Press, Washington DC.

Hayley, J. (1980), *Leaving Home: The Therapy of Disturbed Young People*, McGraw-Hill, New York.

Haythornwaite, C. (2000), 'Online personal networks', *New Media and Society*, 2(2): 195–226.

Healy, K. (2005), *Social Work Theories in Context*, Palgrave Macmillan, New York.

Heap, K. (1977), *Group Theory for Social Workers*, Holywell, Oxford.

Hemming, S., Rigney, D., Wallis, A., Trevorrow, T., Rigney, M., Trevorrow, G., (2007), 'Caring for Ngarrindjeri country: Collaborative research, community development and social justice', *Indigenous Law Bulletin*, May, 6(27): 6–8.

Hepworth, D.H., Rooney, R.H. & Larson, J.A. (1997), *Direct Social Work Practice*, Brooks/Cole, Pacific Grove, CA.

Herman, J.L. (1992), *Trauma and Recovery*, Basic Books, New York.

Hill, K. & Hughes, J. (1998), *Cyberpolitics: Citizen Activism in the Age of the Internet*, Rowman & Littlefield, Lanham, NJ.

Hollinsworth, David (1998), *Race and Racism in Australia*, 2nd ed., Social Science Press, Katoomba.

Hollinsworth, David & Cunningham, Joan (1998), *Indigenous Health: A Cultural Awareness Program for Medical Education*, Yunggorendi First Nations Centre for Higher Education and Research, Flinders University, Adelaide.

Home, A. (1999), 'Group empowerment: An elusive goal', in W. Shera & L.M. Wells (eds), *Empowerment Practice in Social Work: Developing Richer Conceptual Foundations*, Canadian Scholars' Press, Toronto.

Howe, D. (1986a), *Introduction to Social Work Theory*, Avebury, Aldershot.

Howe, D. (1986b), *Social Workers and Their Practice in Welfare Bureaucracies*, Gower Publishing Co., Aldershot, Hants, England; Brookefield VT, US.

—— (1998), 'Relationship-based thinking and practice in social work', *Journal of Social Work Practice*, 12(1): 45–56.

HREOC (Human Rights and Equal Opportunity Commission) (1997), *Bringing Them Home: National Enquiry into the Separation of Aboriginal and Torres Strait Islander Children from Their Families*, AGPS, Canberra.

Hsiung, R. (2000), 'The best of both worlds: An online self-help group hosted by a mental health professional', *CyberPsychology & Behaviour*, 3: 935–50.

323

Hubble, M., Duncan, B. & Miller, S. (1999), *The Heart and Soul of Change: What Works in Therapy*, American Psychological Press, Washington, DC.

Huggins, J. (1991), 'Black women and women's liberation', in S. Gunew (ed.), *A Reader in Feminist Knowledge*, Routledge, London.

Hulsman, R., Mollema, E., Hoos, A., de Haes, J. & Donnison-Speijer, J. (2004), 'Assessment of medical communication skills by computer: Assessment method and student experiences', *Medical Education*, 38: 813–24.

Humphreys, C. & Stanley, N. (eds), (2006), *Domestic Violence and Child Protection: Directions for Good Practice*, Jessica Kingsley Publishers, London.

Hunter, S. & Kottler, J.A. (2007), 'Therapists are socially constructed too', *Psychotherapy in Australia*, 13(2): 22–7.

Hurst, M. (1995), 'Counselling women from a feminist perspective', in W. Weeks & J. Wilson (eds), *Issues Facing Australian Families*, 2nd ed., Longman, Melbourne.

Ife, J.W. (1995), *Community Development: Creating Community Alternatives—Vision, Analysis and Practice*, Longman, Melbourne.

—— (1997), *Rethinking Social Work: Towards Critical Practice*, Addison Wesley Longman, Melbourne.

—— (1999), 'Postmodernism, critical theory and social work', in B. Pease & J. Fook (eds), *Transforming Social Work Practice*, Allen & Unwin, Sydney.

Ivey, A. (1983), *Intentional Interviewing and Counselling*, Brooks/Cole, Pacific Grove, CA.

Ivey, A. & Ivey, M.B. (1999), *Intentional Interviewing & Counselling: Facilitating Client Development in a Multi-Cultural Society*, 4th ed., Brooks/Cole, Pacific Grove, CA.

Jackson, S. & Charble, D. (1980), 'Engagement: A critical aspect of family therapy practice', *Australian and New Zealand Journal of Family Therapy*, 6(2): 65–69.

Jackson, V.H. & Lopez, L. (1999), *Cultural Competency in Managed Behavioral Healthcare*, Manisses Communications Group, Rhode Island.

Jenkins, A. (1990), *Invitations to Responsibility: The Therapeutic Engagement of Men Who Are Violent and Abusive*, Dulwich Centre Publications, Adelaide.

Jesuit Social Services (2006), *Understanding Families*, Jesuit Social Services, Melbourne.

Johnson, D.W. & Johnson, F.P. (1997), *Joining Together: Group Theory and Group Skills*, Allyn and Bacon, Boston.

Ka Tat Tsang, A. & George, U. (1998), 'Towards an integrated framework for cross-cultural social work practice', *Canadian Social Work Review*, 15(1): 73-93.

Kadushin, A. (1990), *The Social Work Interview*, 3rd ed., Columbia University Press, New York.

—— (1997), *The Social Work Interview*, 4th ed., Columbia University Press, New York.

Kanel, K. (1999), *A Guide to Crisis Intervention*, Brooks/Cole, Pacific Grove, CA.

Kaplan, H., Sadock, B. & Grebb, J. (1994), *Kaplan and Sadock's Synopsis of Psychiatry: Behavioral Sciences, Clinical Psychiatry*, Williams and Wilkins, Baltimore, MD.

Keene, J. (2001), *Clients with Complex Needs: Inter-professional Practice*, Oxford, Blackwell Science.

Kenny, M. & McEachern, A. (2004), 'Telephone counseling: Are offices becoming obsolete?', *Journal of Counseling and Development*, 82: 199-202.

Kids Help Line (2007), *Kids Help Line 2006 Overview: Issues Concerning Children and Young People*, www.kidshelp.com.au/upload/18423.pdf.

Kirst-Ashman, K. & Hull, G. (2001), *Generalist Practice with Organizations and Communities*, 2nd ed., Brooks/Cole, Pacific Grove, CA.

Kondrat, M.E. (1999), 'Who is the self in self aware: Professional self awareness from a critical theory perspective', *Social Service Review*, 73(4): 451-77.

Kurzydio, A., Casson, C. & Shumack, S. (2005), 'Reducing professional isolation: Support scheme for rural specialists', *Australasian Journal of Dermatology*, 46: 242-5.

Lago, C. & Thompson, J. (1996), *Race, Culture and Counselling*, Open University Press, Buckingham.

Lawler, V. (1998), *Domestic Violence: The Case for Routine Screening*, Key Centre for Women's Health in Society, Melbourne.

Leaffer, T. & Mickelberg, L. (2006), 'The digital health-care revolution: Empowering health consumers', *The Futurist*, May–June, 53-7.

Lee, J.A.B. (1994), *The Empowerment Approach to Social Work Practice*, Columbia University Press, New York.

—— (2001), *The Empowerment Approach to Social Work Practice: Building the Beloved Community*, 2nd ed., Columbia University Press, New York.

Lehmann, P. & Coady, N. (2001), *Theoretical Perspectives for Direct Social Work Practice*, Springer, New York.

Leon, J. (1999), *Terrific Telephone Techniques*, Terrific Trading, West Leederville, WA.

Lethem, Jane (1994), *Moved to Tears, Moved to Action: Solution Focused Grief Therapy with Women and Children*, BT Press, London.

Lewis, M. (2002), 'Intensive individual psychodynamic psychotherapy', in M. Lewis (ed.), *Child and Adolescent Psychiatry: A Comprehensive Textbook*, Lippincott Williams & Wilkins, Philadelphia, PA.

Lifeline (1999), Telephone Counsellor Training Notes (unpublished), Melbourne.

Lifton, R.J. (1993), *The Protean Self: Human Resilience in an Age of Fragmentation*, Basic Books, New York.

Lischman, Joyce (1994), *Communication in Social Work*, Macmillan, London.

Locke, B., Garrison, R. & Winship, J. (1998), *Generalist Social Work Practice: Context, Story and Partnerships*, Brooks/Cole, Pacific Grove, CA.

Lum, D. (1990), *Culturally Competent Practice: A Framework for Growth and Action*, Brooks/Cole, Thomson Learning, Melbourne.

—— (1999), *Culturally Competent Practice: A Framework for Growth and Action*, Brooks/Cole, Toronto.

—— (2000), *Social Work Practice and People of Color*, 4th ed., Brooks/Cole, Thomson Learning, Melbourne.

Lum, D. & Lu, Y. (2003), 'Skill development', in D. Lum (ed.), *Culturally Competent Practice*, 2nd ed., Brooks/Cole, Thomson Learning, Pacific Grove, CA.

Lynn, R. (1998), *Murri Way! Aborigines and Torres Strait Islanders Reconstruct Social Welfare Practice*, Centre for Social Research, James Cook University, Townsville.

Lynn, R., Thorpe, R. & Miles, D., with Cutts C., Ford, L. & Butcher, A. (1997), 'A yarn, a joke and a cup of tea: Aboriginal and Torres Strait Islander helping styles in social welfare practice', *Social Work Review*, IX(3): 18–23.

McCashen, W. (2005), *The Strengths Approach: A Strengths-based Resource for Sharing Power and Creating Change*, St Luke's Innovative Resources, Bendigo, Vic.

McConnochie, K.R., Hollinsworth, D. & Pettman, J. (1988), *Race and Racism in Australia*, Social Science Press, Wentworth Falls, NSW.

McDonald, C., Marston, G. & Buckley, A. (2003), 'Risk technology in Australia: The role of the Job Seeker Classification Instrument in employment services, *Critical Social Policy*, 23(4): 498-525.

MacKinnon, L.K. (1998), *Trust and Betrayal in the Treatment of Child Abuse*, Guilford Press, New York.

McMahon, M. (1996), *The General Method of Social Work Practice*, Prentice Hall, Englewood Cliffs, NJ.

McPhatter, A. (1997), 'Cultural competence in child welfare: What is it? What happens without it?', *Child Welfare League of America*, LXXVI(1): 255-78.

Maidment, J. (2000), 'Strategies to promote student learning and integration of theory with practice in the field', in Lesley Cooper & Lynne Briggs (eds), *Fieldwork in the Human Services*, Allen & Unwin, Sydney.

Maidment, J. & Cooper, L. (2002), 'Acknowledgment of client diversity and oppression in social work student supervision', *Social Work Education*, 21(4): 397-407.

Mailick M.D. & Vigilante, F.W. (1997), 'The family assessment wheel: Social constructionist perspective', *Families in Society: The Journal of Contemporary Human Services*, July–August, 361-9.

Maluccio, A. (1979), *Learning from Clients*, The Free Press, London.

Maluccio, A., Washitz, S. & Libassi, M. (1999), 'Ecologically oriented, competence-centred social work practice', in *Case Studies in Social Work Practice*, 2nd ed., Brooks/Cole, Toronto.

Marchant, H. & Wearing, B. (1986), *Gender Reclaimed: Women in Social Work*, Hale & Iremonger, Sydney.

Markward, M. (1998), 'Attention deficit hyperactivity disorder', in B.A. Thyer & J.S. Wodarski (eds), *Handbook of Empirical Social Work Practice: Mental Disorders—Vol. 1*, John Wiley, New York.

Marsh, P. & Doel, M. (2005), *The Task-centred Book*, Routledge, London pp. 24-44.

Marsh, P. & Triseliotis, J. (1996), *Social Workers and Probation Officers: Their Training and First Year in Work*, Avebury, Aldershot.

Matahaere-Atariki, D., Bertanees, C. & Hoffman, L. (2001), 'Anti-oppressive practices in a colonial context', in M. Connolly (ed.), *New Zealand Social Work: Contexts and Practice*, Oxford University Press, Auckland.

Matsumoto, D. & Juang, L. (2004), *Culture and Psychology*, 3rd ed., Thomson Wadsworth, Melbourne.

Mayo, M. (1998), *Training and Education in Urban Regeneration: A Framework for Participants*, Policy Press, University of Bristol, Bristol.

Meites, E. & Thom, D. (2007), 'Telephone counseling improves smoking cessation rates', *American Family Physician*, 75(5): 650.

Merrett, L. (2004), 'Closure with clients', in Maidment, J. & Egan, R. (eds), *Practice Skills in Social work and Welfare*, Allen & Unwin, Crows Nest.

Metcalf, L. (1998), *Solution Focussed Therapy: Ideas for Groups in Private Practice, Schools, Agencies, and Treatment Programs*, Free Press, New York.

Middleman, R. & Goldberg-Wood, G. (1990), *Skills for Direct Practice in Social Work*, Columbia University, New York.

Miley, K., O'Melia, M. & DuBois, B. (1998), *Generalist Social Work Practice: An Empowering Approach*, 2nd ed., Allyn & Bacon, Needham Heights, MA.

—— (2001), *Generalist Social Work Practice: An Empowering Approach*, 3rd ed., Allyn & Bacon, Boston.

—— (2007), *Generalist Social Work Practice: An Empowering Approach*, 5th ed., Pearson, Boston.

Miller, J., Donner, S. & Fraser, E. (2005), 'Talking when talking is tough: Taking on conversations about race, sexual orientation, gender, class and other aspects of social identity', *Smith College Studies in Social Work*, 74(2): 377–92.

Miller, R. & Dwyer, J. (1997), 'Reclaiming the mother-daughter relationship after sexual abuse', *Australian and New Zealand Journal of Family Therapy*, 18(4): 194–202.

Miller, S., Hubble, M. & Duncan, B. (1996), *Handbook Of Solution-Focused Brief Therapy*, Jossey-Bass, San Francisco, California, p. 89.

Minuchin, S. (1974), *Families and Family Therapy*, Harvard University Press, Boston.

Moreau, M.J. (1979), 'A structural approach to social work practice', *Canadian Journal of Social Work Education*, 5(1): 78–94.

Morgan, A. (2000), *What is Narrative Therapy?*, Dulwich Centre Publications, Adelaide.

Morley, C. (2003), 'The dominance of risk assessment in child protection: Is it risk?' *Social Work Review*, XV(1 & 2): 33–6.

Mulitalo-Lauta P.T. (2001), 'Pacific peoples' identities and social services in New Zealand: Creating new options', in C. Macpherson, P. Spoonley

& M. Anae (eds), *Tangata O Te Moana Nui. The Evolving Identities of Pacific Peoples in Aotearoa/New Zealand*, Dunmore Press, Palmerston North, NZ.

Mullaly, Bob (1997), *Structural Social Work: Ideology, Theory and Practice*, Oxford University Press, Toronto.

—— (2002), *Challenging Oppression*, Oxford University Press, Toronto.

Munford, R. & Sanders, J. (1999), *Supporting Families*, Dunmore Press, Palmerston North, NZ.

Munson, C. (1993), *Clinical Social Work Supervision*, Haworth Press, New York.

Murphy, L. & Mitchell, D. (1998), 'When writing helps to heal: Email as therapy', *British Journal of Guidance and Counselling*, 26(1): 21–32.

Myers Kurst, P. (2000), *Getting the Most from Your Human Services Internship: Learning from Experience*, Brooks/Cole, Toronto.

Mylan, Trish & Lethen, Jane (1999), *Searching for Strengths in Child Protection Assessment: From Guidelines to Practice*, BT Press, London.

NASW (National Association of Social Workers) (1989), *NASW Standards for the Practice of Clinical Social Work*, NASW Press, Washington, DC.

Newhill, C. (1995), 'Client violence toward social workers: A practice and policy concern for the 1990s', *Social Work*, 40(5): 631–6.

New Zealand Mental Health Commission (2000), *Clinical Assessment of Infants, Children & Youth with Mental Health Problems: Guidelines for Mental Health Services in New Zealand*, NZMHC, Wellington.

—— (2001), *Recovery Competencies for the New Zealand Mental Health Workforce*, NZMHC, Wellington.

Nezu, A.M., Nezu, C.M. & Perri, M.G. (1995), *Problem-solving Therapy for Depression: Theory and Research and Clinical Guidelines*, Wiley, New York.

Nichols, M. (1984), *Family Therapy: Concepts and Methods*, Gardner Press, New York.

Norman, J. (2000), 'Constructive narrative in arresting the impact of post-traumatic stress disorder', *Clinical Social Work*, 28: 303–19.

Nursten, J.P. (1997), 'The end as a means to growth—within the social work relationship', *Journal of Social Work Practice*, 11(2): 73–80.

O'Connor, I., Wilson, J. & Setterlund, D. (2003), *Social Work and Welfare Practice*, Pearson Education, Frenchs Forest, N.S.W.

329

O'Donnell, H. (1998), 'Suicide risk assessment: A challenge for all health care professionals', *Nursing Review*, 16(2): 40–5.

O'Hanlon, B. & Weiner-Davis, M. (2003), *In Search Of Solutions: A New Direction In Psychotherapy*, W.W. Norton, New York.

O'Hanlon, W.H. & Weiner-Davis, M. (1989), *In Search of Solutions*, Norton, New York.

O'Hara, A. (2006), 'The microskills of interviewing', in A. O'Hara & Z. Weber (eds), *Skills for Human Service Practice*, Oxford University Press, Melbourne.

O'Hare, T. (1996), 'Readiness for change: Variation by intensity and domain of client distress', *Social Work Research*, 20(1): 13–18.

Orbach, S. (1999), *Towards Emotional Literacy*, Virago, London.

Owen, J. (1993), *Programme Evaluation Forms and Approaches*, Allen & Unwin, Sydney.

Palincsar, A. & Herrenkohl, L. (2002), 'Designing collaborative learning contexts', *Theory into Practice*, 41(1): 26.

Papell, C. (1996), 'Reflections on issues in social work education', in N. Gould & I. Taylor (eds), *Reflective Learning for Social Work*, Arena, Aldershot.

Parfitt, B.A. (n.d.), 'Rural Family Violence Risk Indicator Tool', unpublished.

Parton, N. (1996), 'Social work, risk and the "blaming system"', in N. Parton (ed.), *Social Theory, Social Change and Social Work*, Routledge, London.

Parton, N. & O'Byrne, P. (2000), *Constructive Social Work: Towards a New Practice*, Macmillan, Basingstoke.

Paterson, T. (1996), 'Leaving well alone: A systemic perspective on the therapeutic relationship', in C. Flaskas & A. Perlesz (eds), *The Therapeutic Relationship in Systemic Therapy*, Karnac Books, London, pp. 15–33.

Patford, J. (2002), 'Dilemmas for social workers in secondary settings', in P. Swain (ed.), *In the Shadow of the Law*, Federation Press, Sydney.

Payne, M. (1997), *Modern Social Work Theory*, 2nd ed., Macmillan, London.

Pease, B. & Fook, J. (1999), 'Postmodern critical theory and emancipatory social work practice', in B. Pease & J. Fook (eds), *Transforming Social Work Practice: Postmodern Critical Perspectives*, Allen & Unwin, Sydney.

Pentony, P. (1981), *Models of Influence in Psychotherapy*, Collier Macmillan, London.

Perlman H.H. (1957), *Social Casework: A Problem Solving Process*, University of Chicago Press, Chicago.

—— (1970), 'The problem solving model in social case work', in R. Roberts & R. Nee (eds), *Theory of Social Casework*, University of Chicago Press, Chicago.

Perry, B.D. (2001), 'Violence and childhood: How persisting fear can alter the developing child's brain', in D. Schetsky & E. Benedek (eds), *Textbook of Child and Adolescent Forensic Psychiatry*, American Psychiatric Press, Washington, DC.

Phillips, M.H. & Cohen, C.S. (2000), 'Strength and resiliency themes in social work practice with groups', in E. Norman (ed.), *Resiliency Enhancement: Putting the Strengths Perspective into Social Work Practice*, Columbia University Press, New York.

Pine, D.W. (1996), 'Postmodernist analysis: A valuable tool for feminists', *Refractory Girl*, 51: 4-7.

Potocky-Tripodi, M. (2002), *Best Practices for Social Workers with Refugees and Migrants*, Columbia University Press, New York.

Povey, D. (2002), *How Much is Enough? Life Below the Poverty Line in Dunedin 2002*, Presbyterian Support, Otago, NZ.

Prochaska, J. (1999), 'How do people change, and how can we change to help many more people change?', in M. Hubble, B. Duncan & S. Millar (eds), *The Heart and Soul of Change: What Works in Therapy*, American Psychological Association, Washington, DC.

Prochaska, J. & DiClemente, C. (1986), 'Toward a comprehensive model of change', in W. Miller & N. Heather (eds), *Treating Addictive Behaviours*, Plenum Press, New York.

Puckett, T.C. and Cleak, H. (1994), 'Caution—helping may be hazardous: Client abuse threats and assaults', *Australian Social Work*, 47(1): 3-10.

Quintana, S.M. (1993), 'Toward an expanded and updated conceptualization of termination: Implications for short-term, individual psychotherapy', *Professional Psychology: Research and Practice*, 24: 426-32.

Quinton, D. (2004), *Supporting Parents: Messages from Research*, Jessica Kingsley Publishers, London.

—— (2005), 'Themes from a UK research initiative on supporting parents', in J. Scott & H. Ward (eds), *Safeguarding and Promoting the Well-being of Children, Families and Communities*, Jessica Kingsley Publishers, London.

Ramon, S. (1999), 'Collective empowerment: Conceptual and practice issues', in W. Shera & L.M. Wells (eds), *Empowerment Practice in*

Social Work: Developing Richer Conceptual Foundations, Canadian Scholars' Press, Toronto.

Rapp, C.A. (1998), *The Strengths Model: Case Management with People Suffering from Severe and Persistent Mental Illness*, Oxford University Press, New York.

Rawson, S. & Maidment, J. (forthcoming), 'Email counselling with young people in Australia', *Qualitative Social Work*.

Reese, R., Conoley, Collie W. & Brossart, D.F. (2006), 'The attractiveness of telephone counselling: An empirical investigation of client perceptions', *Journal of Counseling and Development*, 84: 54-60.

Reid, W. & Caswell, D. (2005), 'A national telephone and online counselling service for young Australians', in R. Wootton & J. Batch (eds), *Telepediatrics: Telemedicine and Child Health*, Royal Society of Medicine Press, London.

Relph, A. (1985), 'The last time: A metaphor for leaving', *Australian and New Zealand Journal of Family Therapy*, 6(3): 123-7.

Rey, L.D. (1996), 'What social workers need to know about client violence', *Families in Society*, 77(1): 33-9.

Reynolds, Henry (1987), *Frontier*, Allen & Unwin, Sydney.

Rigney, D., Wallis, L., Trevorrow, T., Rigney, M. & Trevorrow, G. (forthcoming), 'Caring for country: Collaborative research, community development and social justice', *Indigenous Law Bulletin*.

Ritvo, R.Z. & Ritvo, S. (2002), 'Psychodynamic psychotherapy', in M. Lewis (ed.), *Child and Adolescent Psychiatry: A Comprehensive Textbook*, Lippincott Williams & Wilkins, Philadelphia, PA.

Roberts, R. (1990), *Lessons from the Past: Issues for Social Work Theory*, Tavistock/Routledge, London.

Robson, D. & Robson, M. (1998), 'Intimacy and computer communication', *British Journal of Guidance and Counselling*, 26(1): 33-41.

Rønnestad, M.H. & Skovholt, T.M. (2003), 'The journey of the counselor and therapist: Research findings and perspectives on professional development', *Journal of Career Development*, 30(1): 5-44.

Rosenfield, M. & Smillie, E. (1998), 'Group counselling by telephone', *British Journal of Guidance and Counselling*, 26(1): 11-19.

Rossiter, A (2000), The professional is political: An interpretation of the problems of the past in solution focussed therapy, *American Journal of Orthopsychiatry*, 70(2): 150-61.

Royal Commission into Aboriginal Deaths in Custody (RCIADIC) (1991), *National Report: Overview and Recommendations*, AGPS, Canberra.

Rubin, I. & Campbell, T. (1998), *The ABCs of Effective Feedback: A Guide for Caring Professionals*, Jossey-Bass, San Francisco.

Russell, A. & Perris, K. (2003), 'Telementoring in community nursing: A shift from dyadic to communal models of learning and professional development', *Mentoring and Tutoring*, 11(2): 227–37.

St John, S. (2008), 'Child poverty and family incomes policy in New Zealand', in K. Dew & A. Matheson (eds), *Understanding Health Inequalities in Aotearoa New Zealand*, Otago University Press, Dunedin.

Saleebey, D. (ed.) (1992), *The Strengths Perspective in Social Work Practice*, Longman, New York.

—— (1996), 'The strengths perspective in social work practice: Extensions and cautions', *Social Work*, 41(3): 296–305.

—— (1997), *The Strengths Perspective in Social Work Practice*, 2nd ed., Longman, New York.

—— (2001a), *Human Behavior and Social Environments: A Biopsychosocial Approach*, Columbia University Press, New York.

—— (2001b), 'Practicing the strengths perspective: Everyday tools and resources', *Families in Society: The Journal of Contemporary Human Services*, 82(3): 221–2.

Schore, A.N. (2002), 'Disregulation of the right brain: A fundamental mechanism of traumatic attachment and the psychopathogenesis of posttraumatic stress', *Australian and New Zealand Journal of Psychiatry*, 36: 9–30.

Schorr L.B. (1993), 'What works: Applying what we already know about successful social policy', *The American Prospect*, 13, November 30, 2002.

Schwartz, W. (1971), 'Groups in social work practice', in W. Schwartz & S. Zalba (eds), *The Practice of Group Work*, Columbia University Press, New York.

Scott, D. (2006a), *RE: Best Interests Paper*, unpublished email to R. Miller.

—— (2006b), 'Sowing the seeds of innovation and sustaining hope in the protection of children', paper presented at Every Child Every Chance launch, Melbourne, 13 April.

Scott, D. & O'Neill, D. (1996), *Beyond Child Rescue: Developing Family Centred Practice at St Luke's*, Allen & Unwin, Sydney.

Seden, Janet (1999), *Counselling in Social Work Practice*, Open University Press, Buckingham.

Sheppard, M. (1998), 'Practice validity, reflexivity and knowledge for social work', *British Journal of Social Work*, 28: 763–81.

Shonkoff, J.P. (2006), 'Closing the gap between what we know and what we do', conference paper presented at Putting Children First: Their Future, Our Future conference, Melbourne, 3 March.

Shulman, L. (1991), *Interactional Social Work Practice: Toward an Empirical Theory*, F.E. Peacock, Itasca, IL.

—— (1992), *The Skills of Helping: Individuals, Families and Groups*, F.E. Peacock, Itasca, IL.

—— (1993), *Interactional Supervision*, National Association of Social Workers Press, Washington, DC.

Simon, M. (2008), Originally from DeNeen Brown, 'Canadian government apologizes for abuse of Indigenous people', *Washington Post*, reprinted in *The Age*, 13 June, p. 13.

Siporin, M. (1975), *Introduction to Social Work*, Macmillan, New York.

Smallgood, M. (1996), 'This violence is not our way: An Aboriginal perspective on domestic violence', in R. Thorpe & J. Irwin (eds), *Women & Violence: Working for Change*, Hale & Iremonger, Sydney.

Smith, Linda Tuhiwai (1998), Towards the New Millenium: International Issues and Projects in Indigenous Research, paper presented to Te Oru Rangahua conference, Maori Research and Development, Massey University, New Zealand, July.

Stanley, J. & Goddard, C. (2002), *In the Firing Line: Violence and Power in Child Protection Work*, John Wiley & Sons, Melbourne.

Stanley, N. & Manthorpe, J. (1997), 'Risk assessment: Developing training for professionals in mental health work', *Social Work and Social Sciences Review*, 7(1): 26–38.

Starling, J. & Dossetor, D. (2005), 'Child and adolescent telepsychiatry', in R. Wootton & J. Batch (eds), *Telepediatrics: Telemedicine and Child Health*, Royal Society of Medicine Press, London.

Stople, G. & Chechele, P. (2004), 'Online counseling skills, part II', in R. Kraus, J. Zack & G. Stricker (eds), *Online Counselling: A Handbook for Mental Health Professionals*, Elsevier, London.

Stratigos, S. 2000, 'Domestic violence screening and pregnancy', in *The Way Forward: Children, Young People and Domestic Violence Conference Proceedings*, Commonwealth of Australia, Melbourne.

Strom-Gottfried, Kim (1999), *Social Work Practice*, Pine Forge Press, Thousand Oaks, CA.

Suler, J. (2004) 'The psychology of text relationships' in R. Kraus, J. Zack, & G. Stricker (eds), *Online Counselling: A Handbook for Mental Health Professionals*, Elsevier, London.

Taft, A. (2001), 'To screen or not to screen: Is this the right question? Quality care, intervention and women's agency in health care responses to partner violence and abuse', *Women Against Violence: An Australian Feminist Journal*, 10: 41–6.

Tait, A. (1999), 'Face-to-face and at a distance: The mediation of guidance and counselling through the new technologies', *British Journal of Guidance and Counselling*, 27(1): 113–22.

Te Puni Kokiri (2002), Ministry of Maori Development, www.tpk.govt.nz.

Thoburn, J. Lewis, A. & Shemmings, D. (1995), *Paternalism or Partnership: Family Involvement and Child Protection Policies*, HMSO, London.

Thompson, N. (2001), *Anti-discriminatory Practice*, Palgrave, New York.

Timms, N. & Timms, R. (1977) *Perspectives in Social Work*, Routledge and Kegan Paul, London.

Timmreck, T. (1995), *Planning, Programme Development, and Evaluation*, Jones and Bartlett, London.

Tobin, J.J. & Friedman, J. (1984), 'Intercultural and developmental stresses confronting South East Asia refugee adolescents', *Journal of Operational Psychiatry*, 15: 39–45.

Tomm, K. (1988), 'Interventive interviewing', *Family Process*, 27: 1–15.

Trevithick, P. (2000), *Social Work Skills*, Open University Press, Buckingham.

Trotter C. (1999), *Working with Involuntary Clients*, Allen & Unwin, Sydney.

—— (2002), 'Worker style and client outcome in child protection', *Child Abuse Review*, 11: 38–50.

Trudgen, R. (2000), *Why Warriors Lie Down and Die*, Aboriginal Resource and Development Services Inc., Darwin.

Trute, B. (1997), *Integration of Quantitative and Qualitative Approaches in Family Research: The Need for Ecumenism in Epistemology and Method*, Pre-publication draft, Centre for Applied Family Studies, McGill University, Montreal, Canada.

Turnell, A. (2006), *Working with Denied Child Abuse: The Resolutions Approach*, Open University Press, Maidenhead.

Turnell, A. & Edwards, S. (1999), *Signs of Safety: A Solution and Safety Oriented Approach to Child Protection Casework*, W.W. Norton, New York.

Turney, D. (1997), 'Hearing voices, talking difference: A dialogic approach to anti-oppressive practice', *Journal of Social Work Practice*, 11(2), 115-25.

Valtonen, K. (2001), 'Social work with immigrants and refugees: Developing a participation-based framework for anti-oppressive practice', *British Journal of Social Work*, 31: 955-60.

Van der Kolk, B.A. (2005), 'Developmental trauma disorder: Toward a rational diagnosis for children with complex trauma histories', *Psychiatric Annals*, 35(5): 401-8.

Wald, M.S. & Woolverton, M. (1990), 'Risk assessment: The emperor's new clothes?' *Child Welfare*, 69: 483-511.

Walker, Ranginui (1990), *Ka Whawhai Tonu Matou—Struggle Without End*, Penguin, Auckland.

Walsh, D. (1999),'A risk assessment for practitioners when working with disclosures of domestic violence', *Advances in Social Work and Welfare Education*, 2(2): 139-50.

Walsh, D. & Weeks, W. (2004), *What a Smile Can Hide*, Royal Women's Hospital, Melbourne.

Walsh, F. (1998), *Strengthening Family Resilience*, Guilford Press, New York.

Walsh, P. (1999), *Solution Focussed Child Protection: Towards a Positive Frame for Social Work Practice*, Department of Social Studies Occasional Paper No. 6, Trinity College, University of Dublin, Dublin.

Ward, D. (1998), 'Groupwork', in R. Adams, L. Dominelli & M. Payne (eds), *Social Work: Themes, Issues and Critical Debates*, Macmillan, London.

Waterson, J. (1999), 'Redefining community care social work: Needs or risks led?', *Health and Social Care in the Community*, 7(4): 276-9.

Weaver, H.N. (1999),'Indigenous people and the social work profession: Defining culturally competent services', *Social Work*, 44(3): 217-25.

Webb, S. (2006), *Social Work in a Risk Society*, Palgrave Macmillan, Houndmills.

Weeks, W. & Quinn, M. (2000), *Issues Facing Australian Families: Human Services Respond*, Longman, Melbourne.

Weick, A., Rapp, C., Sullivan, W.P. & Kisthardt (2001), 'A strengths perspective for social work practice', *Social Work*, July 1989, reprinted 2001.

Weisz, A., Tolman, R. & Saunders, D. (2000),'Assessing the risk of severe domestic violence', *Journal of Interpersonal Violence*, 15(1): 75-90.

Welsh, J. (2006), *Theories for Direct Social Work Practice*, Thompson Brookes/Cole, Belmont.

West, M. (1994), *Effective Teamwork*, British Psychological Society, Leicester.

Westcott, J., Dafforn, T. & Sterne, P. (1993), 'Escaping victim life stories and co-constructing personal agency', in S. Gilligan & R. Price, (eds), *Therapeutic Conversations*, W.W. Norton, New York, pp. 258–76.

Westermeyer, J. (1991b), 'Special considerations', in J. Westermeyer, C.L. Williams & A.N. Nguyen (eds), *Mental Health Services for Refugees*, DHHS, US Government Printing Office, Washington, DC.

White, M. (1988), 'Saying hello again: The incorporation of the lost relationship in the resolution of grief', *Dulwich Centre Newsletter*, Spring, pp. 7–11.

—— (1989), *Selected Papers*, Dulwich Centre Publications, South Australia.

—— (1995), *Re-authoring lives: Interviews and essays*, Dulwich Centre Publications, Adelaide.

—— (1999), 'Reflecting teamwork as definitional ceremony revisited', Gecko, 2: 55–82.

—— (2002), 'Addressing personal failure', *The International Journal of Narrative Therapy and Community Work*, 3: 33–52.

White, M. & Epston, D. (1990), *Narrative Means to Therapeutic Ends*, W.W. Norton, New York.

Wiles, D. (1998), *Human Services: A Discussion Paper*, Edith Cowan University, Perth.

Willett, J. & Manheim, R. (1976), *Bertolt Brecht Poems 1913–1956*, Eyre Methuen, London.

Williams, B. & Grant, G. (1998), 'Defining "people-centredness": Making the implicit explicit', *Health and Social Care in the Community*, 6(2): 84–94.

Winnicott, D. (1965), *The Family and Individual Development*, London, Tavistock.

Wood Goldberg, G. & Middleman, R. (1989), *The Structural Approach to Direct Practice in Social Work*, Columbia University Press, New York.

Wootton, R. & Batch, J. (eds) (2005), *Telepediatrics: Telemedicine and Child Health*, Royal Society of Medicine Press, London.

World Internet Usage Statistics (2007), Retrieved from www.internet worldstats.com/stats.htm [9 July 2007].

Yalom, I. with Leszcz, M. (1995), *The Theory and Practice of Group Psychotherapy*, Basic Books, New York.

Yllo, K. (1990), 'Political and methodological debates in wife abuse research', in K. Yllo & M. Bograd (eds), *Feminist Perspectives of Wife Abuse*, Sage, Newbury Park, CA.

INDEX